Picture Dictionary of Popular Flowering Plants

by A. G. L. Hellyer

Hamlyn
London · New York · Sydney · Toronto

Colour Illustrations

Contents

Introduction to Gardening

To be a good gardener two things are necessary: a love of plants and mastery of a few basic techniques. If the would-be gardener simply intends to grow plants without making any attempt to increase them, the techniques he will have to master are extremely simple. But if, as is more probable, he decides to try his hand at propagation, he will find his skill a little more extended.

Soil preparation

boom cultivator

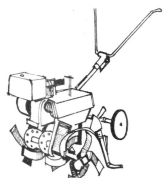

drag-shoe cultivator

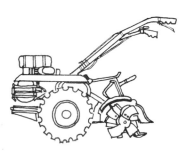

wheel-driven cultivator

First essentials are a knowledge of soil preparation and of planting methods. Soil needs to be broken up to let in air, which is necessary for fertility and to make it reasonably soft and workable. Digging with spade or fork is the traditional method and is still as good as any, though where large areas are involved, ploughing or mechanical rotary cultivation may be substituted. In any event the aim is to get at least a 9 in. depth of soil—more if possible—well broken up, and either to remove weeds to a heap in which they will in time rot down into good compost, or to turn them well down under the soil so that they rot where they lie. This second method is quite satisfactory with annual and shallow-rooting weeds such as groundsel, chickweed and dead nettle, but is not recommended for permanent deep-rooting weeds such as dandelion, dock and bindweed (wild convolvulus). These have an awkward habit of reappearing weeks or months later, even when they have been well buried in the soil.

It is desirable, though not essential, that soil cultivation be completed some weeks or even months before planting or sowing is attempted. This is partly to enable soil to settle again after disturbance and partly to give weeds a chance to rot. Soil cultivation should not be attempted when soil is very wet or frozen. The ideal time is when it is sufficiently moist for a spade to be driven into it easily but not so wet that soil clings badly to the spade.

Manures and fertilisers Plants live largely on air and water, but they also require very small quantities of chemicals from the soil. These chemicals are not always present in sufficient amounts or in the right proportions for healthy growth, and the object of manuring is to replenish the stocks.

Animal manures, such as those from the farmyard, stable or poultry house, contain all, or almost all, the essential chemicals, and in addition improve the texture of soil, particularly if they have been prepared with plenty of straw, peat or other litter. Texture is important, because it enables a soil to hold water without becoming waterlogged and also because it enables the soil to be worked easily most of the year. But too much animal manure may do harm by making the soil sour, injuring the roots of plants or encouraging very vigorous growth at the expense of flowers and fruits. Farmyard and stable manure can usually be applied quite safely at rates up to a hundredweight (a good wheelbarrow load) to ten square yards, but not more than a bucketful of the richer poultry manure will be needed for the same area.

Chemical fertilisers supply the plant's requirements in even more concentrated forms—so concentrated, indeed, that with some no more than the lightest of dustings can be given with safety. But for a good average compound fertiliser (one that provides the three chemicals most likely to be in short supply, namely nitrogen, phosphorus and potash) a dressing of 3 to 4 ounces to the square yard is usually about right.

Some plant foods are prepared from animal products, three of the most important being bonemeal, hoof-and-horn meal and dried blood. These approximate more closely in use and application to chemical fertilisers than to the bulky animal manures and are used at rates varying from 1 to 6 ounces to each square yard according to type and requirements.

The bulky manures are generally turned into the soil when it is dug, forked, ploughed or rotary tilled. Mixed with the soil in this way they soon become a part of it, giving to it all their virtues. Chemical fertilisers, by contrast, are usually applied as topdressings, scattered over the surface of the soil and at most only raked or lightly forked in. This type of application is best delayed until a few days before seeds are sown or plants are planted except in the case of some slow-acting fertilisers, such as basic slag and bonemeal, which can be applied several months in advance.

Fertilisers may also be sprinkled lightly round plants in growth to give them an extra fillip or to keep them growing vigorously in the same ground even when they have occupied it for years. Care must be taken to apply the chemical direct to the soil and keep it off stems and leaves which it may burn.

Bulky manures are also used, spread on the surface, to feed established plants, a process known as mulching, and the same precautions regarding direct contact with foliage must be observed. One merit of mulching is that it helps to keep the soil cool and moist in hot weather.

planting bulbs with a trowel

putting in young plant

Planting and aftercare

The basic rule in all planting is to return the plant to the soil in as nearly similar a 'posture' as that in which it was originally growing, that is to say the roots should be at the same depth below soil level and, with the exception of container-grown plants, the roots should be spread out as they are when growing naturally. As a rule this involves making a fairly wide hole, for it is only a few plants, such as hollyhocks and gypsophila, that send their roots straight down into the soil. These tap-rooted plants may be planted with a pointed stick or dibber, but most plants should be planted with a trowel or spade, whichever is more convenient.

It is not so easy to generalise about depth, but often the soil mark on the plant (the mark on the stem left by the soil in which the plant was formerly growing) will give the best guide. It should be just covered by the new soil, as there is sure to be some sinking of the soil later on. Many bulbs are happy if covered with their own depth of soil, for example, a bulb measuring 2 inches from top to bottom will need a 4-inch-deep hole. There are some important exceptions to this which are mentioned in the notes on particular plants.

Plants with roots should have fine soil worked around and between the roots; this can be accomplished by shaking the plant gently so that the soil fills in the space between roots. Almost all plants like to be planted firmly. When most of the soil has been returned around them it should be pressed all round, with the knuckles for small plants, the feet for large ones.

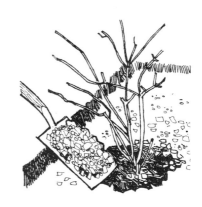

The two principal planting seasons are spring and autumn. In spring all herbaceous (that is soft-stemmed) plants can be transplanted and also most rock plants and the summer-flowering bulbous-rooted plants such as the gladiolus and montbretia. Early autumn is also a good time for planting many herbaceous plants and the spring-flowering kinds of bulbs such as the daffodil (narcissus), snowdrop and crocus. A little later in the autumn is ideal for tulips and hyacinths and for deciduous trees and shrubs, including roses and fruit trees, bushes and canes. Evergreen trees and shrubs are best planted in early autumn or spring. Planting should be attempted only when the soil is in good condition, moist but not so wet that it sticks badly to feet and tools.

If plants are well established in containers, so that their roots bind all the soil into firm balls, it is possible to transplant them at any time when the

planting container-grown shrub

driving in a stake

spreading

firming in

soil is in workable condition. To do this successfully plants must be removed carefully from the containers without injury to their roots or disturbance of the soil around them, so that the root ball remains intact, and be replanted immediately in holes the right size to receive them. Then if the larger plants are securely staked so that they cannot be disturbed by wind, and all plants are watered for a few weeks whenever the soil looks like getting dry, they will receive little check to growth and will re-establish themselves even when planted in summer. All manner of containers may be used including tin cans, earthenware and plastic pots and polythene bags.

Staking Only the taller herbaceous plants need staking and the method used can vary according to the type of growth they make. Plants with long spikes of bloom such as delphiniums or hollyhocks may need one cane or other support to each stem. Plants with a more branching or spray-like habit may be allowed to grow up through large mesh wire or plastic netting or special wire hoops which can be purchased for this purpose. Alternatively, twiggy branches such as those sold as support for culinary peas can be thrust into the soil around the plants in spring so that the stems grow up through them. As far as possible the aim should be to get the plants to conceal the supports as they grow.

Trees require more substantial support when young, but after a few years stakes can be discarded as the trees will be well established and quite capable of supporting themselves. Posts as much as 2 inches square and 7 feet long may be required for standard trees. They should be driven well into the soil, if possible into the centre of the hole prepared for planting before the tree is placed in position. Then the main stem can be made secure to the stake, preferably with one of the special plastic tree ties sold for the purpose as these are unlikely to damage the bark and can be progressively let out as the trunk increases in girth. Care should be taken to ensure that the bark is not damaged by rubbing against the stake or by allowing ties to bite into it.

Small shrubs do not as a rule require staking but larger shrubs, and in particular evergreens which present a big surface of leaves to the wind, may require support at least for the first year. Similar instructions to those already given for trees apply except that the stakes may be shorter and thinner. The one-inch square, 5- to 6-foot long stakes sold for supporting standard roses will serve equally well for many shrubs.

Protection Two kinds of protection may be considered in the garden, temporary and permanent. Temporary protection is particularly useful for things newly planted, and evergreens often benefit greatly from it because their leaves lose a lot of water and can easily shrivel and die if exposed to drying winds after being transplanted.

Temporary protection can be obtained with evergreen branches pushed into the soil around each plant to break the force of the wind; with screens made of hessian or other material; with wattle hurdles or woven wood fencing panels, or very simply for fairly small plants by cutting the bottoms off large plastic bags (old fertiliser or cattle food bags are ideal) and dropping one of these over each plant and supporting it by three or four canes firmly pushed into the soil. White or transparent bags are to be preferred to black bags which tend to cut off too much light.

Permanent protection is for plants that are a little too tender to be completely safe when growing fully exposed in that particular locality. In every garden there are some places that are colder or draughtier or wetter than average and some that are warmer or more sheltered or drier. A border at the foot of a south or west facing wall, or best of all in the angle between two walls one facing south the other west, is likely to provide a particularly warm and sheltered place in which shrubs such as ceanothus and fuchsia, climbers such as passiflora or campsis and bulbs such as nerine and amaryllis can be grown successfully in areas which might otherwise be too cold for them. Evergreen trees also provide useful shelter for some shade-loving plants, and it is notable that the more tender rhododendrons can often be grown successfully in such an environment (provided that the shade is not too dense) in localities where they would certainly fail if fully exposed.

Watering When water is required it is best given straight from the spout of a watering-can held close to the ground so that the gush of water is not too violent, or from a sprinkler attached to a hose. If a watering-can fitted with a rose is used there is danger that insufficient water will be applied since it is essential that it should soak several inches into the soil where the roots are. If a sprinkler is used it should be left in place for an hour or more according to its rate of delivery. In fact, the slower this is the better as it will cause less puddling of the surface, though it does also mean that the sprinkler must be left running for a longer time. Evening watering is economical since it is then relatively cool and little water is lost by evaporation, but contrary to popular belief daytime watering is not harmful, even when there is bright sunshine. Soil should not be kept sodden for long periods as this checks or even kills roots. The aim should be to wet the soil well and then let the water drain away and give no more until the soil appears to be getting dry again.

protection from wind

Kinds of plants

Most garden plants can be put into one of three groups, annuals, biennials or perennials.

Annuals are plants that complete their life cycles in one year, germinating, flowering, setting seed and then dying. This does not necessarily take place in a calendar year, as it is possible to sow seeds of many annuals in autumn to flower the following spring or summer. From the gardener's point of view, annuals are subdivided into a further three groups—hardy, half-hardy and tender. The hardy ones can be sown and grown out of doors at any time of the year without protection, examples being clarkia, cornflower, godetia and calendula. Half-hardy annuals, by contrast, can be grown out of doors only in warm weather, and must usually be started under glass and then planted outdoors to flower, although occasionally, as with Ten-week Stocks, annual asters, French and African marigolds and zinnias, the need for protection can be dispensed with if they are sown fairly late in the spring. Tender annuals need the protection of a greenhouse for most of the time, and are in general unsuitable for growing out of doors. All annuals are discarded after flowering.

Biennials are plants that take approximately two years to germinate, grow, flower and produce seed and then die. Examples of these are Canterbury bells and foxgloves, but many other plants, such as hollyhocks, Sweet Williams, wallflowers and double daisies, although strictly speaking perennials, are in gardens usually treated as biennials.

Perennials are plants that continue to live for an indefinite number of years and to flower time and time again. Some, such as lupins, which rarely live for more than 5 or 6 years, are short-lived perennials, others such as peonies are long-lived perennials. Both these are herbaceous perennials (plants of soft growth), but trees and shrubs with woody growth are perennials as well. Bulbs, corms and tubers are herbaceous perennials with fleshy storage organs which enable them to survive long periods without growth.

Perennials, like annuals, may be hardy, half-hardy or tender. The fully hardy kinds can be grown out of doors in all parts of the British Isles and the tender kinds need protection in all parts except possibly in summer. It is the half-hardies about which it is impossible to generalise since there are many different climates in a country such as Britain and even in the

Canterbury Bell

9

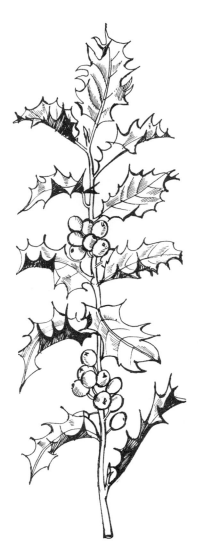

same locality the weather can vary greatly from one season to another. Even the half-hardy perennials themselves differ greatly in their susceptibility to cold, some being killed by only a degree or so of frost and some surviving temperatures several degrees below freezing point, particularly if they are fairly dry.

Hardiness is also affected by many conditions in addition to temperature. Plants in active growth are usually less hardy than when they are dormant or nearly so. Growth that has been well ripened by warmth and sunshine is often hardier than growth that is poorly ripened. Bright sunshine occurring with frost seems sometimes to aggravate damage. Wind can also increase frost damage, but a good covering of snow may protect low-growing plants from frost. Many plants that can survive a few degrees of frost continuing for no more than a day or so at a time are injured or killed by a similar frost that persists for days or weeks. For the purpose of this book 'severe frost' may be defined as temperatures below −10°C. (14°F.), and 'prolonged frosts' as frost continuing for more than two days without break, but it must be understood that these are only rough and ready guides. There is no real substitute for trial on the spot and local information can be very useful. Even within a garden there may be microclimates, i.e. differences in temperature, moisture, exposure, sunshine etc., so that slightly tender plants may succeed in one position but fail in another. All one can say with certainty is that half-hardy plants will grow out of doors much of the time but that many must be protected in winter especially in cold places.

Evergreen and deciduous With trees and shrubs another important subdivision must be made between evergreen and deciduous kinds. Evergreens retain their leaves all the winter, typical examples being holly and yew. Deciduous trees and shrubs lose all their leaves each autumn and produce a fresh lot the following spring. In consequence evergreens retain a rather similar appearance throughout the year except when flowering or bearing berries or other fruits. Deciduous trees and shrubs, by contrast, are constantly changing in appearance from the first appearance of the leaves, often pale in colour, through their gradual development to maturity and the brilliant colour changes that occur in some kinds in autumn and then to the bare tracery of branches in winter. It is by taking these features into account and making good use of the contrasts between evergreens and deciduous plants that some of the best garden effects can be achieved.

Greenhouses and frames

span-roofed greenhouse

The Greenhouse A greenhouse enables the gardener to provide plants with a controlled environment to suit their needs, though the degree of control will depend upon the facilities provided, especially for heating. Only in the mildest parts of the British Isles will an unheated greenhouse exclude frost at all times and since it only takes a little freezing to kill frost-tender plants, this limits the uses to which an unheated greenhouse can be put.

Even where heating is introduced there are limits to what can be grown according to the temperatures that can be maintained. In this respect it is convenient to consider greenhouses in four categories to be known respectively as cold greenhouses, cool greenhouses, intermediate greenhouses and warm greenhouses, and this is the classification used in this book to describe the temperature requirements of plants grown under glass.

A cold greenhouse is one that has no artificial heating of any kind so that in winter the temperature inside it may at times drop well below freezing point. At this season a cold greenhouse is only suitable for hardy plants such as various herbaceous perennials, alpines and bulbs. From about April to October it may be possible to maintain quite warm temperatures by sun heat alone and so grow a range of tender plants for this limited period. A warm propagator inside a cold greenhouse may make it possible to start plants into growth earlier and they can be transferred to the greenhouse staging as night temperatures rise sufficiently.

A cool greenhouse is one with sufficient heating to maintain a minimum winter temperature of 7°C. (45°F.). In such a greenhouse artificial heat will not be required constantly in winter since much of the time the outside temperature will be above 7°C. (45°F.) and even when it is not sun heat may raise the inside temperature to the required level or even considerably higher. For these reasons it is a great economy to have the heating apparatus controlled by a thermostat which can be set at about 8°C. (47°F.) so that the artificial sources have time to take effect before the temperature drops too low. In spring and summer a temperature range of 13 to 18°C. (56 to 65°F.) is ideal for such a greenhouse though in warmer weather it will inevitably go higher since it is not usual (or indeed necessary) in Britain to provide apparatus to keep greenhouses at lower than outside temperatures. All the same, shading and ventilation should be used to prevent the temperature reaching far above 18°C. (65°F.) as it can do very early on sunny days. In a cool greenhouse artificial heat is unlikely to be required from about mid-April to mid-October, when temperature control can be entirely by ventilation and shading.

lean-to greenhouse

An intermediate greenhouse is one with a winter minimum temperature of 13°C. (56°F.) and a spring and summer range of 16 to 21°C. (61 to 70°F.). Simila remarks apply to the management of this type of house as to the cool g eenhouse except that some artificial heat is likely to be required most of the winter and also at times in May and September. As a result the cost of heating such a house is several times greater than that of heating a comparable cool greenhouse.

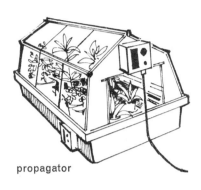

propagator

A warm greenhouse is for the cultivation of tropical plants and is likely to need heating at periods throughout the year. In winter the minimum temperature should be 18°C. (65°F.), and the spring and summer range should be between 21 and 27°C. (70 to 81°F.) which may rise to as much as 32°C. (90°F.) with direct sun heat. But for most tropical plants these high temperatures must be accompanied by a humid atmosphere and some shade from direct sunshine.

Frames Frames are of many different types but are alike in being relatively low so that the plants growing in them must be tended from outside. Sometimes they are constructed entirely of glass or plastic but more commonly they have wooden, brick or concrete sides with removable glass or plastic 'lights'. Like greenhouses, frames can be heated and it would be quite possible to arrange for different levels of heating to suit particular types of plant, as described for the four greenhouse categories. But more generally, frames are used as temporary homes for plants to protect them in the early stages of growth or to help them to adjust to the difference in climate between a heated greenhouse and the open air. This last function is known as 'hardening off' and is an important stage in the cultivation of most half-hardy plants which are raised in greenhouses or are kept in greenhouses in winter but are planted out of doors in summer. If these plants can be transferred to frames for the last three or four weeks and be given increasing ventilation, with the protective lights removed altogether during mild days, their leaves and stems will toughen and they will be far less susceptible to weather damage when they are planted out. For this hardening off artificial heating is rarely necessary and many frames have no provision for heating.

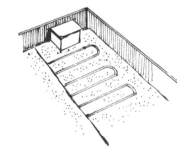

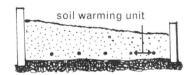

soil warming unit

Yet another alternative to air heating is soil warming. Where a mains supply of electricity is available this is easily effected by burying special soil-warming cable in a layer of sand, 3 to 6 inches beneath the surface of the soil. Soil warming is economical, especially if thermostatically controlled, and with it a frame can be used for a great deal of the early seed raising that would otherwise be done in cool or intermediate greenhouses, and also for rooting cuttings and growing some of the shorter tender plants.

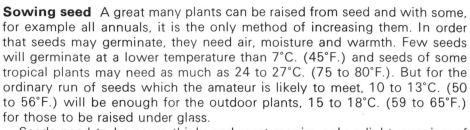

Increasing plants

Sowing seed A great many plants can be raised from seed and with some, for example all annuals, it is the only method of increasing them. In order that seeds may germinate, they need air, moisture and warmth. Few seeds will germinate at a lower temperature than 7°C. (45°F.) and seeds of some tropical plants may need as much as 24 to 27°C. (75 to 80°F.). But for the ordinary run of seeds which the amateur is likely to meet, 10 to 13°C. (50 to 56°F.) will be enough for the outdoor plants, 15 to 18°C. (59 to 65°F.) for those to be raised under glass.

Seeds need to be sown thinly and most require only a light covering of soil. Out of doors the most favourable times for sowing are spring, late summer and early autumn. The soil should be crumbly and reasonably fine and the seeds are usually sown in drills (little furrows drawn with the corner of a hoe or a rake). These drills may be 1 to 1½ inches deep for the biggest seeds such as sweet peas and lupins, but no more than ½ inch deep for most small seeds. The displaced soil is then drawn back over the seeds with a rake or scuffled over them with the feet, a method which has the advantage of making the soil reasonably firm at the same time.

In some cases it is more convenient to sow seed broadcast—to scatter it as evenly as possible all over the surface of the soil. If this method is adopted out of doors, the seed is usually covered by raking the soil carefully first in one direction then in another.

When seeds are sown in boxes, pots or pans, they are almost always broadcast, and then they are usually covered by sprinkling a little fine soil over them. Usually the containers are covered with sheets of glass and of paper, the first to trap as much moisture as possible, the second to exclude light and prevent the soil drying out too rapidly. But such coverings must be removed as soon as seedlings appear or they will become weak and spindly.

Pricking out Even when seeds are sown thinly the seedlings usually come up too thickly to be left undisturbed. Sometimes they are thinned out, surplus seedlings being pulled out and thrown away, sometimes they are transplanted, a process known as pricking out and generally applied to seedlings raised under glass.

Pricking out requires care. It is usually done as soon as the seedlings can be handled, and the only tools required are a dibber, which can be made by rounding the end of a stick about the length and thickness of a fountain pen, and a notched stick, made from a seed label, and used for handling very small seedlings. The seedlings are gently eased out of the soil without breaking their roots. Then they are very carefully separated and replanted singly in holes made by pushing the dibber into the soil. The dibber is used to press the soil firmly around the roots.

After pricking out, seedlings should be given the same temperature as before, at any rate for a few days. Later on, if they are to be planted out eventually, the temperature can be lowered gradually and more ventilation given, the process already described as hardening off. Always the aim should be to avoid any sudden changes to treatment or climate.

Soil for seed raising Soil for seed raising and pricking off must be fairly fine, reasonably rich and porous. One of the best mixtures is that known as the John Innes Seed Compost often referred to as JIS. It is prepared with medium loam (that is, good soil containing the partly decayed roots of grass), granulated peat and coarse river sand with the addition of very small quantities of powdered chalk or limestone and a fertiliser called superphosphate of lime. The proportions are: 2 parts by bulk of loam, 1 part of peat and 1 part of sand. To each bushel of this mixture ¾ oz. of ground chalk or limestone and 1½ oz. of superphosphate of lime are added.

All the ingredients must be thoroughly mixed together and if possible the loam should first be sterilised by heating it, preferably by steam, to a temperature of about 93°C. (200°F.) and maintaining it at this for half an hour. For seed composts this loam should then be rubbed through a sieve with a $\frac{1}{4}$-in. mesh. John Innes Seed Compost already prepared from properly sterilised loam and ready for immediate use can be purchased from most dealers in horticultural sundries.

An alternative to JIS is soilless compost usually based on peat with or without the addition of other ingredients such as sand, powdered clay and fertilisers. There is no generally accepted formula and soilless composts are usually prepared ready for use and are sold under brand names. They can be entirely satisfactory provided they are used strictly in accordance with manufacturers' instructions.

Potting As young plants grow, many are transferred singly to small pots, a process known as potting. Greenhouse plants are usually grown in pots throughout their lives and, as they get bigger and bigger, must be moved on into larger and yet larger pots. This is called potting on.

All pots must be quite clean inside and out. There must be a hole, or holes, in the bottom of each pot to allow surplus water to escape, and these holes may be covered with one or more pieces of broken pot to prevent soil washing down into them and blocking them up. The broken pieces of pot are called crocks and the whole process of providing a pot with drainage material is known as crocking.

However, thanks to the improvement of seed and potting composts and the introduction of plastic pots, crocking is seldom considered necessary nowadays by commercial growers and has been dropped by many good private gardeners.

An excellent soil mixture for potting is that known as the John Innes Potting Compost. It is prepared in much the same way as the seed compost, the ingredients being: 7 parts by loose bulk of loam, 3 parts of peat and 2 parts of sand. To each bushel of this mixture is added $\frac{3}{4}$ oz. of ground chalk or limestone, and 4 oz. of a base fertiliser prepared from 2 parts by weight of superphosphate, 2 parts of hoof-and-horn meal and 1 part of sulphate of potash. As for the seed compost, it is essential that all ingredients are well mixed and desirable that the loam should be sterilised. For small plants loam may be rubbed through a sieve with a $\frac{1}{2}$-in. mesh. For large ones it is usually sufficient to pull the lumps of loam apart by hand.

The mixture described is the basic John Innes Potting Compost, usually referred to as JIP.1. It is suitable for all young plants and many older ones, but some strong-growing or hungry plants may appreciate richer compost especially when growing in pots 4 inches or more in diameter. Four successive grades are recognised. JIP.1 as above, JIP.2 with double quantities of chalk and fertilisers, JIP.3 with triple quantities and JIP.4 in which the quantities are quadrupled. These terms are often used when describing cultural methods for pot plants.

Soilless potting composts are also available and like the seed compost equivalents are mainly branded preparations to be used in accordance with manufacturers' instructions.

To pot a plant in a soil-based compost a little of this should first be put into the pot. Then the plant is held in position with one hand and with the other soil is run in around its roots. When the pot is nearly full of soil the pot is given a sharp rap on some firm surface (a stout wooden bench is ideal) to settle the soil and it is then further firmed with fingers, particularly around the edge of the pot. For very large plants a piece of old broom handle or similar thick stick, known as a rammer, is used instead of the fingers to firm the soil. Usually after potting, plants are given a good soaking of water from a can fitted with a rose, the object being to freshen up the plants and still further settle the soil.

When a plant has been correctly potted, its uppermost roots should be just covered with soil and the surface of the soil should be a little below the rim of the pot—about $\frac{1}{4}$ inch in small pots, as much as 1 inch in large ones. The object is to allow room for water to be poured into the pot when watering is necessary.

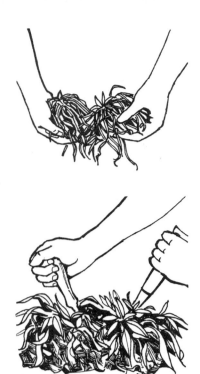

A slightly different method is required with soilless composts since these must never be made very firm. Gentle pressure with the fingers and several sharp raps of the compost-filled pot on a hard bench, followed by a thorough watering from a can fitted with a coarse rose is usually sufficient to settle the compost around the roots.

Dividing plants Many soft-stemmed perennial plants are increased by dividing the roots instead of by sowing seed. This is a very simple method of propagation, all that is necessary being to lift a strong plant and pull the root apart into several pieces. If this cannot be done with the fingers two forks may be thrust back-to-back through the centre of the clump and levered apart. Each division must have both roots and shoots, or at least buds from which shoots can grow later. The divisions are replanted at once exactly as if they were plants.

Stem cuttings Some perennial plants cannot be divided and even with some which can be it is too slow a method of getting a large number of new plants. Cuttings are then often used as a means of increase. A stem cutting is a shoot, or a piece of a shoot, which is severed from the plant and induced to form roots. It may be anything from an inch to a foot in length according to the kind of plant from which it is taken.

There are three main types of stem cutting—soft, half-ripe and ripe or hard-wooded. Soft cuttings are generally taken in winter or spring, half-ripe in summer and hard-wooded in autumn.

As a rule, soft and half-ripe cuttings must be given some form of protection—in a frame, under a cloche of some kind, inside a polythene bag, in a special plant propagator or under special mist apparatus—until they form roots. The object of this is to restrict the circulation of air, keep the atmosphere very moist and so prevent the cutting from collapsing while it is without roots. Hard-wooded cuttings can usually be rooted in the open because they are taken at a time of year when plants are losing moisture very slowly.

The usual way of preparing a cutting is to cut off a suitable shoot, remove the lower leaves, if any, with a sharp knife or razor blade, and then cut the bottom of the shoot cleanly through just below a joint—the point at which a leaf has been attached or a bud is situated. The joints on a stem are usually quite easily seen. The base of each cutting may be dipped in hormone rooting powder, which can be purchased from any garden shop ready for use, but this is not essential. The cutting is then inserted, right way up, in rather sandy soil or in a substance, such as vermiculite, which holds moisture well. With soft and half-ripe cuttings it is only necessary to insert them sufficiently deeply to hold them erect, usually $\frac{1}{2}$ to 1 inch, but hard-wooded cuttings are inserted at least two-thirds of their length in the ground out of doors.

Soft cuttings are made from young shoots that are still quite soft. Half-ripe cuttings, usually of shrubs, are made from young shoots that are firm, at any rate at the base, though they have not quite completed their growth. Plenty of suitable material can generally be found in July and early August. Hard-wooded cuttings of trees or shrubs are always made from fully grown stems at the end of their season of growth. Those from deciduous trees or shrubs may be nearly or completely without leaves.

Soft cuttings will usually form roots in a few weeks and are then treated much like seedlings, being transplanted to pots or nursery beds. Half-ripe cuttings may take a month or so to root and are then treated in the same way. Hard-wooded cuttings are seldom properly rooted until the following year and are generally allowed to remain undisturbed for a full twelve months.

Root cuttings A few perennial plants can be increased by root cuttings. These are pieces of root laid in soil and encouraged to form shoots. Thick roots, such as those of hollyhock, anchusa and verbascum, are cut into 2-in.-long pieces making a slanting cut at the bottom of each to indicate the position of the base. These pieces are then pushed into soil, right way up, until they are just covered. Thinner roots, such as those of phlox and gaillardia, are usually strewn thinly on the surface of soil and then covered with a further $\frac{1}{2}$ inch of soil. Most root cuttings are taken in winter and are ready to be planted in a nursery bed or potted singly to grow on by the following May or June.

root cuttings

Layering Layering is a very convenient method of increasing some perennial plants, particularly shrubs. Pliable branches are bent down to soil level and either ringed or partially slit with a knife or given a sharp twist where they touch the soil. This injured portion is then buried a few inches deep and held securely in position with a peg or a heavy stone. In time roots form from the wounded areas, and when there are enough of these, the layered stem can be severed from the parent plant, dug up and treated as an ordinary plant. Shrub layering is usually done in May or June and the layers are well rooted by the autumn of the following year.

Layering is also used to increase border carnations. The work is done in July, non-flowering shoots are used, and an incision is made in each through a joint in such a way as to form a tongue which will open when that part of the shoot is bent down into the ground. Carnation layers are generally held in position with wire pegs like large hairpins, and they should be well rooted in eight or ten weeks.

carnation layering

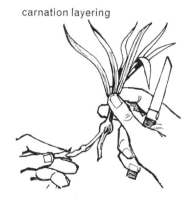

Pests and diseases

In general, pests and diseases are less troublesome in the ornamental garden than they are to vegetables and fruits, and it is only with a few plants, notably roses, that regular spray programmes are necessary. All the same it is wise to be on one's guard and ready to take action should it become necessary. A relatively few remedies will meet most requirements.

Pests may be insects, mites or other small creatures or they may be much larger animals such as mice, rats, rabbits, squirrels and some birds. Obviously no one method of control will suffice for the lot and the remedy chosen must fit the need.

Similarly, diseases may be caused by fungi, bacteria, viruses or nutritional deficiencies and again correct diagnosis is required, followed by the use of an appropriate remedy. None of this need prove too difficult to apply except in a very few cases in which expert advice should be sought.

Insect pests are of two main kinds, the suckers and the biters. Into the first group come all the aphids, a name which covers the familiar greenfly and blackfly as well as numerous other allied pests. Capsid bugs and scale insects are other suckers, the former active little creatures which can seldom be caught at work, the latter clinging motionless like tiny limpets or mussels to stems or leaves. Thrips, which are thread like and can be seen scampering about if flowers or leaves on which they are feeding are sharply tapped over a sheet of white paper, are also suckers and so are red-spider mites, which are so small that a hand lens may be needed to see them. All this group of insects puncture the tender young shoots or leaves and draw sap from them without leaving any visible wounds. They are most likely to be troublesome in warm weather and occasional spraying from May to September with derris will take care of most of them. An alternative is to use a systemic insecticide such as menazon, dimethoate or formothion about once a month during this period. Derris and other contact insecticides such as malathion and lindane (BHC) must actually touch the pests in order to kill them, but systemics penetrate leaves, stems or roots, are distributed in the sap and so poison the food of the suckers. When using insecticides it is very important to follow the manufacturers' instructions.

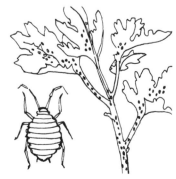

aphid

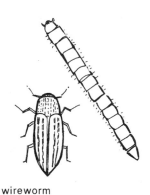

capsid bug

wireworm

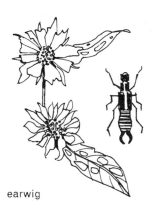

earwig

black spot

Although sucking pests can be seen often the first indication that they are at work may be the distinctive damage they cause. Aphids make leaves curl and cockle and lose some of their healthy green colour. Capsid bugs cause even more severe cockling with some parts of the leaf failing to develop and possibly splitting as a result. Thrips and red-spider mites produce severe leaf mottling, more streaky and sometimes black or silvery with thrips, grey or bronze with red-spider mites. Scale insects cover stems and leaves with a sticky substance on which black mould usually grows making plants extremely unsightly.

The biting pests actually eat leaves, stems or fruits making holes in them or stripping them completely so that the damage they do is much more obvious. They are caterpillars, sawfly larvae and other grubs, also weevils (which look like beetles but have long snouts), slugs and snails. Some of them attack roots or stems at or near soil level and these include leather-jackets, cutworms, wireworms and millepedes.

Again derris will take care of many of the biters above ground, and BHC will kill both those above ground, if applied as a spray or dust, and those below ground if used as a soil powder well raked in. But very often in the flower garden hand picking is sufficient or trapping with pieces of carrot or orange peel just buried in the soil and examined daily. Earwigs, which can damage the flowers of chrysanthemums and dahlias quite seriously, can be trapped in empty match boxes slightly opened and hung among the stems.

Slugs and snails are not insects and are not killed by the ordinary run of insecticides. Special chemicals must therefore be used against them, the two most popular being metaldehyde and methiocarb. Both can be purchased as prepared baits ready to be sprinkled around plants likely to be attacked. Metaldehyde is also available in liquid form to be further diluted with water and applied from a watering-can fitted with a rose wherever slugs or snails are likely to lie concealed.

Mice and rats can be trapped or poisoned. Moles, which can be a nuisance burrowing under lawns and in seed beds, are nevertheless good friends to the gardener because of the soil insects they devour. Naphthalene balls buried about 3 inches deep and 3 inches apart in a complete ring or rectangle will usually keep them out of any particular plot of land, but in severe cases it may be necessary to trap them. Grey squirrels, rabbits and troublesome birds are best shot, but are only likely to be a real nuisance in country gardens.

A great many common diseases are caused by fungi and can be controlled by occasional spraying with a good fungicide such as thiram or a copper fungicide. For some more difficult diseases like rose black spot other chemicals may be required such as maneb or Milfaron, the last a systemic which enters the sap and can actually kill the fungus after it has penetrated the leaf skin.

Diseases caused by bacteria and viruses are much more difficult to control and it is usually wise to destroy all infected plants. The symptoms are varied but some bacteria cause soft decay of stems and crowns and one, known as crown gall, causes large tumour-like swellings on stems or tree trunks, often near soil level. Oddly enough, though very disfiguring this disease seldom seems to do much damage to the plants and can usually be ignored.

Symptoms of virus infection also vary greatly from yellow mottling of leaves or dry brown spotting to severe leaf and stem distortion and dwarfing of the whole plant. Dahlias are particularly susceptible to virus infection and a sharp watch should be kept for it especially on plants which are to be used for propagation. Many viruses are spread by sucking insects, especially aphids.

Deficiency diseases may occur in very acid or very alkaline soils and also in some other soils short of particular chemicals. Lack of iron or manganese results in yellowing of the leaves, shortage of magnesium can produce purple or brown patches in the centres of the leaves, potash deficiency can cause grey or brown margins to leaves and boron deficiency can cause the tips of shoots to wither as if burned. Since these symptoms can be easily confused with those due to other causes it is wise to seek expert advice when chemical deficiencies are suspected.

Plant Dictionary

A

abutilon

ABUTILON. Deciduous shrubs. 3 to 10 ft. Various colours. Mostly summer flowering. Abutilons are mainly grown in the greenhouse or as bedding plants to be placed out of doors in summer but given greenhouse protection from October to May. Two fine kinds, however, are hardy enough to be grown out of doors winter and summer in mild or sheltered places. One is a tall shrub with upright branches, greenish-grey leaves and lovely soft mauve flowers (white in one variety) in May or June. It is known as the Vine-leaved Abutilon, *Abutilon vitifolium*, because of the shape of its leaves. The other is the Brazilian Abutilon, *A. megapotamicum*, a very different plant with thin, rather sprawling stems which need to be tied to a support, and drooping crimson and yellow flowers that are produced for quite a long time in summer.

The most popular of the more tender kinds for summer bedding is Thompson's Abutilon, *A. striatum thompsonii*, with green maple-shaped leaves mottled with yellow, but there are also some attractive hybrids with green leaves and white, yellow, orange or chestnut-red bell-shaped flowers produced over a long season.

All abutilons like sun and can be grown in any reasonable soil. They can be increased by cuttings of firm young shoots in spring, summer or autumn. Pruning, to get rid of frost-damaged stems and to keep the plants well balanced, can be carried out in spring.

ACACIA (Mimosa). Half-hardy evergreen trees and shrubs. 8 to 30 ft. Yellow flowers mainly in winter and spring. These Australian trees and shrubs are nearly all too tender to be grown out of doors except in the mildest parts, but one, usually known by gardeners as Mimosa, *Acacia dealbata*, will often succeed in a warm, sheltered place such as against a south or west wall. Where it can be so grown it will quickly make a sizeable tree. It has ferny grey-green leaves and fluffy-looking sprays of small yellow flowers each like a tiny pompon and produced in March or April.

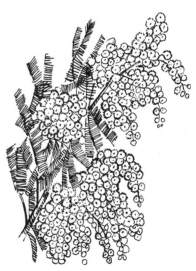

Acacia dealbata

Mimosa and several of the more tender acacias such as Drummond's Acacia, *A. drummondii*, can be grown in large pots or tubs in a frostproof greenhouse in JIP.2 or equivalent compost. The root restriction will slow their growth and in addition they can be pruned after flowering, but eventually they will become too large and will have to be replaced.

All acacias like sun and thrive in fairly light, well-drained soils. They can be raised from seed sown in spring in a greenhouse or frame with a temperature of 15 to 18°C. (59 to 65°F.), and cuttings can also be rooted in summer in a frame inside the greenhouse. Some kinds produce suckers freely and these can be dug up in autumn or early spring with roots attached and can be replanted elsewhere.

Acacias, which are known as wattles in their country of origin, must not be confused with the hardy False Acacias (robinia) which are often used for street planting in towns.

ACANTHUS (Bear's Breeches). Hardy herbaceous perennials. 3 to 5 ft. Purple and white flowers in late summer. All acanthus are grown as much for the beauty of their very large shining green, rather thistle-like leaves, as for their strange stiff spikes of dull purple and white flowers. They are very easy plants to grow, thriving in practically any soil and sunny or

Acanthus mollis

achillea

achimenes

acidanthera

partly shaded places. They throw up fresh plants from the roots and so can be easily increased by division—in fact, when plants are dug up new ones often appear spontaneously from broken roots left in the soil.

The two best kinds are the Soft Bear's Breeches, *Acanthus mollis*, with broadly-lobed leaves, and the Spiny Bear's Breeches, *A. spinosus*, with more deeply and sharply divided leaves.

ACHILLEA (Yarrow). Hardy herbaceous perennials and rock plants. Prostrate to 4 ft. White or yellow flowers in spring and summer. One of the commonest yarrows is a troublesome lawn weed, *Achillea millefolium*, but it has produced one or two forms with brightly coloured flowers which are worth growing in the herbaceous border. The best of these grows 18 in. high, has carmine flowers in summer and is known as Cerise Queen.

The Fernleaf Yarrow, *A. filipendulina*, has flat heads of yellow flowers, one of the best varieties being appropriately known as Gold Plate. This is a fine summer-flowering herbaceous plant growing about 4 ft. tall. Another with smaller flower heads produced all summer on 3-ft. stems is Coronation Gold. Still shorter are *A. taygetea* and a variety or hybrid of it named Moonshine. Both are 18 to 24 in. high, have ferny grey-green foliage and flat heads of primrose-yellow flowers for most of the summer but Moonshine is probably the better garden plant. Yet another distinctive kind, *A. ptarmica*, has white flowers which last well when cut, the best varieties being The Pearl and Perry's White. In both these the flowers are double, like little white buttons.

There are also some useful prostrate yarrows for the rock garden or dry wall, such as *A. tomentosa*, with flattish clusters of sulphur-yellow flowers all the summer, and *A. ageratifolia*, with finely divided silvery leaves and white flowers in summer.

Most of these yarrows are hardy, indestructible plants which will grow anywhere but the grey-leaved varieties like well-drained soil and sunny places. All can be increased by pulling the clumps apart in spring or autumn.

ACHIMENES (Hot Water Plant). Tender perennials. Trailing or to 1 ft. White, pink, red, purple or violet flowers from June to September. Achimenes get their popular name because some people think they like to be watered with hot water. In fact, they will thrive with the ordinary treatment given to rather tender greenhouse plants—a temperature of at least 16°C. (60°F.) while they are growing and fairly frequent watering with water at about greenhouse temperature. Achimenes make small tuberous roots which can be stored dry in a frostproof place in winter and can be repotted and started into growth in successive batches from January to May. The stems are rather weak and the flowers, which are produced continuously for several months, are brightly coloured. These plants are often grown in hanging baskets but are equally happy in pots. They can be raised from seed sown in a well-warmed greenhouse in spring or they can be increased by separating the tubers in late winter and spring.

ACIDANTHERA. Half-hardy corm. 3 ft. White and maroon flowers from August to September. This beautiful plant, with white maroon-blotched, sweetly-scented flowers, is closely related to the gladiolus and requires similar treatment. The corms are planted in April or May to a depth of 3 in. in well-drained soil and a warm sheltered position. Acidantheras need to be watered well in dry weather. In early November the corms should be lifted and stored in a dry, cool but frostproof place until Eastertime when they can be replanted.

ACONITUM (Monkshood). Hardy herbaceous perennials. 3 to 6 ft. Purple, blue or yellow, sometimes with white, flowers from July to September. The popular name refers to the hooded flowers which look a little like the cowls sometimes worn by monks. All monkshoods are hardy herbaceous plants and most have blue or purple flowers, though there is one which is yellow and some which are splashed with white. The flowers are borne in long narrow spikes a little like those of a delphinium.

One of the best garden monkshoods is known as Spark's Variety and is a particularly deep purple form of the Common Monkshood, *Aconitum napellus*. Bressingham Spire is an improved variety about 3 ft. high with closely set violet-blue flowers in July and August. Another fine plant, flowering late in the summer and with lighter blue flowers, is *A. fischeri*. *A. wilsonii* is one of the tallest and latest, 6 ft. and September to October flowering.

All will grow in any ordinary but not dry soil and sunny or partly shady position. Increase is by division of the roots in spring or autumn or by seed sown in spring.

aconitum

AETHIONEMA (Stone Cress). Rock plants. 6 to 12 in. Pink flowers from May to June. These are really tiny shrubs, but they are so small and slender that one always thinks of them as plants of the rock garden or dry wall. In time they will make foot-wide mounds of slender stems and narrow leaves surmounted in spring by clusters of small pink flowers. One of the finest varieties is known as Warley Rose, which is neater in habit than most and has brighter pink flowers. This variety must be raised from cuttings inserted in a frame or propagating box in July, but most stone cresses can be easily raised from seed sown in spring. All like rather light well-drained soils and sunny places.

AGAPANTHUS (African Lily). Fleshy-rooted perennials. 2 to 5 ft. Blue or white flowers throughout the summer. *Agapanthus africanus* is the blue clustered 'lily'—it is not really a lily at all—that is so frequently grown in tubs or large ornamental vases for summer decoration in the garden. It can equally well be grown as a greenhouse pot plant but it requires a large pot, or better still a tub, as it makes a big clump with masses of fleshy roots. There is a white-flowered variety.

Another kind, *A. mooreanus*, can be grown out of doors where frosts are not severe or prolonged. The Headbourne Hybrids are also hardy and have flowers in various shades from white to deep blue-violet.

All African lilies like sun and well-drained soils. They can be increased very readily by dividing the roots in spring or from seed sown in spring, though it will be several years before seedlings make big flowering plants.

Aethionema grandiflorum

AGERATUM. Half-hardy annuals. 6 to 18 in. Blue, purple or white flowers throughout the summer. This is one of the most popular of dwarf summer bedding plants and a particular favourite for edging beds. It has masses of small fluffy-looking, pale blue, lavender, purple or white flowers and keeps on producing them all the summer. There is also a taller kind, up to 18 in. high, with flowers in a similar range of colours.

Ageratum is best grown as a half-hardy annual, seed being sown in a greenhouse or frame, temperature 15 to 18°C. (59 to 65°F.), in March and the seedlings planted out in late May where they are to flower. For a really good display, space dwarf varieties 6 in. apart and the tall kind 9 in. They will grow practically anywhere.

AGROSTEMMA (Corn Cockle). Hardy annual. 3 to 4 ft. Mauve flowers in July and August. The variety commonly grown is Milas. It has slender but wiry stems bearing flowers rather like mauve pinks or single carnations and it is first class for cutting. Seed can be sown out of doors in spring or late summer where the plants are to flower. The soil should be well drained and the position sunny. Thin the seedlings 6 to 9 in. apart.

AJUGA (Bugle). Hardy herbaceous perennials. 3 to 12 in. Purple flowers in May and June. *Ajuga reptans* is a native British plant, creeping in habit with green leaves spread flat on the soil and little spikes of purple

agapanthus

Allium ostrowskianum

flowers. It is varieties of this rather than the common form that are cultivated as ground cover or in rock gardens. *A. r. atropurpurea* has bronzy-purple leaves, Rainbow (or *multicolor*) combines bronze, purple, pink and yellow, and *variegata* is green and cream. Another kind, *A. pyramidalis*, has dark green leaves and purple flowers.

All will grow readily in most soils, in sun or shade, and can be increased by division at almost any time.

ALLIUM (Ornamental Onion). Hardy bulbs. 9 in. to 4 ft. White, yellow, purple or blue flowers from March to August. Though the kitchen garden onion has little decorative value there are numerous ornamental onions. Notable are *Allium moly*, with roundish heads of buttercup-yellow flowers on 1-ft. high stems in May, and *A. rosenbachianum*, which has much larger globular heads of purplish flowers carried on 3- to 4-ft. stems in May. Both are perfectly hardy and are easily grown, in fact, *A. moly* often makes itself so much at home that self-sown seedlings soon appear.

Other good kinds are *A. albopilosum* with large globular heads of lilac flowers on 2-ft. stems in June; *A. caeruleum* with slender 2-ft. stems bearing small heads of blue flowers in June and July; *A. giganteum*, 4 ft. high, with big globular heads of mauve flowers also in June and July; *A. karataviense*, 8 in. high, with very handsome blue-green and bronzy-red leaves and nearly white flowers in May and June; *A. neapolitanum* with loose clusters of white flowers on 12-in. stems from March to May, and *A. ostrowskianum* with heads of pink flowers on 9-in. stems in May and June.

Alliums thrive in ordinary soil and most prefer a sunny position though *A. moly* will grow in shade. Increase by separating the bulb clusters in September and October, which is also the best planting season.

Allium neapolitanum

ALSTROEMERIA (Peruvian Lily). Herbaceous perennials, hardy or nearly so. 3 ft. Orange, pink, apricot or flame flowers in July. These are neither true lilies nor have they bulbs. Their roots are thickened and fleshy and need to be planted at least 5 in. deep in good, well-drained soils and warm, sunny places. The flowers are carried in loose heads and are bright orange in *Alstroemeria aurantiaca* and various shades of pink, salmon, apricot and flame in the Ligtu Hybrids.

All the Peruvian lilies can be raised from seed sown in a greenhouse or frame in spring, but it is sometimes a little difficult to transplant the Ligtu Hybrid seedlings successfully to the open ground. Perhaps the best method is to sow two or three seeds in a 3-in. pot, let the seedlings grow in this for the first year and transplant the whole potful the following March. Peruvian lilies like warmth, sunshine and good drainage. They are excellent for cutting.

althaea

ALTHAEA (Hollyhock). Hardy herbaceous perennials, biennials and annuals. 5 to 8 ft. White, pink, mauve, red, crimson and yellow flowers in July and August. The Hollyhock is botanically named *Althaea rosea*. Though this is a perennial it is often grown as a biennial, that is to say it is raised from seed sown one year, flowers the next year and is then thrown away. This is because older plants are often killed in winter by a combination of wet and cold. In well-drained sandy or gravelly soils they are more permanent, though seldom long lived. They like sunny places.

Seed is sown in May out of doors and seedlings are transplanted to their flowering quarters in autumn. There are double-flowered as well as single-flowered varieties in a wide range of colours and usually 7 or 8 ft. tall, though there are varieties which can be grown as annuals and these are shorter, usually about 5 ft. Seed of these annual varieties can be sown in a cool or intermediate greenhouse in February or March and hardened off for planting out in May. Alternatively, they can be sown outdoors in early April.

Another species, the Fig-leaved Hollyhock, *A. ficifolia*, is similar in habit but has deeply lobed leaves. It is less susceptible to rust disease than the common hollyhock and has been used in the breeding of rust-resistant strains.

Where this disease is troublesome such varieties should be grown and plants should be sprayed occasionally with a copper fungicide.

ALYSSUM. Hardy annuals and herbaceous perennials. 4 to 12 in. White, purple or yellow flowers from May to September. The two most popular alyssums are very different plants. The Sweet Alyssum, *Alyssum maritimum*, is a low-growing annual with white or purple scented flowers produced during summer. It is a favourite edging plant, often used with blue lobelia, and it is raised from seed sown in April or early May where the plants are to flower. Alternatively, seed may be sown in a greenhouse in early March, the seedlings being pricked out into boxes in April and planted out in May.

The other common kind, *A. saxatile*, is a perennial with golden-yellow flowers (lemon in the variety *citrinum*) in spring. It is often known as Gold Dust or Yellow Alyssum. This plant likes a sunny rock garden or wall, or it may be planted at the front of a border. Single-flowered varieties can be raised from seed sown out of doors in May, the seedlings flowering the following year, but the double-flowered variety, which makes an even better display, must be grown from cuttings rooted in spring in a frame.

Alyssum saxatile

AMARANTHUS (Love-lies-bleeding, Prince's Feather, Joseph's Coat). Hardy and half-hardy annuals. 2 to 4 ft. Red, crimson or lime-green flowers in July and August. There are several quite different kinds of amaranthus, two grown for their flowers and one for foliage. *Amaranthus caudatus* is probably better known as Love-lies-bleeding, a remarkably decorative hardy annual 2 to 3 ft. high with long tassel-like trails of crimson or lime-green flowers. It is sometimes called the Tassel Flower. A second kind, *A. hypochondriacus*, or Prince's Feather, has similar tiny crimson flowers but arranged in erect much-branched spikes. It grows from 2 to 4 ft. tall. Both these kinds can be raised from seed sown out of doors in spring where the plants are to flower, seedlings being thinned out to 9 to 12 in. apart. Alternatively, seed can be sown in a greenhouse or frame and seedlings pricked out into boxes or potted singly for planting out in May or June after proper hardening off. Plants enjoy good soil and a sunny place.

The third kind, *A. tricolor*, or Joseph's Coat, is grown for its green, red and yellow leaves. It is a half-hardy annual to be raised from seed sown in spring in a temperature of 15 to 18°C. (59 to 65°F.). Seedlings are potted singly in not too rich soil—JIP.1 is ideal—and can be moved on to 4-in. pots as they get larger or be planted out of doors in June.

amaryllis

AMARYLLIS (Belladonna Lily, Jersey Lily). Half-hardy bulbs. 1½ to 2 ft. Pink or white flowers in September and October. Although the Belladonna or Jersey Lily, *Amaryllis belladonna*, is not a true lily, the pink or white flowers are trumpet shaped like those of many lilies and the plant makes large bulbs. Amaryllis should be given a warm sunny position near the foot of a wall and the bulbs should be only just covered with soil since deep planting can check flowering. However, in cold places the bulbs should be further protected from November to March with a good covering of sand, peat or leafmould. Alternatively, bulbs can be grown in fairly large pots in JIP.2 compost. If pot grown, no water should be given from June to about mid-August, and during this period of rest and ripening the plants should be stood in the warmest, sunniest place available.

The Belladonna Lily likes well-drained but fairly rich soil and should be disturbed as little as possible. The very fragrant flowers are produced in early autumn before the leaves.

AMELANCHIER (Snowy Mespilus). Hardy deciduous trees or shrubs. 8 to 25 ft. White flowers in April and May. One of the best kinds for general planting is *Amelanchier laevis* which eventually makes a shapely, round-headed tree 20 to 25 ft. high. It flowers in April or early May and requires no pruning. *A. canadensis* is shorter and more shrub like, usually 10 to 15 ft. high and with similar flowers to those of *A. laevis*. The two kinds

amelanchier

Anchusa italica

have been much confused and *A. laevis* may be listed in catalogues as *A. canadensis*. Both succeed best in well-drained but not dry soils and open sunny places. The foliage usually colours brilliantly in autumn. Increase is by seed sown in a frame or out of doors in spring.

ANAGALLIS (Pimpernel). Half-hardy annuals. 6 to 8 in. Blue or red flowers from June to August.. The cultivated pimpernels are all varieties of *Anagallis linifolia*, a sprawling plant with small but brilliantly coloured blue or scarlet flowers. It makes an effective edging or ground cover.

Seed should be sown in spring in a temperature of 15 to 18°C. (59 to 65°F.), seedlings being pricked out into boxes and hardened off for planting out of doors in late May or June. Plant about 6 in. apart in well-drained soil and a sunny position.

ANCHUSA (Alkanet). Hardy herbaceous perennials. 1 to 5 ft. Blue flowers from May to June. All the anchusas have blue flowers rather like forget-me-nots though often much larger. The giant of the family is the Italian Alkanet, *Anchusa italica* (or *azurea*), which grows 3 to 5 ft. high and has flowers 1 in. across. There are numerous garden varieties of this differing in height and the precise shade of blue. A much smaller plant, only about 1 ft. high and suitable for the front of a border, is *A. angustissima* (sometimes erroneously named *caespitosa*). The flowers are in scale with the plant, intensely blue and freely produced in May and June.

All anchusas like sun and well-drained soils and can be raised from seed, but good forms of the Italian Alkanet are usually increased by root cuttings in a frame or greenhouse in winter as seedlings may vary a little in colour. *A. angustissima* can be divided in spring.

ANDROSACE (Rock Jasmine). Rock plants. 2 to 6 in. Pink or white flowers in June and July. Androsaces are delightful alpines, some trailing, some cushion forming, but all have neat, rounded, pink or white flowers like pieces of confetti. They like sun and sharp drainage, and are never so happy as when sprawling over the face of a terrace wall or hugging close to a boulder in the rock garden. Two of the best for general planting are *Androsace lanuginosa*, a trailing plant, and *A. sarmentosa*, which increases its soft hummocks of growth by pushing out small runners in all directions. Both flower in June and July and can be increased by division in spring.

Androsace sarmentosa

ANEMONE (Windflower). Hardy herbaceous perennials, some with tuberous roots. 4 in. to 4 ft. Flowers in all colours occurring in all seasons. This is one of those families of plants that can be confusing because it is so big and contains so many members totally unlike one another except to the trained eye of the botanist. At one extreme is our own native Wood Anemone, *Anemone nemorosa*, a lowly but lovely plant which carpets woodlands in spring with its finely-divided leaves and fragile, white (or very pale blue) flowers; at the other is the Japanese Anemone (it may be called *A. elegans*, *A. hupehensis* or *A. japonica*) which flaunts its white to rose-pink flowers in September on stems 2 to 4 ft. high according to variety. These Japanese anemones have rather tough fibrous roots, do not really like being disturbed and so are best planted where they can be left to spread for years. They will grow in most soils in sun or shade and are increased by division in spring.

The Wood Anemone makes little tubers which are often sold dry in early autumn as are the tubers of *A. apennina* and *A. blanda*, two very similar low-growing plants producing fragile, blue, pink, white or white and rose flowers in March and April. All will grow in shade but *A. apennina* and *A. blanda* flower most freely in a more open situation than the Wood Anemone. All should be planted 2 in. deep and a few inches apart and can be left alone for years.

The Flame Anemone, *A. fulgens*, with much larger scarlet flowers on 12-in. stems in spring, is planted in a similar manner but must have a sunny place.

Anemone japonica

This is also best for the Poppy Anemone, *A. coronaria*, of which there are several strains, some with single and some with double flowers on 18-in. stems and in a variety of shades of pink, red, blue and purple, occasionally with white. These are first-class plants for cutting and by varying the time of planting—putting in some tubers in the autumn and some in the spring—the flowering season can be extended from spring to early summer. This anemone can also be grown from seed sown out of doors in May or June when the seedlings will flower the following spring if left undisturbed. Either way it is customary to lift poppy anemones every year (about August) and replant as required, storing them dry in a frostproof place if some are to be kept until the spring.

Anemone blanda

ANGELICA. Hardy biennial. 4 to 5 ft. Greenish-white flowers in summer. This is grown both as a herb—the stems and leaf stalks to be candied and used as edible decorations for cakes—and as a handsome plant with fine leaves and big flat heads of small greenish-white flowers. It is a biennial which dies after ripening its seed, but it often grows freely from self-sown seedlings and then all that is necessary is to thin out or transplant the seedlings about 1 ft. apart. To make a start sow seed out of doors in April or May in good soil and an open situation and thin the seedlings well. The young plants can be transplanted, if necessary, in early autumn or spring.

Anemone apennina

ANTHEMIS (Chamomile, Golden Marguerite). Hardy herbaceous perennials. 9 in. to 3 ft. White or yellow flowers from May to September. All anthemis have finely-divided, strongly aromatic leaves and one, *Anthemis nobilis*, the Chamomile, is occasionally planted thickly and clipped to make a fragrant lawn. It is readily raised from seed sown out of doors in spring. This species has white flowers which are double in the variety *A. n. flore pleno*. Another kind, *A. cupaniana*, is grown for its ferny grey leaves and large white daisy flowers in May and June. It is a sprawling plant about 9 in. high.

There are several good varieties of *A. tinctoria*, a bushy plant 2 to 3 ft. high producing yellow daisy flowers on long stems during most of the summer, E. C. Buxton and Wargrave are pale yellow, Loddon and Grallagh Gold are deep yellow. *A. sancti-johannis* is very similar with deep yellow flowers.

Anthemis enjoy light, well-drained soils and warm, sunny places and may prove impermanent in wet, cold gardens. All varieties are easily increased by cuttings in late summer, and if a few cuttings are rooted in a frame or greenhouse each year and over-wintered under glass they will provide replacements against possible losses.

Anthemis tinctoria

ANTHERICUM (St Bernard's Lily). Hardy herbaceous perennials. 1½ to 2 ft. White flowers from May to August. These are not really lilies though they do look rather like them with their grassy leaves and slender stems carrying starry white flowers from May to August according to variety. The two kinds usually grown are *Anthericum liliago*, which is early flowering and *A. ramosum*, which is later. Both are herbaceous plants of great elegance, not fussy about soil but liking an open situation. They can be easily increased by division in spring or summer.

ANTIRRHINUM (Snapdragon). Half-hardy herbaceous perennials usually grown as half-hardy annuals. 6 in. to 3 ft. Flowers in all colours except blues and purples and occurring from June to September. The antirrhinums are among the most popular of all summer bedding plants that can be raised easily from seed. The popular name snapdragon refers to the peculiar pouched flowers which can be opened like mouths if they are pinched at the sides, though the penstemon-flowered and double varieties have lost this characteristic. There are dwarf, medium and tall varieties from 6 in. to 3 ft. in height, and with flowers in a wide colour range, including some very bright shades of scarlet and flame as well as pink, yellow, apricot, orange and white.

antirrhinum

Aponogeton distachyus

aquilegia

Arabis albida
flore pleno

arctotis

Antirrhinum seed is usually sown in a greenhouse or frame, temperature 15 to 18°C. (59 to 65°F.), in January or February, the seedlings being pricked out into boxes in March or early April and gradually hardened off for planting out in May. Alternatively, seed sown in September will give seedlings that can be over-wintered in an unheated frame and planted out in April. Antirrhinums succeed best in a sunny, open place and a well-drained soil. If rust disease is troublesome, as it may be in hot, dry places, plants should be sprayed frequently with thiram or a proprietary copper fungicide.

APONOGETON (Water Hawthorn). Hardy herbaceous perennials for pools. Floating. White flowers from April to October. *Aponogeton distachyus* is an easily grown water plant with narrow floating leaves and short spikes of scented white flowers that project above the water. It will grow in water from about 6 in. to 2 ft. deep and can be planted in a mound of good loamy soil on the bottom of the pool or in a soil-filled basket sunk in the pool. There are few water plants that have such an extended flowering season.

Plants can be increased by division in late spring or early summer.

AQUILEGIA (Columbine). Hardy herbaceous perennials. 1 to 3 ft. Flowers in all colours from May to June. The most popular aquilegias are the Long-spurred Hybrids. These are exquisitely graceful flowers, with long, nectar-filled spurs which add to their charm. By contrast, the old-fashioned Columbine, *Aquilegia vulgaris*, has short-spurred flowers which may be single or double.

All aquilegias are hardy herbaceous perennials, though often they are not very long lived. However, they can be raised very easily from seed sown out of doors in spring or summer and frequently appear in great numbers as self-sown seedlings around old plants. Colours are varied and usually delicate, though there are quite strong blues and reds. As a rule, mixed colour strains are grown, two of the best known being the Mrs Scott Elliott Hybrids and McKana Giant Hybrids. All will grow in sun or partial shade and are not fussy about soil provided it is not badly drained.

ARABIS (Rock Cress). Hardy herbaceous perennials. Trailing. White or pink flowers from March to May. *Arabis albida* is one of the most popular of all white-flowered trailing plants. It flowers in spring and makes a first-rate companion for the blue or pink aubrietas when grown on sunny walls, rock gardens or banks. There is a double-flowered variety which is even more effective than the more common single. The single can be raised from seed sown in a frame in spring but the double produces no seed and must be raised from cuttings taken in May or June. There is also a pink-flowered variety and another with white flowers and cream-variegated leaves.

ARCTOTIS (African Daisy). Half-hardy annuals. 1 to 2 ft. White, yellow, orange, red or purple flowers from June to August. These are some of the loveliest of South African daisies, mostly with long stems which make them useful for cutting. Almost all the best-known kinds are treated as half-hardy annuals and are raised each year from seed which is sown in a greenhouse or frame, temperature 15 to 18°C. (59 to 65°F.), in March, the seedlings being pricked out into boxes early in April and planted out of doors in a sunny place and rather porous soil in May.

Arctotis grandis has flowers which are silvery white above and very pale blue beneath. There are also hybrid strains with flowers of various colours.

ARENARIA (Sandwort). Hardy herbaceous perennials. Prostrate to 9 in. White flowers from May to July. Most arenarias are grown for their close carpets or hummocks of tiny green or golden leaves rather than for their starry white flowers, but one kind, *Arenaria montana*, has quite large white flowers freely produced on trailing stems. This is a really good plant for a sunny rock garden or bank in any reasonably well-drained soil. Like other arenarias it can be readily increased by division in the spring.

ARMERIA (Thrift). Hardy herbaceous perennials. 2 to 18 in. Pink, crimson or white flowers in May and June. The thrifts are tufted plants with narrow grass-like leaves and heads of small flowers. The Common Thrift, *Armeria maritima*, is a seaside plant found in stony places and with stems no more than 6 in. high. It flowers in spring and has red and white flowered varieties as well as the familiar rather pale pink form. It is admirable for a sunny place in the rock garden and will survive in quite stony dry places.

A much bigger plant, known as Bees' Ruby, is useful for the front of the herbaceous border and carries its heads of carmine flowers on 18-in. stems in May and June. The smallest armeria is *A. caespitosa*, the very pale pink flower clusters of which sit closely on the tuft of grassy leaves. It is a rock garden plant for particularly sunny, well-drained places. All can be increased by division in spring.

Armeria caespitosa

ARTEMISIA. Hardy herbaceous or semi-shrubby plants. 1 to 5 ft. White or greenish flowers from July to September and often with silvery leaves. There are a great many artemisias with numerous popular names and in general they are a rather confused and unattractive lot. But there are notable exceptions and some of the best grey-leaved plants are among them. The names of these are apt to be unreliable and it is advisable to choose them at the nursery whenever possible. Most are 1 to 2 ft. high and are perennials preferring sunny places and well-drained soils.

Kinds to look for are *Artemisia absinthium*, 2 to 3 ft. with ferny foliage; *A. ludoviciana*, 2 ft. and narrow leaves; *A. schmidtiana nana*, 6 in. with lacy foliage and *A. stelleriana*, 2 to 3 ft. and silvery leaves. A much taller and very different plant is *A. lactiflora* which has green leaves and elegant sprays of small creamy-white flowers in August and grows 5 ft. tall. It is an excellent border plant.

Most can be increased by division in spring but some are more shrubs than herbaceous plants and must be increased by cuttings in early summer.

Armeria maritima

ARUNCUS (Goat's Beard). Hardy herbaceous perennials. 5 to 6 ft. Creamy-white flowers in June and July. The only kind grown, *Aruncus sylvester*, has finely-divided leaves and great plumes of tiny creamy-white flowers, like those of an astilbe, in June and July. It is sometimes listed as *Spiraea aruncus*.

Aruncus grows 5 or 6 ft. high and will thrive almost anywhere in sun or shade. It can be easily increased by division in spring or autumn and also by seed and is sometimes spread in the garden by self-sown seedlings.

ASTER, PERENNIAL (Michaelmas Daisy). Hardy herbaceous perennials. 9 in. to 6 ft. Blue, purple, pink, crimson or white flowers from June to October. The perennials which gardeners call Michaelmas daisies are mostly varieties of two North American perennial asters. The garden varieties produced from these vary greatly in character from very dwarf plants like Audrey, mauve, and Margaret Rose, pink, which can be used to edge the herbaceous border, to tall plants like Climax mauve, Marie Ballard, blue and Ernest Ballard, rose, for the middle or back of the border. Some have double flowers, some single. The main flowering season is in September, but the Amellus varieties, which are of quite different origin having been developed from a European aster, flower a month earlier, and are all single flowered and usually about 18 in. high. King George is the most popular of these and has large blue flowers. *Aster frikartii* is very similar to the last and one of the best of this type of Michaelmas daisy.

Other useful kinds are *A. acris* with close-packed clusters of small starry blue flowers in August and September, the whole plant being about 3 ft. in height; *A. alpinus*, a much shorter plant with quite large purple, pink or white flowers borne singly on 9-in. stems in July; *A. subcaeruleus*, not unlike the last with purplish-blue flowers in June and *A. linosyris*, sometimes listed as Goldilocks, with packed clusters of small yellow flowers on 2-ft. stems in September. Botanists do not agree that this last plant is really an aster, some

Aster alpinus

astilbe

aubrieta

Azalea indica

saying that its correct name is *Linosyris vulgaris* and others that it should be *Crinitaria linosyris* and it may be listed in catalogues under any of these names.

There is similar confusion over another plant often sold as *Aster hybridus luteus* but correctly named *Solidaster luteus*, under which name it is also sold. It is a showy plant, 2 to 3 ft. high, producing masses of small yellow daisy flowers in August to September.

All asters are easily grown in almost any soil and can be increased by division. With many of the new large-flowered varieties it pays to divide the plants every spring. This treatment does not suit the Amellus varieties or *A. frikartii* which are best left undisturbed for several years and should then be moved in spring only, as losses may follow autumn planting.

ASTILBE. Hardy herbaceous perennials. 6 in. to 3 ft. White, pink and crimson flowers in June and July. These plants are sometimes wrongly called spiraeas in gardens but the true spiraeas are shrubs. The astilbes die down to ground level each winter, throw up a fresh lot of ferny leaves in spring and quickly follow up with feathery plumes of flowers which may be white, pink or crimson. They like damp soil and are often grown at the waterside, though they can be planted in ordinary beds or borders provided these are not too dry. They also make excellent pot plants, for which purpose strong roots are potted in autumn and kept in a frame or cool greenhouse for a month or so, after which they can be gently forced in a temperature of 15 to 18°C. (59 to 65°F.). They must be well watered.

The most popular varieties are garden raised hybrids with fancy names such as Gertrude Brix, crimson, Salmon Queen, pink, White Queen, white, and so on. All these are fairly tall plants but *Astilbe simplicifolia*, with pink flowers, is a wild Japanese plant only 6 in. high and suitable for the rock garden. The hybrids listed as *A. crispa* are almost as short and in various shades from white to rose. All astilbes are best increased by division of the roots in spring or autumn.

AUBRIETA. Hardy herbaceous perennial. Trailing. Purple, lavender, pink or crimson flowers from March to June. This is one of the most popular of spring-flowering trailing plants for sunny rock gardens or dry walls and is an excellent companion for white-flowered arabis and golden alyssum. The aubrieta is typically a plant with lavender-blue flowers but there are also pink, purple and crimson flowered varieties.

Plants can be easily raised from seed sown in spring in a frame or greenhouse but seedlings vary in colour. For this reason selected varieties are usually increased by cuttings of young shoots inserted in a frame about mid-summer. Aubrietas like sunny places and thrive best in soils containing lime or chalk, though there are few soils in which they cannot be grown successfully.

AZALEA. Hardy and half-hardy deciduous and evergreen shrubs. 2 to 8 ft. White, yellow, orange, red, pink and mauve flowers from December to June. All the plants known as azaleas are, in fact, rhododendrons and they need the same lime-free (or chalk-free) soils as the rest of the rhododendrons. They will thrive in sun or partial shade.

There are two quite distinct types of azalea—the evergreen varieties and those that lose their leaves in winter. The evergreens are further subdivided into two groups, one of which, often known as the Indian Azalea, requires greenhouse protection in winter, whereas the other is hardy enough to be grown out of doors. The popular Kurume azaleas from Japan are of this second group and are free-flowering shrubs, spreading in habit but not tall. The most usual varieties are pink, scarlet and magenta, but there are also mauve, lavender and white kinds. They flower in April and May.

The deciduous azaleas mostly flower a little later continuing into June, make larger and more open bushes and have bigger flowers, which are sometimes very fragrant. The colour range is largely in yellow, orange, red and pink. There is a great number of varieties available.

The greenhouse or Indian azaleas are compact shrubs with large double flowers. They make fine pot plants and are sold in great quantities by florists from Christmas until spring. They need greenhouse protection in winter but can be planted out of doors from May to October, during which period they must be freely watered and frequently syringed.

The evergreen azaleas can be raised from cuttings of firm young shoots rooted in a frame in July and so can the deciduous kinds, but with much more difficulty. As a rule these are raised from seed sown in peaty soil in a frame or greenhouse in spring. The seedlings usually start to flower in their third or fourth year and may vary in colour.

BARTONIA. Hardy annual. 2 ft. Yellow flowers from June to August. *Bartonia aurea*, more correctly known as *Mentzelia lindleyi*, is an easily grown annual with showy bright yellow flowers freely produced on well-branched plants about 2 ft. high. Seed should be sown in spring where the plants are to flower and seedlings thinned to about 9 in. apart. Bartonia likes well-drained soil and sunny places.

BEGONIA. Half-hardy and tender herbaceous perennials, some grown as half-hardy annuals. 6 in. to 3 ft. White, pink, red, yellow and orange flowers produced throughout the year. There are a great many different kinds of begonia, and no one system of cultivation can be applied to all, but they are fairly tender plants, certainly requiring greenhouse protection for part of the year—some kinds for the whole year round.

Very popular are the summer-flowering tuberous-rooted begonias usually with large double flowers in a variety of colours from pink to crimson, pale yellow to orange and white. The tubers can be stored dry in a frostproof place from autumn until late winter or early spring. In January, February or early March (according to the time at which they are required to flower) the tubers are put into shallow boxes filled with damp peat and are placed in a green-house with a temperature of 10°C. (50°F.) or more. When leaves appear the tubers are potted singly and may either be grown on to flower in 5- or 6-in. pots, or be planted out of doors in early June as summer bedding plants. If grown under glass all summer they should be shaded from May to September. Tuberous-rooted begonias can also be grown from seed sown in a greenhouse, temperature 15 to 18°C. (59 to 65°F.), between January and March but the seed is dust like and should not be covered except with a sheet of glass or polythene. The tuberous-rooted pendulous begonias are grown in just the same way except that, once started, they are placed in hanging baskets or in pots stood up on inverted pots, so that the plants can hang down.

The summer-flowering fibrous-rooted begonias are mainly grown from seed as bedding plants, though they can be used as pot plants and in a moderately heated greenhouse will continue to flower for most of the year. Seed is sown in February or early March in a temperature of 15 to 18°C. (59 to 65°F.), the seedlings are pricked out, hardened off and eventually planted out in early June after the danger from frost is over. Flowers are small, freely produced all summer and are white, pink or crimson. Some varieties have green and some bronze coloured leaves.

Winter-flowering fibrous-rooted begonias are rather similar in general appearance but make larger plants and flower under glass in December and January. They like a really warm greenhouse and are usually raised from cuttings taken after flowering.

Rex begonias have very large, handsomely-marked leaves. They are grown in fairly warm greenhouses, shaded in summer, and should be kept growing winter and summer. They are increased by dividing the fibrous roots in March, or by leaf cuttings taken in spring or summer.

Begonia rex

tuberous-rooted begonia

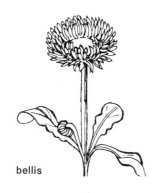
bellis

Beloperone guttata

Berberis
darwinii

BELLIS (Double Daisy). Hardy herbaceous perennials often grown as hardy biennials. 3 to 6 in. White to crimson flowers from March to May. The Common Daisy, *Bellis perennis*, which is such a troublesome weed of lawns, has produced numerous double-flowered varieties which are excellent garden plants. The smallest flowered is Dresden China, a delightful plant with rosebud-pink flowers. It can be used as an edging to beds and is increased by division at almost any time. The largest flowered types may be listed in seed catalogues as *Bellis monstrosa* or simply as Giant Red, Giant Pink or Giant White and are readily raised from seed sown out of doors in May or June. The plants are popular for spring bedding, sometimes as a carpet for taller flowers such as tulips, and are usually thrown away after flowering, though they can be split up, replanted and kept for further use if required.

BELOPERONE (Shrimp Plant). Tender herbaceous perennial. 1 to 2 ft. Pinkish-brown and white or yellowish-green flowers produced throughout the year. *Beloperone guttata* is known as the Shrimp Plant because of the colour and shape of its little curling spikes of flowers. It makes an excellent pot plant for the cool or intermediate greenhouse or for a sunny room. It can be grown in any reasonably good soil, such as JIP.1, and should be watered fairly freely from April to September, moderately from October to March and can be repotted when overcrowded in March. Increase is by cuttings in spring. When well grown this plant is seldom without flowers.

BERBERIS (Barberry). Hardy evergreen and deciduous shrubs. 2 to 10 ft. Yellow or orange flowers from April to June and coral, scarlet or purplish-black berries from September to November. This very large family includes some of the finest deciduous berry-bearing shrubs for the garden, several of the best flowering evergreens and also some excellent foliage shrubs. In the first category a typical variety is *Berberis wilsoniae*, which makes a dense spiny bush usually only 3 ft. high with yellow flowers in summer, followed by abundant coral-red berries. There are many other kinds, differing in height and habit.

The finest evergreens are *B. darwinii* and *B. stenophylla*. The first has tiny holly-like leaves and orange flowers in late April, and makes a big compact bush; the second, looser and more arching in habit, has narrow leaves and golden-yellow honey-scented flowers in early May. Both make large bushes eventually as much as 10 ft. high and through. *B. verruculosa*, with glossy green leaves and golden-yellow flowers, is much slower growing and usually not over 5 ft. and *B. candidula*, yet another evergreen berberis with yellow flowers, is around 3 ft. high when fully grown. It is, therefore, especially suitable for small gardens.

For foliage one of the best is the purple-leaved form of *B. thunbergii*, a spiny bush not unlike *B. wilsoniae* in style but with reddish leaves. It is deciduous and the green-leaved form often colours brilliantly before the leaves fall in the autumn.

All these barberries will grow in almost any soil and reasonably open place. They can be increased by seed, but cuttings taken in July are to be preferred for selected forms such as the purple-leaved variety. *B. stenophylla* can also be increased by division in November.

The mahonias are sometimes known as barberries, but are dealt with here under Mahonia.

BERGENIA (Large-leaved Saxifrage). Hardy herbaceous perennials. 1 to 1½ ft. Pink to carmine and also white flowers from March to May. These plants are sometimes called megasea and sometimes saxifrage. They differ from the true saxifrages in having very large leathery leaves, which are handsome enough to justify the plants being grown for this feature alone, and all produce clusters of flowers on thick stems very early in the year. Among the best kinds are *Bergenia cordifolia*, pink and its variety *purpurea*, reddish-purple; *B. crassifolia*, pink to purple with very large leaves; *B. ligulata*, white to carmine; *B. stracheyi*, pink and Silver Light, blush pink.

Bergenias are hardy herbaceous plants suitable for the front of the border and may be grown in practically any soil or place, even in shade. All can be increased by division in spring or autumn.

BILLBERGIA. Tender herbaceous perennials. 1½ ft. Green and pink flowers from June to August. *Billbergia nutans* is the most useful kind, an attractive pot plant for the cool or intermediate greenhouse or for a sunny room. It has long narrow leaves and slender arching flower stems bearing unusual nodding green and pink flowers.

This plant will grow well in JIP.1 or an equivalent compost and needs to be watered moderately from April to September, sparingly from October to March. Increase is by division in March or April which are also the best months for repotting overcrowded plants.

Billbergia nutans

BOUGAINVILLEA. Tender climber. Magenta, pink or orange flowers from July to September. Visitors to Mediterranean countries will be familiar with the bougainvillea draping walls with its vivid magenta 'flowers', which are, in fact, not true flowers but coloured bracts surrounding the quite insignificant flowers. It will thrive in a cool greenhouse either planted in large pots or tubs in a compost such as JIP.2 or, a better way, planted in a bed of good soil on the greenhouse floor. Either way it should have the sunniest place possible and plenty of room to climb on wires strained a few inches below the rafters. Plants should be watered freely in spring and summer, moderately in autumn and scarcely at all in December and January. In March all weak shoots should be cut out and others shortened to within a few inches of the main vines.

There are a number of garden varieties or hybrids, one with white-variegated leaves, another, Mrs Butt, with pink bracts, yet others, such as Orange King, with orange bracts. These are probably better for pot cultivation than the common magenta variety.

bougainvillea

BRACHYCOME (Swan River Daisy). Half-hardy annual. 1 ft. Blue, pink or white flowers from June to August. This delightful little Australian annual has finely-divided leaves and dainty blue, pink or white daisy flowers produced all summer on a compact plant. It is not fully hardy, so seed should be sown in a greenhouse or frame, temperature 15 to 18°C. (59 to 65°F.), in March, seedlings being pricked out and hardened off for planting out of doors in late May or early June. Alternatively, seed may be sown in early May out of doors where the plants are to flower. In either case they should have a sunny place, preferably in light well-drained soil.

BRODIAEA (Spring Star Flower). Moderately hardy bulbs. 8 in. Blue flowers in April and May. The kind usually grown is *Brodiaea uniflora*, but it is sometimes listed under other names such as ipheion, milla and triteleia which can be confusing. It is a pretty little plant with grassy leaves and starry pale blue flowers carried singly on slender stems. It enjoys a sunny place and well-drained soil and is a suitable plant for the rock garden or the front of a sheltered bed. Brodiaea is a native of Australia, can be killed by heavy frost and so is not recommended for areas where frosts are severe or prolonged.

The bulbs should be planted in September or October, 2 in. deep, and the plants can be left undisturbed for years. When overcrowded, lift and divide the bulb clusters in August or September.

Browallia speciosa

BROWALLIA. Tender annual. 1 to 1½ ft. Blue or white flowers from July to December. The kind usually grown, *Browallia speciosa major*, has large bright blue flowers and makes an excellent pot plant for a cool or intermediate greenhouse. There is also a white-flowered variety. Another kind sometimes grown is *B. viscosa* with blue white-eyed flowers.

If seed is sown in February or March plants will flower from July to September and if it is sown in May or June they will flower in the autumn.

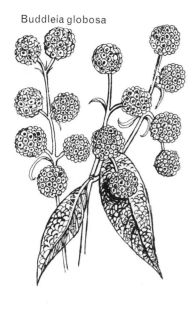
Buddleia globosa

Seedlings should be potted singly in 4-in. pots in JIP.1 or equivalent compost and the tips of the young shoots should be pinched out occasionally to make plants more bushy. Water fairly freely throughout.

BUDDLEIA (Butterfly Bush). Hardy deciduous shrubs. 6 to 12 ft. Lavender, purple, orange or white flowers from May to August. The most popular kind is *Buddleia davidii*, sometimes known as the Butterfly Bush because it attracts butterflies when it is in bloom in late summer. It is an easily grown deciduous shrub which often produces self-sown seedlings freely. The colour varies from pale lavender to deep reddish-purple and there are also white-flowered forms. All can be pruned hard back each March if space is limited or large flower spikes are required but such pruning is not essential.

Another kind, *B. alternifolia*, is a more graceful but less showy shrub, with long slender arching stems wreathed in small lavender flowers in June. *B. globosa*, often known as the Orange Ball Tree, produces its orange-yellow flowers in small clusters in June.

Buddleias are quick-growing shrubs. They are not at all fussy about soil and *B. davidii* succeeds very well on chalk. All are raised from seed sown in spring or by cuttings in early autumn.

BUTOMUS (Flowering Rush). Hardy herbaceous water plant. 3 ft. Pink flowers from July to September. *Butomus umbellatus* is found growing wild in the shallow water at the edges of lakes and slow-moving streams in some parts of Britain and is a handsome plant for the garden pool. It has rush-like leaves and stiff flower stems surmounted by heads of pink flowers.

Butomus is perfectly hardy, grows best in a 2- or 3-in. depth of water in good loamy soil. Plant in May and leave undisturbed until overcrowded when it can be lifted, divided and replanted, also in May.

Butomus umbellatus

CALCEOLARIA. Hardy and tender herbaceous plants and half-hardy semi-shrubs. 3 in. to 2 ft. Yellow, orange, red or crimson flowers from April to September. The curiously pouched and often rather luridly coloured flowers of these plants never fail to attract attention. Nowadays the most familiar are the large-flowered greenhouse varieties derived from *Calceolaria crenatiflora*, but years ago the small-flowered nearly hardy kinds derived from the shrubby calceolaria, *C. integrifolia* (sometimes listed as *C. rugosa*), were quite as popular and were used in summer bedding schemes almost as freely as geraniums and marguerites. There are two principal varieties of this plant, one with yellow, the other with chestnut-red flowers. Both can be easily increased by cuttings in August or September and should be over-wintered in a frame, though in the milder parts where frosts are not severe or prolonged plants may survive for years out of doors if planted in a sunny, sheltered place.

The greenhouse calceolarias are treated as biennials and are raised from seed each year. Seed is sown in June or July, the seedlings are pricked out into boxes and later potted singly, first into small pots, but finally, early in March, into 5-in. (or bigger) pots in which they will flower in April and May. Throughout they need cool greenhouse treatment, plenty of ventilation except in cold weather, an average temperature of 10°C. (50°F.) or a little more, and careful watering. Particular care should be taken to prevent water lodging at the base of large leaves where it may cause decay. There are numerous strains differing in height, habit and size of bloom. The Multiflora varieties have medium-size flowers on plants about 1 ft. high, the Giant-

calceolaria

flowered or Grandiflora varieties have very large flowers on plants about 18 in. high. There are also dwarf varieties little more than 6 in. high.

In addition, there are one or two small hardy herbaceous calceolarias suitable for cool shady places out of doors. Two of the best of these are *C. darwinii*, only 3 in. high with quite large yellow and chestnut-red flowers, and *C. polyrrhiza*, 6 in. with yellow, purple-spotted flowers. Both flower in summer, need plenty of leafmould or peat and protection from slugs in winter. They are not the easiest plants to grow.

calendula

CALENDULA (Pot Marigold). Hardy annual. 1½ to 2 ft. Yellow or orange flowers from June to September. This familiar orange 'daisy' is often referred to simply as a marigold, but it is less confusing to use its proper name, calendula, to distinguish it from the African and French marigolds which are not only very different in appearance but need different treatment in the garden. These are described under Tagetes.

The calendula is one of the hardiest of annuals; a plant that once admitted to the garden is likely to reproduce itself year after year from self-sown seed. This will germinate equally well in spring or autumn, the only difference in results being that the autumn seedlings start to bloom earlier. However, for best results, self-sown seedlings should be discouraged and a fresh start made each year from good purchased seed or seed carefully selected from flowers of good quality. There are yellow as well as orange varieties and the best have fully double flowers with either broad and flat or quilled petals. Seedlings should be thinned to 9 in. and plants discarded after flowering before they start to distribute their ripe seed.

CALLISTEPHUS (Annual Asters). Half-hardy annuals. 1 to 2 ft. Flowers of all colours from July to September. Correctly, the showy annuals which most gardeners know as asters are callistephus to the botanists, and the botanists' asters are what gardeners call Michaelmas daisies.

There are a great many varieties of callistephus, some with single, some with double flowers. The doubles are further subdivided according to the character of their flowers, the very shaggy, narrow-petalled kinds being known as Ostrich Plume Asters, the neater and broader-petalled kinds as Comet Asters. There are also miniatures as well as varieties with very compact flowers. All are raised from seed sown in a greenhouse or frame in March or out of doors in April or May. Greenhouse-raised seedlings are pricked out into boxes and hardened off for planting out in May. Seedlings from outdoor sowings are usually thinned to about 9 in. apart and left to grow where they are without the check of transplanting. The single-flowered varieties are best for outdoor sowing and these will also tolerate some shade, but in general annual asters like open places. They are not fussy about soil. Almost all make excellent cut flowers.

Caltha palustris

CALTHA (Marsh Marigold, Kingcup). Hardy herbaceous perennial. 1 to 2 ft. Yellow flowers in April and May. This lovely waterside plant is also known as Kingcup. Its buttercup-like flowers and shining green leaves may often be seen in spring in damp meadows or beside streams in Britain. Even this common wild form, *Caltha palustris*, is worth transplanting to the garden, but there are others much more desirable including one with fully double flowers like golden pompons—*C. p. flore-pleno*. A Russian species, *C. polypetala*, has extra large single flowers and is a strong-growing plant about 2 ft. high.

All calthas are easily increased by division and should be planted in wet but reasonably open places.

CAMASSIA. Hardy bulbs. 2 to 3 ft. Blue or white flowers from May to June. All the camassias make clumps of long narrow leaves and have narrow spikes of quite large starry flowers. They are distinctive and easily grown plants that are not as well known as they deserve to be. Good

Camassia esculenta

kinds are *Camassia cusickii*, 2 ft., pale blue; *C. leichtlinii*, 2 ft., deep blue or white and *C. quamash* (sometimes listed as *C. esculenta*), 2 to 3 ft., violet blue.

Bulbs should be planted in September, with 2 in. of soil over them, in any reasonably good soil and open, sunny place. Plants can be left undisturbed for years until they get overcrowded when they can be lifted and divided in September.

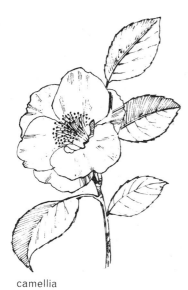

camellia

CAMELLIA. Hardy and slightly tender evergreen shrubs. 6 to 10 ft. Flowers from white to crimson and produced from October to May. The flowers of many of the garden camellias have an almost artificial perfection of form with row upon row of petals superimposed with geometric precision. Others are more informal like small peonies or with a circle of large petals and a central mound of much smaller petals or petal segments. There are also wild camellias with single flowers, less showy but in some respects more graceful and certainly worth planting in woodland gardens where informality is preferred. All are evergreen shrubs and almost all are quite hardy though for years they were believed to require greenhouse protection.

The greatest number of garden varieties has been produced from *Camellia japonica*, which flowers in early spring and has a colour range from white and palest pink to deep red. There is also a fine race of hybrids between varieties of *C. japonica* and a Chinese species named *C. saluenensis*. Collectively these hybrids are known as *C. williamsii* and there are numerous named varieties of which J. C. Williams, with single pink flowers, and Donation, with semi-double dark pink flowers, are two of the most popular. All are excellent garden plants with the useful habit of dropping their faded flowers so that they require no 'dead heading' such as the *C. japonica* varieties frequently do.

Campanula cochlearifolia

Yet other varieties are derived from *C. sasanqua* and flower in winter but they are less hardy and more suitable for places where frosts are not severe or prolonged, as are the varieties of *C. reticulata*. The last are noted for the size of their flowers.

All camellias thrive in lime-free soils like those that suit rhododendrons and azaleas and enjoy similar conditions. They will grow in full sun though they are usually happier in partial shade. No pruning is required but overgrown bushes can be cut back in May.

Camellias can be increased by cuttings in July, or by well-grown leaves cut with a growth bud attached and pushed, stalk end first, into peaty soil in a frame or propagating box in the greenhouse.

CAMPANULA (Bellflower, Canterbury Bell). Hardy herbaceous perennials, rock plants, hardy and half-hardy biennials. Prostrate to 5 ft. Blue, purple, pink or white flowers from June to August. The name bellflower, though highly appropriate, has never caught on, and most gardeners know these flowers simply as campanulas. A few kinds have open starry flowers but most are bell shaped and nodding. Habit varies from completely prostrate rock plants to tall plants for the herbaceous border.

All the familiar kinds are easily grown and most will stand a certain amount of shade, though they will thrive equally well, perhaps even better, in full sun. The dwarf rock garden types mostly flower in June or July after the main flush of rock plants is over and are doubly valuable to prolong the season. Good kinds are *Campanula cochlearifolia* (also known as *C. pusilla*), white or blue; *C. garganica*, blue or violet; *C. portenschlagiana* (also listed as *C. muralis*), mauve blue and *C. poscharskyana*, light blue.

campanula

The herbaceous types are also summer flowering. Some, such as the Peach-leaved Campanula, *C. persicifolia*, with blue or white, double or single flowers in slender spikes, others such as the Milky Campanula, *C. lactiflora*, with loose sprays of white, blue or mauve flowers that are exceptionally elegant. The Tussock Bellflower, *C. carpatica*, is well described by its popular name—a plant forming low clumps 6 to 9 in. high

Camellias are hardier shrubs than is often thought. Here,
Inspiration, one of the *C. williamsii* hybrids, makes a fine display

The November-flowering, anemone-centred chrysanthemum,
Raymond Mounsey, needs greenhouse protection

with fairly large upward-facing blue or white flowers. It is suitable for the rock garden or for the front of a border. The Clustered Bellflower, *C. glomerata dahurica*, is taller, about 1 ft., with closely packed heads of violet-purple flowers and is another good front row plant for the border.

Campanula pyramidalis, the Chimney Bellflower, is a biennial with tall spikes of white or blue flowers in July. This is a slightly tender plant and more suitable for an unheated or cool greenhouse than for cultivation out of doors. It must be raised from seed sown annually in May or early June, the seedlings being pricked out and potted in JIP.2 or an equivalent soil in 5-, 6- or 7-in. pots.

The Canterbury Bell, *C. medium*, is also a biennial which must be renewed from seed annually. This is sown in May or early June, preferably in a frame though it can be sown out of doors. The seedlings should be pricked out a few inches apart into a nursery bed to grow on into sturdy plants to be placed in their flowering quarters in October. Space them at least 1 ft. apart and give them rather good soil and a fully sunny or partially shaded position. They will flower the following June and are usually about 3 ft. tall. The flowers are long, bell shaped, with a curious saucer-like appendage in the cup-and-saucer varieties, and are borne in very broad spikes. Colours are blue, mauve, pink and white and there are a number of double-flowered varieties.

All campanulas except *C. pyramidalis* and *C. medium* can be increased by division in spring or autumn.

Campanula persicifolia

CAMPSIS (Trumpet Vine). Hardy climbers. Red or orange flowers in August and September. These very showy climbers are sometimes listed as tecoma and occasionally as bignonia. *Campsis radicans* climbs by aerial roots like an ivy and has clusters of narrowly trumpet-shaped orange and scarlet flowers. *C. grandiflora* has larger, more widely open orange-red flowers and needs the support of wires, trellis or something of the kind. So does the hybrid between these two species named *C. tagliabuana*, the best form of which, Madame Galen, has large salmon-red flowers.

All like very warm, sunny places and are most satisfactory in milder parts where frosts are not severe or prolonged. Without adequate warmth they will grow but produce few flowers. Campsis will thrive in any reasonably good soil and can be increased by seed sown in spring, summer cuttings or layers. Regular pruning is not essential but if plants get too big they can be cut back in March.

campsis

CANNA (Indian Shot). Half-hardy herbaceous perennials. 3 to 7 ft. Red, crimson, orange or yellow flowers from July to September. Cannas are handsome plants with broad, tropical-looking leaves often deep red in colour, though some varieties are green leaved, and with spikes of large gaudy flowers in summer. They are more familiar in the elaborate bedding schemes seen in public parks than in private gardens, but there is no reason why they should not be more widely grown, as they are not difficult to manage provided the fleshy roots can be started in a warm greenhouse each spring. At this stage they like a temperature of around 16°C. (60°F.) and plenty of water. They must be removed to a frame in May and hardened off for planting out of doors in a sunny place in June. Before frost occurs in autumn the plants must be lifted, brought back into the greenhouse and gradually dried off. From about November until March they can be kept in their pots without water and with no more heat than is needed to ensure complete protection against frost. Division of the roots in spring is the easiest way to increase cannas, as seed needs a lot of heat for satisfactory germination.

Most cultivated cannas are garden hybrids but two species are sometimes seen—*Canna iridiflora* and *C. indica*, the Indian Shot. The first is extra tall, to 7 ft. or even more, and the madder-red flowers hang down in clusters from the tall, stiff stem. *C. indica* is much shorter, 3 to 4 ft., and has short spikes of relatively small orange-red flowers.

canna

Cassia corymbosa

Catalpa bignonioides

catananche

CARYOPTERIS (Blue Spiraea). Hardy deciduous shrubs. 2 to 3 ft. Blue flowers in August and September. These are small bushy shrubs with clusters of fluffy-looking blue flowers in August and September. Despite their popular name they have no connection with the true spiraeas. The kind commonly grown, *Caryopteris clandonensis*, is a hybrid and it is rather variable in the quality and colour of its flowers. Selections have, therefore, been made and given distinctive names such as Arthur Simmonds, Ferndown and Kew Blue.

The stems of caryopteris are rather soft and often get damaged in winter but the plants usually break out freely from the firmer wood at the base. They are useful for their late flowering and comparatively dwarf habit; if pruned hard each March they are unlikely to exceed 2½ ft. Caryopteris like sunny places and well-drained soils and can be increased by cuttings of firm young shoots in summer in a frame.

CASSIA. Half-hardy evergreen shrubs. 10 ft. Yellow flowers from June to October. The kind most commonly seen, *Cassia corymbosa*, is a loosely branched shrub which can be easily trained against a wall and it is in this way that it is usually grown. It covers itself in summer and early autumn with large clusters of bright yellow flowers and is highly decorative. Unfortunately it is not fully hardy and can only be grown out of doors in the mildest parts not subject to severe or prolonged frosts and, even then, must usually be planted against a sunny wall. Elsewhere it can be grown in a cool or intermediate greenhouse, preferably planted in a bed of soil on the greenhouse floor though it can be grown in tubs or large pots in JIP.1 compost. Water freely from April to September, moderately from October to March. Regular pruning is not essential but if plants get too big they can be cut back in March.

Cassias can be increased by seed sown in a greenhouse, temperature 18 to 20°C. (65 to 68°F.), in spring or by cuttings of firm young growth taken in summer and inserted in sandy soil in a propagating frame.

CATALPA (Indian Bean Tree). Hardy deciduous tree. 20 to 30 ft. White flowers in July and August. The kind commonly grown, *Catalpa bignonioides*, is a very handsome tree with large roundish light green leaves (golden yellow in the variety *aurea*) and flower spikes rather like those of the Horse Chestnut in shape. Each spike is composed of cup-shaped white flowers spotted with yellow and purple. These are followed by long hanging seed pods which give the popular name Bean Tree.

Catalpa makes a very broad rounded tree, grows well in most soils and is an excellent town tree. Regular pruning is not essential but if necessary branches can be cut hard back each March. This will keep the tree much smaller and result in even larger leaves though it will probably prevent flowering. One drawback of the Indian Bean Tree is that it comes into leaf very late, usually not before the end of May.

The green-leaved form can be raised from seed, the golden-leaved variety from cuttings of either firm young shoots or of roots.

CATANANCHE (Cupid's Dart). Hardy herbaceous perennial. 2 ft. Blue flowers from June to September. *Catananche caerulea* is a pretty blue-flowered perennial rather like a cornflower in appearance. It is quite hardy and can be grown in any sunny place provided the soil is reasonably well drained. The flowers appear in summer and are useful for cutting as they last well. Stock can be increased by dividing roots, preferably in the spring.

CEANOTHUS (Californian Lilac). Hardy or nearly hardy evergreen and deciduous shrubs. 3 to 8 ft. Blue or pink flowers from May to October. The evergreen varieties of ceanothus are all a little tender, appreciating the protection of a sunny wall except in very mild districts. They make densely branched bushes which may grow taller if trained against a wall. One of the most popular for this purpose is *Ceanothus veitchianus*, which has neat shining green leaves and thimble-like heads of powder-blue flowers in May and June. Others of similar character are *C. burkwoodii*, which produces bright blue flowers for most of the summer; *C. impressus*, with deep blue flowers in May and a widely spreading habit of growth; *C. prostratus*, which has trailing stems and bright blue flowers in May; *C. rigidus*, with stiff erect stems and purplish-blue flowers in May and *C. thyrsiflorus*, one of the hardiest and tallest of the evergreen kinds with bright blue flowers in May and June.

There are also deciduous kinds flowering in late summer which are, in general, hardier and make fine bushes in the open. Good varieties are Gloire de Versailles, blue; Topaz, violet and Perle Rose, pink. These varieties flower later than most of the evergreen kinds, roughly from July to October, and benefit from fairly hard cutting back each March. The evergreen kinds only need light pruning after flowering to keep them in shape. All can be increased by cuttings in July.

celosia

CELOSIA (Prince of Wales' Feather, Cockscomb). Half-hardy annuals. 1 to 2½ ft. Cream, yellow, orange, pink to crimson flowers in July and August. The small primrose, yellow, orange, carmine or crimson flowers of *Celosia plumosa*, the plant popularly known as Prince of Wales' Feather, have a silken sheen and are carried in elegant plumes like those of an astilbe but on a much-reduced scale. This plant is easily raised from seed sown in February or early March provided that it can be given a minimum temperature of 18°C. (65°F.). The seedlings are pricked out into small pots filled with JIP.1 or equivalent compost and are either removed to a frame in May to be planted out of doors in a warm sunny place in June, or are repotted into 4-in. pots to be grown on in a cool or intermediate greenhouse. Stock must be renewed each year from seed.

The Cockscomb is a special form of this plant usually listed as *C. cristata*. In place of the elegant plumes of flowers it has a mass of creamy-white, yellow, orange, pink, salmon-bronze or crimson flowers crowded together in a twisted head not unlike a cock's comb. It is grown in the same way as *C. plumosa* but always as a greenhouse pot plant and not for planting out of doors in summer.

CENTAUREA (Cornflower, Sweet Sultan). Hardy herbaceous perennials and hardy annuals. 1 to 3 ft. Blue, yellow, pink, mauve, red or white flowers from May to August. The Common Cornflower, *Centaurea cyanus*, with its rich blue flowers in summer, is a hardy annual easily grown in any fairly open place from seed sown in March, April or September where the plants are to flower. All that is necessary afterwards is to thin the seedlings to about 9 in. apart and stick a few twiggy branches around them for support. In addition to the blue there are pink and white varieties. There are also dwarf varieties which need no support and can be grown 6 in. apart.

Centaurea montana

The perennial cornflower most closely resembling the annual cornflower is *C. montana*, an easily-grown plant about 18 in. high with grey leaves and blue flowers in May and June. The much larger yellow flowers of *C. macrocephala* are thistle like in form, handsome and carried erect on stout 3-ft. stems from June to August. *C. dealbata* also has thistle-like blooms but pink in colour and borne on 2-ft. stems from June to August. All these perennials will grow in any reasonably good and well-drained soil and open, preferably sunny place. They can be increased by division in spring.

In addition to the perennial cornflowers cultivated mainly for their flowers there are other kinds grown for their grey or silvery leaves. Since these are mostly Mediterranean plants, they are not very hardy and may need frame protection in winter in cold districts or on poorly drained soils. Their main use is in summer bedding schemes as a foil to the bright colours of geraniums, salvias and other bedding plants. Principal kinds are *C. gymnocarpa*, *C. ragusina* and *C. rutifolia*, the last is often listed as *C. cineraria*.

Centaurea moschata

Cerastium
tomentosum

The botanical name of Sweet Sultan is *C. moschata* and it may be listed under either name in catalogues. Its flowers have a similar thistle-like form to those of the cornflower and come in shades of pink, lavender, purple, yellow and white. The plants like sunny places and well-drained soils and can be difficult in cold and heavy soils. Seed may be sown in March, April or September, seedlings being thinned to about 9 in. This is a pretty, hardy annual and all varieties are excellent for cutting.

CENTRANTHUS (Red Valerian). Hardy herbaceous perennial. $1\frac{1}{2}$ to 2 ft. Red, pink or white flowers in June and July. Though *Centranthus ruber* can be found growing wild on rocks or walls in many parts of the country, it is well worth cultivating in the garden because of its hardiness, its long flowering season and its ability to thrive in the stoniest places. The clusters of small pink, red or white flowers in June or July make a fine show and it is an excellent companion for the blue catmint thriving in similar sunny places and poor well-drained soils. Increase is by careful division in spring, by cuttings in spring or early summer or by seed. Once established it usually spreads freely by self-sown seedlings.

CERASTIUM (Snow-in-summer). Hardy herbaceous perennials. 6 to 8 in. White flowers in May and June. The cerastiums make dense, rapidly spreading carpets of slender stems bearing grey leaves and, in May and June, smothered in white flowers similar to those of the stitchworts to which they are related. They will thrive in the poorest soils and hottest, driest places and are excellent for covering sunny banks and terrace walls, but they are invasive and, if not frequently restricted, can quickly overrun less vigorous plants. They are readily increased by division at almost any time of the year.

The two species commonly grown, *Cerastium tomentosum* and *C. biebersteinii*, do not differ much in appearance but some gardeners consider that *C. biebersteinii* is a little less rampant and therefore a more desirable garden plant.

Ceratostigma plumbaginoides

CERATOSTIGMA (Leadwort, Hardy Plumbago). Hardy herbaceous perennials or shrubs. 6 in. to 3 ft. Blue flowers from July to October. Two kinds of ceratostigma are commonly grown in gardens and both used to be known as plumbago, a name under which they are still occasionally listed. Both have rich blue, rather phlox-like flowers produced in late summer and autumn, and both have a mixture of woody stems and soft shoots, that is to say they are part shrubby and part herbaceous. But *Ceratostigma plumbaginoides* leans strongly towards the herbaceous side and is between 6 and 12 in. high whereas *C. willmottianum* is much more shrubby and can be 3 ft. high.

Both these plants like warm, sunny, rather dry places and *C. plumbaginoides* is particularly suitable for planting on walls or rock gardens whereas *C. willmottianum* is more suitable for the front of shrub or herbaceous borders. Both can be increased by summer cuttings.

Quite frequently the stems of *C. willmottianum* are killed to ground level in winter but as a rule it will shoot up again from the roots. If wished, it can be cut hard back each spring.

Cercis siliquastrum

CERCIS (Judas Tree). Hardy deciduous tree. 12 to 18 ft. Rosy-purple flowers in May and June. Judas Tree is the common name for *Cercis siliquastrum* and it may be found listed under either name in catalogues. The popular name derives from the legend that Judas hanged himself on this tree. It has attractive rounded light green leaves and small, rosy-purple or magenta pea-type flowers borne freely along the stems in May and June. It likes warm, sunny, sheltered places and well-drained soil and is an excellent tree to plant in a rather hot, dry place. No regular pruning is required.

The Judas Tree is easily raised from seed but seedlings may vary quite a lot in the quality of their colour so it is worthwhile to select plants when they are in bloom.

CHAENOMELES (Japanese Quince, Japonica, Cydonia). Hardy deciduous shrubs. 4 to 5 ft. Red, pink or white flowers from March to May. These popular, early-flowering shrubs were formerly known as cydonia and may be still found under that name in some catalogues. In the open they make dense, spiny bushes but they are more commonly seen trained against walls, for which purpose they should be secured to trellis work or wires, outward pointing shoots which cannot conveniently be tied back being shortened to an inch or so in June. Chaenomeles grow in any aspect and are not particular about soil.

The flowers of the commonest varieties are scarlet, but there are also white, pink and crimson forms which are equally beautiful. One of the finest varieties is Knap Hill Scarlet, others being *simonii*, crimson and rather shorter than most; Phylis Moore, semi-double, salmon pink; *moerloosei*, pale pink and *nivalis*, white.

CHEIRANTHUS (Wallflower). Hardy herbaceous perennials commonly grown as biennials. 1 to 1½ ft. Yellow, orange, coppery or bronze-red, crimson, purple or mauve flowers from March to June. Cheiranthus is the botanical name of the wallflowers and they are listed under this in some catalogues. All are perennials but the Common Wallflower, *Cheiranthus cheirii*, used for spring bedding is usually treated as a biennial. Seed is sown each May, the seedlings are pricked out in a nursery bed for the summer, are planted in late summer or early autumn where they are to flower and, after flowering, are pulled out and thrown away. This is because they tend to get straggly with age and are then frequently destroyed by wet and cold in winter. There are numerous colours, including yellow and blood red (the two most popular), light chestnut red and purplish-mauve. All grow best in sunny places and well-drained soils and have a special liking for soils containing lime or chalk.

The Siberian Wallflower, *C. allionii*, flowers a little later and goes on flowering for a longer time than the Common Wallflower. Another notable point of difference is that its vivid orange flowers are scarcely scented. It is grown in exactly the same way.

In addition there are several hardier and more compact wallflowers which are commonly grown as perennials being planted and allowed to remain undisturbed for a number of years. One of the best of these is Harpur Crewe, which has double yellow flowers in spring. Another is Moonlight, a very compact plant with primrose-yellow flowers, but this belongs to an allied genus and may be listed under its correct name—*Erysimum alpinum* Moonlight. These perennials are increased by cuttings taken soon after flowering. They like very well-drained soils and warm, sunny places and are good plants for rock gardens and dry banks.

cheiranthus

CHIMONANTHUS (Winter Sweet). Hardy deciduous shrub. 8 to 10 ft. Pale yellow and maroon flowers from December to February. The pale yellow and maroon flowers of this vigorous deciduous shrub are not very conspicuous and have a curious, semi-transparent appearance, but they make their presence known by their extremely sweet perfume which fills the air for many yards around. Chimonanthus is a fairly hardy shrub but the flowers are readily damaged by frost, so it is wise to plant it in a sheltered place, preferably against a wall facing south or west. It is not in the least fussy about soil and will submit to a little pruning each spring after flowering to keep it tidy. Increase is by seed sown in spring or by layering the younger stems in spring.

Chimonanthus praecox

CHIONODOXA (Glory of the Snow). Hardy bulbs. 6 in. Blue, pink or white flowers from March to April. These are delightful bulbous-rooted plants producing loose sprays of starry flowers at the same time as the daffodils and crocuses are in bloom. Chionodoxas are normally blue with a white eye though there are also pink and wholly white varieties. *Chionodoxa luciliae* is light blue, *C. sardensis* is a deeper blue with a smaller white eye.

single chrysanthemum

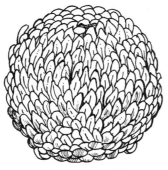

anemone

exhibition incurved

Korean

They are excellent for the rock garden, border or shrub garden and will succeed in full sun or partial shade. The small bulbs should be planted 3 in. deep in September or October. They are readily increased by lifting and dividing the clusters of bulbs at planting time.

CHOISYA (Mexican Orange Blossom). Hardy evergreen shrub. 4 to 6 ft. White flowers in May and June. *Choisya ternata* is a fine evergreen shrub with shining green leaves, a well-branched, rounded habit of growth and fragrant white flowers, at their best in May and early June though some may be produced spasmodically throughout the summer. It is a little tender when young but becomes hardier as it matures and can certainly be planted out of doors with safety in most parts of the British Isles. Choisya is not fussy about soil but does best in a warm, sunny situation, though it will also grow in partial shade. No pruning is normally required. It is increased by cuttings taken between July and September.

CHRYSANTHEMUM (Moon Daisy, Marguerite, Shasta Daisy). Hardy and half-hardy herbaceous perennials and hardy annuals. 6 in. to 6 ft. Flowers in all colours except blue produced from June to January. This is a very large family of plants which from the garden standpoint must be considered in several quite distinct sections. What most gardeners think of first as chrysanthemums are the 'Florist chrysanthemums', originally derived from Chinese and Japanese varieties but now raised all over the world and including thousands of varieties to which more are added annually. They are half-hardy or nearly hardy herbaceous plants. All the varieties that flower before October can normally be grown out of doors, though it may be necessary to lift some plants in late October and put them in a frame or greenhouse during the winter. This is more a protection against damp and slugs than against cold. The autumn- and winter-flowering chrysanthemums require greenhouse protection after the end of September to prevent the flowers or flower buds being damaged by frost. Enough artificial heat will be needed to keep out frost and, if cuttings are being rooted, to maintain a temperature of 10 to 12°C. (50 to 55°F.).

All these chrysanthemums are increased by cuttings of young shoots (preferably of shoots growing directly from the roots) taken as they become available between November and May. The cuttings are rooted in sandy soil in a frame or greenhouse and are then potted singly in good compost such as JIP.1. The outdoor varieties are planted in their flowering beds in early May but the greenhouse varieties are usually grown on in pots, reaching those of 8- to 10-in. diameter by mid-May. From then until late September the pots are usually stood out of doors in a sheltered but sunny spot. Some gardeners prefer to plant out in good soil and then to lift the plants carefully in autumn and transplant them to a border within the greenhouse. They like rather rich but reasonably well-drained soil and should be given as much sun and light as possible and plenty of water in summer.

If large flowers are required, the number of stems to each plant is restricted, occasionally to one, though more usually to between three and twelve. In addition, only one flower bud is permitted to remain on each stem, all other buds being removed at the earliest possible date. The alternative is to allow all buds to develop in sprays of smaller flowers.

Florist chrysanthemums are divided into a number of groups according to their flower size and shape and their time of flowering. Thus there are Incurved types with ball-like flowers; Reflexed varieties with petals curling outwards; Intermediates, in which the central petals curl inwards and the outer petals curl outwards; Singles, Anemone-centred varieties; Pompons with button-like flowers; Charm varieties with masses of small single flowers and Cascades, similar to the last but lax in habit so that they can be trained downwards. Some of these classes are further split up as Early-flowering (or Border), October-flowering and Late (or Greenhouse) and may also be grouped according to flower size, particularly for exhibition purposes. Charm and Cascade varieties are often grown from seed sown in a frame or greenhouse in March or April. They are usually discarded when flowering is over.

The hardy perennial chrysanthemums are popularly known as Moon Daisies or Shasta Daisies and are mostly derived from two species, *Chrysanthemum maximum* and *C. leucanthemum*. They are the big white daisies that come in mid-summer and are so useful both for cutting and for the border. All are hardy but a few of the double-flowered kinds, such as Esther Read and Horace Read, are not quite so robust as the singles and do not greatly relish cold, wet soils in winter. Apart from this all are perfectly easily grown in any open place and reasonable soil. All can be increased by division in spring.

The Korean and Rubellum chrysanthemums stand midway between these hardy perennial kinds and the florist chrysanthemums, to which they are closely related. They have mainly single flowers in a wide range of colours, are very bushy in habit and flower in late summer and autumn. In good, well-drained soil and fairly sheltered places they will over-winter out of doors, especially if protected from slugs, but in many gardens they are better raised annually from cuttings, like the florist chrysanthemums, or from seed, like the Charm and Cascade types.

pompon chrysanthemum

The hardy annual chrysanthemums must be renewed annually from seed, which may be sown out of doors where the plants are to flower or be raised in boxes and planted out later. Seed can be sown in March, April or September. There are three major races of the annual kind, the Tricolor or Carinatum varieties with single or double flowers banded in several colours such as white, yellow and red; the Coronarium or Garland varieties, also single or double but in various shades of yellow and the Segetum or Corn Marigold with single yellow flowers, sometimes with a dark centre. The Tricolor and Coronarium chrysanthemums are mostly about 2 ft. high, the Segetum varieties a little shorter, around 18 in. Still shorter is *C. multicaule*, an attractive much-branched plant only 6 in. high with small single yellow flowers freely produced all summer.

The Marguerites are half-hardy perennials and are varieties of a species of chrysanthemum named *C. lutescens*, but their use and treatment is very different from that of other chrysanthemums. They are primarily used as summer bedding plants and their large white or pale yellow flowers make an admirable foil for the more brilliant colours of bedding pelargoniums and salvias. Marguerites are bushy, quick-growing plants, easily raised from cuttings taken at almost any time (spring and late summer are most usual). They are not quite hardy, though they will survive the winter out of doors in some maritime or otherwise mild localities. Elsewhere, plants or rooted cuttings should be placed in a frostproof frame or greenhouse from October to May. This is also an excellent plant for window-boxes and hanging baskets.

Chrysanthemum lutescens

CINERARIA. Half-hardy perennials grown as tender annuals. 1 to 2 ft. Blue, purple, pink, red, crimson and white flowers from November to May. Cinerarias have very showy daisy flowers and make good pot plants for the slightly heated greenhouse. The plants have big rather coarse leaves and large loose sprays of flowers in a wide range of colours, including many shades of blue, purple, pink and crimson, often with bands of white for contrast. There are large-flowered and small-flowered races, the latter are often called Star cinerarias.

All cinerarias are treated as annuals, seed being sown in JIS in a slightly heated greenhouse some time between April and July according to the time that flowers are required—before Christmas from the earliest sowings, in May from the latest. Seedlings are potted singly into JIP.1 and moved on gradually until they reach the 6- to 8-in. pots in which they will flower. They like a good porous soil and rather careful watering. From June to early October the plants are really happier in a frame than in a greenhouse for they are nearly hardy. Even in mid-winter they need only enough heat to keep out frost.

CISTUS (Rock Rose). Hardy or nearly hardy evergreen shrubs. 2 to 6 ft. White, pink or magenta flowers in June and July. These showy shrubs thrive well in sunny places and well-drained soils, but some kinds are

cineraria

clarkia

only fully safe in the mildest areas and by the sea. The flowers are rather like single roses, very freely produced though individually they do not last long. One of the hardiest kinds is *Cistus laurifolius*, 5 or 6 ft. high with pure white flowers. Similar, but with purple blotches on its petals, is *C. cyprius. C. purpureus* has rose-coloured flowers with a maroon blotch on each petal and also grows to 5 or 6 ft., but the lovely kind known as Silver Pink, soft pink throughout, is shorter, rarely exceeding 3 ft. Other relatively short kinds are *C. corbariensis*, white, 3 ft.; *C. crispus* (also known as Sunset and *pulverulentus*), grey leaves, magenta flowers, 2 ft.; *C. obtusifolius*, white, 18 in. and *C. populifolius*, poplar-like leaves, white flowers, 3 ft.

All cistus bloom in June and July. No regular pruning is required but shoots damaged by frost should be cut out in spring. Most can be increased easily by seed and also by cuttings in July.

CLARKIA. Hardy annuals. 1½ to 2 ft. Purple, red, pink and white flowers from June to August. These are pretty annuals which are readily raised from seed sown in March, April, May or September where the plants are to flower. The seedlings should be thinned to 6 or 8 in. apart. Clarkias produce slender spikes of double flowers in many shades from white to reddish-purple. They will grow in full sun or in partial shade and in practically any soil.

CLEMATIS. Hardy evergreen and deciduous climbers and hardy herbaceous perennials. Flowers in all colours from April to October. Clematis thrive best in rather chalky or limy soils. The climbing varieties like to be placed so that their roots are a little shaded, as by a wall, a building or an evergreen shrub, though their stems should be free to scramble up into full sunshine. The stems of all climbing clematis are very slender and rather brittle and often trouble occurs through accidental breakage. They should be given a good, firm support such as a trellis or a dead tree.

Clematis montana

There are a great many different kinds of clematis grown in gardens, some are species and others garden hybrids. Species particularly recommended are *Clematis montana*, a very vigorous climber with masses of small white or pink flowers in May; *C. armandii*, with quite large evergreen leaves and small white flowers in April; *C. macropetala*, with hanging skirt-like purple or mauve-pink flowers in May and *C. tangutica*, with hanging bell-shaped yellow flowers from August to October accompanied by silken seed heads.

There are many spectacular hybrids and almost all have large or fairly large flat flowers in a variety of colours. Some flower early, in May and June, some later, from July to September, and some more or less continuously all the summer. It is the flowering season that determines the best time and method of pruning. The May-June clematis should be pruned moderately in February or early March, dead or damaged growths being removed and the remaining healthy shoots shortened a little to the first pair of strong growth buds. The more good growth that can be retained the better since it is from this that the flowering shoots will be produced. By contrast, the late-flowering kinds can be cut back much more severely, to within 2 or 3 ft. of the ground, since it is on the new growth that flowers will be produced and hard pruning, plus some feeding, encourages strong new growth. Clematis with an extended flowering season can be pruned either way according to whether the emphasis is on early or late bloom, but generally light pruning proves most satisfactory. The early-flowering species are best pruned immediately after flowering when all shoots that have flowered can be cut out.

Climbing clematis often die back suddenly due to attack by a disease known as wilt. Plants should be sprayed each spring with Bordeaux mixture or a copper fungicide, all dead or dying shoots cut out and each small wound treated with a good wound dressing to prevent re-infection. All kinds can be increased by layering in late spring or early summer and some can be raised from seeds.

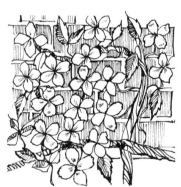
Clematis macropetala

The herbaceous clematis are neither so numerous nor so popular. But some, such as *C. heracleifolia*, 3 ft., with blue tubular flowers and *C. recta*, 3 to 5 ft., with sprays of small white fragrant flowers, are attractive and easily grown plants for open places and ordinary soils. Both flower in August and can be increased by division in spring.

CLEOME (Spider Flower). Half-hardy annual. 3 ft. Pink or white flowers in July and August. Cleome is an unusual and attractive plant which is grown from seed sown in a greenhouse or frame, temperature 15 to 18°C. (59 to 65°F.), in February or March. The seedlings are pricked out into boxes or small pots and are later placed in a frame so that they can be hardened off in readiness for planting out in a sunny place in late May. They should be spaced about 18 in. apart. The plants produce heads of pink (or occasionally white) flowers, notable for their narrow petals and long stamens which give them a curiously spidery appearance.

cleome

CLERODENDRUM. Hardy deciduous shrubs or small trees, tender shrubs and climbers. 4 to 10 ft. White to red flowers from July to September. There are several different clerodendrums, so distinct in appearance and in cultural requirements that one would scarcely guess they were related. Two are shrubs on the borderline of hardiness, but suitable for sunny, sheltered places. One, *Clerodendrum trichotomum*, makes a big shrub or small tree to about 10 ft. and has clusters of small white and red flowers in late summer followed by turquoise-blue berries. The flowers are sweetly scented but the leaves have an unpleasant smell when bruised. This characteristic is even more marked in *C. bungei*, which has handsome dome-shaped heads of light purple flowers on 4- to 6-ft. stems in August and September, but suffers from the drawback that it usually dies back to ground level every winter. Both plants make suckers freely, and these can be detached with roots when increase is required.

Quite different is *C. fallax*, a plant for the intermediate or warm greenhouse and one that is usually renewed from seed every year and treated as an annual. The vivid scarlet flowers are borne in fine showy heads—in autumn if seed is sown in February, or in summer if seed is sown in August. The plants like plenty of warmth, the house should never fall below 10°C. (50°F.) and 18°C. (65°F.) is a better average.

Lastly there is *C. thomsoniae*, a very showy twining plant with loose sprays of crimson and white flowers in summer. Once it was very common in greenhouses, either trained beneath the rafters or over large crinoline-like frames of wire, but, like *C. fallax*, it needs plenty of warmth and so is less seen nowadays. It can be grown in a large pot or tub in JIP.2 or similar soil, or planted in a border within the greenhouse. It should be watered freely from April to September, sparingly from October to March. After flowering it can be pruned as necessary to keep it within bounds. Propagation is by cuttings of young growth taken in spring and rooted in a propagator with bottom heat.

Clerodendrum trichotomum

CLIANTHUS (Lobster Claw, Parrot's Bill, Glory Pea). Half-hardy deciduous or semi-evergreen climbers. Red or white flowers in May and June. The most popular kind is *Clianthus puniceus*, a shrub with long sprawling stems which needs to be trained to trellis, wall or fence. It has showy scarlet or white flowers shaped rather like a lobster's claw or parrot's bill (hence the popular names), and it can be grown out of doors in mild areas not subjected to prolonged or severe frosts if trained in a sunny sheltered place. Elsewhere, it is best grown in a cool greenhouse in JIP.1 or equivalent soil in large pots or tubs, or planted in a bed on the floor of the house. It should be watered freely from April to September, rather sparingly from October to March.

The other kind grown, *C. dampieri*, the Glory Pea, has flowers of similar shape but scarlet and black. The whole plant is weaker in growth, sprawling and even more in need of warmth and sunshine. Its place is in the cool or intermediate greenhouse and it should be watered very sparingly in winter. It can be grown in a hanging basket or in a pot placed on the edge of the staging so that it can hang over.

Both plants can be raised from seed sown in a temperature of 18°C. (65°F.)

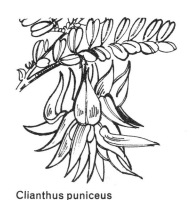

Clianthus puniceus

in spring and both are sometimes grafted on to seedlings of *Colutea arborescens*. *Clianthus dampieri* is often grown as an annual and discarded after flowering.

clivia

CLIVIA. Tender perennial. 1 to 1½ ft. Yellow or orange flowers from March to May. This is an easily grown greenhouse plant with bulb-like fleshy roots. Clivias have trumpet-shaped flowers in clusters on stiff stems and are at their best in March and April. The commonest variety is reddish-orange but there are numerous variations in yellow and orange. Roots should be potted in February and the plants grown in a cool greenhouse throughout the spring and removed to an unheated frame (or left in the greenhouse without heat) for the summer. From November to January they should be returned to the greenhouse and will need little water, but at other times should be watered fairly freely according to their state of growth. They can be increased by dividing the roots at potting time.

COBAEA (Cathedral Bells, Cup-and-saucer Vine). Half-hardy climber usually grown as an annual. Purple and white flowers from July to September. *Cobaea scandens*, the only species grown, is a very quick-growing climbing plant with purple and green or white flowers shaped like those of a Canterbury Bell. It is usually treated as a half-hardy annual, seed being sown in a greenhouse, temperature 15 to 18°C. (59 to 65°F.), in February or March and the seedlings potted singly and removed to a frame to be hardened off for planting out of doors in late May. The stems are slender and the plant climbs by tendrils which need wires, trellis or something of the kind on which to cling.

Cobaea likes sun and warmth but is not fussy about soil. In very mild districts or in a greenhouse it may survive for many years and grow into a large plant for it is really a perennial but not fully hardy.

cobaea

COLCHICUM (Meadow Saffron, Autumn Crocus). Hardy bulbs. 4 to 6 in. Pink, mauve or white flowers in September and October. Despite the extraordinary superficial resemblance of its flowers to those of a crocus, this plant is not a crocus nor are the two related. It makes a very big bulb which should be planted in July or August and be covered with 2 in. of soil. The pink, mauve or white flowers appear in September and October, before the large leaves. There are double-flowered varieties.

Colchicums can be naturalised in grass but are really happiest in rock gardens or at the front of shrubberies and herbaceous borders, in good, rich, loamy soil and a fairly sunny position. They can be increased by dividing the bulb clusters at planting time, but it is unnecessary to lift and replant the bulbs annually. In the right place they will continue for years, each cluster increasing in size all the time.

COLLINSIA. Hardy annual. 9 to 12 in. Lavender and white flowers from June to September. *Collinsia bicolor* is a pretty annual with clusters of small lavender and white flowers in summer. It is easily grown from seed sown in March, April, May or September where the plants are to flower. The seedlings should be thinned to 5 or 6 in. Collinsia likes a sunny place but is not fussy about soil.

CONVALLARIA (Lily of the Valley). Hardy herbaceous perennials. 6 to 9 in. White or pink flowers in May and June. Convallaria is the botanical name of the Lily of the Valley and it will be found listed under either name in catalogues. The fragrant white bells of this plant are among the best loved of all flowers. The plant is a hardy perennial thriving in cool, shady places and rather rich, moist soils. In thin woodland it will often establish itself so firmly as to become almost a weed. It makes close mats of fleshy roots just below the surface, and care should be taken not to damage these by forking or careless hoeing. There is a pink-flowered variety but the colour is very washy and ineffective.

colchicum

Convallaria can be increased by lifting and carefully dividing the plants in March or October. When replanting, spread the roots out horizontally and cover them with only about 2 in. of soil. Do not disturb established beds unnecessarily as the flower display improves with age.

Lily of the Valley is also forced in greenhouses for early flowers. For this purpose specially retarded crowns (roots that have been kept for many months in cold store to prevent them from growing) are packed fairly closely together in pots or boxes in a peaty compost and kept in a dark, cool place for a few weeks. At the same time the water supply should be gradually increased until they are well started into growth and are showing flower stems. They are then removed to a warm, light greenhouse to hurry them on into bloom. Such forced crowns can be planted out of doors later on but are no use for forcing a second time.

annual convolvulus

CONVOLVULUS (Morning Glory). Hardy annual and hardy (or slightly tender) shrubs. 1 to 2 ft. Blue, purple, pink or white flowers from May to August. Two kinds of convolvulus are commonly grown in gardens, one a hardy annual, sprawling in habit and with blue, purple or pink flowers usually with a white or yellow centre in summer; the other a neat silvery-leaved bush no more than 2 ft. high and with white, widely funnel-shaped flowers in May.

The annual is *Convolvulus tricolor*, also sometimes called *C. minor* and popularly known as the Dwarf Morning Glory. It is grown from seed sown in March, April or September where the plants are to flower. It likes a sunny place and any ordinary soil. The seedlings should be thinned to 9 in.

The shrub is *C. cneorum* and it is suitable for a sunny, rather warm place (it is none too hardy) and well-drained soil. It does well on a rock garden or on top of a dry wall and can be increased by cuttings in July or August in a frame.

The climbing morning glories are closely allied to these plants and have similar flowers but belong to a different genus, Ipomoea, under which they are usually listed in catalogues and will be found in this book.

COREOPSIS (Calliopsis, Tickseed). Hardy annuals and hardy herbaceous perennials. 1½ to 2 ft. Yellow and crimson flowers from June to September. The annual kinds have showy, broad-petalled flowers, mainly yellow, though usually more or less blotched with crimson, sometimes so heavily as to appear almost entirely crimson. They like sun but are not fussy about soil and are raised from seed sown in March, April, May or September where the plants are to flower. The seedlings should be thinned to 9 in.

annual coreopsis

The perennial kinds should be planted in spring or autumn, and can be increased by division at these seasons or by seed sown in May. *Coreopsis grandiflora* has large yellow flowers freely produced from June to September. There are several varieties of it differing chiefly in size and quality of bloom. *C. auriculata* is similar but there is a crimson blotch at the base of each yellow petal. *C. verticillata* has very narrow almost fern-like leaves and small but abundant yellow flowers on 2-ft. stems. All these perennial kinds like sunny places and well-drained soils and can prove rather impermanent in cold, heavy, poorly drained soil.

CORNUS (Dogwood, Cornelian Cherry). Hardy deciduous trees and shrubs. 5 to 15 ft. White, pink, or yellow flowers from February to June. Some kinds are grown for their small flowers, others for showy bracts surrounding insignificant flowers and yet others for coloured bark or variegated leaves.

The best of the first group is *Cornus mas*, the Cornelian Cherry, so called because of its red, cherry-like fruits which are edible. However, it is grown primarily for its little clusters of yellow flowers very freely produced on the bare branches in February and March. It makes a freely suckering shrub or small tree to about 15 ft. and is very easily grown in almost any soil and place. It can be increased by seed, cuttings or rooted suckers.

Cornus mas

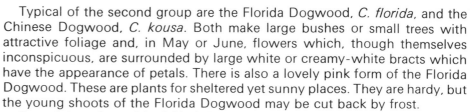

Typical of the second group are the Florida Dogwood, *C. florida*, and the Chinese Dogwood, *C. kousa*. Both make large bushes or small trees with attractive foliage and, in May or June, flowers which, though themselves inconspicuous, are surrounded by large white or creamy-white bracts which have the appearance of petals. There is also a lovely pink form of the Florida Dogwood. These are plants for sheltered yet sunny places. They are hardy, but the young shoots of the Florida Dogwood may be cut back by frost.

Best of the coloured-bark kinds is the Red-barked Dogwood, *C. alba*, which has red stems. A particularly brightly coloured form is known as the Westonbirt Dogwood or *C. alba sibirica*. There is also a lovely form known as Spaeth's Variegated Dogwood, *C. alba spaethii*, in which the light green leaves are heavily marked with cream. All these plants will grow anywhere, though they have a preference for moist soils. To get the very best colour the stems should be cut hard back each spring.

All dogwoods can be increased by cuttings in autumn or by layering in early summer. The Red-barked Dogwood usually makes plenty of suckers which can be detached in autumn with roots.

Cornus kousa

CORTADERIA (Pampas Grass). Hardy perennial grass. 4 to 7 ft. Silvery-white flowers from August to November. The botanical name of the Pampas Grass is *Cortaderia argentea*, under which it will be found in some catalogues. It is a vigorous grass thriving in warm, sunny places and succeeding in most soils but with a preference for those that are well drained. It dislikes disturbance and if left alone will gradually make a large clump of long narrow leaves and produce each autumn increasing numbers of its elegant silken flower plumes carried on stiff straight stems 4 to 7 ft. high according to variety. Cortaderia is best planted in spring and can be increased by division then or by seed sown in spring, preferably in a greenhouse or frame.

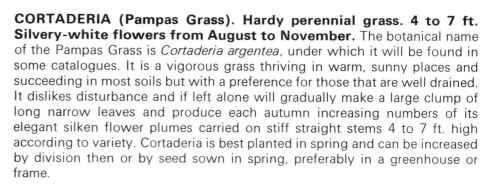

CORYDALIS (Yellow Fumitory). Hardy herbaceous perennial. 1 ft. Yellow flowers from May to August. *Corydalis lutea* is a pretty little British wild plant well worth growing in the garden. It has elegant fern-like foliage and sprays of yellow flowers all summer. Corydalis is often found growing wild on old walls and this is the kind of place in which it should be planted. It usually establishes itself, spreading rapidly by self-sown seedlings and sometimes proving rather a nuisance, but it is a charming wall or rock-garden plant where there is room for it to spread.

cosmos

COSMOS (Cosmea). Half-hardy and hardy annuals. 1½ to 4 ft. Pink, crimson, white, yellow or orange flowers from July to September. *Cosmos bipinnatus* is a popular half-hardy annual with fine fern-like foliage and daisy flowers in shades of pink, rose, purplish-red and white. It should be given a fully open and sunny position, as in shade it is apt to produce a great quantity of foliage and few flowers. Seed is sown in a greenhouse or frame, temperature 15 to 18°C. (59 to 65°F.), in February or March and the seedlings are pricked out and later hardened off for planting out 1 ft. apart in late May. The plants grow 3 to 4 ft. tall and flower in late summer and autumn.

There are also yellow- and orange-flowered cosmeas derived from a different species named *C. sulphureus*. These are shorter and stiffer in habit, 1½ to 2 ft. high on average, some varieties with semi-double flowers. They are grown in exactly the same way as varieties of *C. bipinnatus*.

Yet other varieties are derived from *C. diversifolius*, a species with small starry yellow flowers on plants 2 to 3 ft. high. These are hardy annuals to be sown out of doors in March or April where they are to flower and thinned to about 9 in. apart.

COTINUS (Venetian Sumach, Smoke Tree, Wig Tree). Hardy deciduous shrubs. 7 to 12 ft. Pinkish-fawn flowers from June to July. The Venetian Sumach is frequently listed in catalogues under its old name *Rhus cotinus* but is correctly known as *Cotinus coggygria*. It is a

Cotinus coggygria

remarkable shrub, spreading widely by suckers, with rounded leaves which colour well in the autumn and with flowers and seeds enveloped in long, pinkish-fawn filaments or hairs which become grey as they age, hence the popular names Smoke Tree and Wig Tree. In some varieties, such as Royal Purple, the leaves are purple throughout the year.

Cotinus succeeds in most reasonably well-drained soils, enjoys sunny places and can be increased by summer cuttings, layering or by digging up rooted suckers in autumn.

Cotoneaster cornubia

COTONEASTER. Evergreen and deciduous flowering and berry-bearing shrubs and small trees. Prostrate to 15ft. White flowers from May to June, red or black berries in autumn and winter. This is a big family and from the garden standpoint a most useful one since there are cotoneasters to meet many different requirements from ground or wall cover to the provision of large and shapely specimens. One of the most popular is the Fishbone Cotoneaster, *Cotoneaster horizontalis*, a deciduous shrub which has close parallel rows of thin branches like the skeleton of a fish. The leaves are small and round, the flowers white, the berries abundant. Planted in the open it will spread out horizontally; against a wall it will grow vertically to a height of several feet.

Completely different is the Willow-leaved Cotoneaster, *C. salicifolius*, an evergreen with slender arching branches, which may reach a height of 10 to 12 ft., long narrow shining leaves and clusters of berries. *C. franchetii* and its variety *sternianus* (often listed as *C. wardii*) are similar but not always fully evergreen.

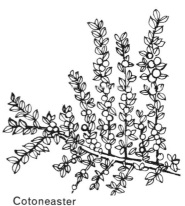
Cotoneaster horizontalis

The Himalayan Cotoneaster, *C. frigidus*, is the largest of them all, really a small deciduous tree around 15 ft. high, with big clusters of berries. Other similar kinds are *C. watereri* and Cornubia, both of which are semi-evergreen (fully so in sheltered places and mild winters).

The lowest growing of all is *C. dammeri* which hugs the ground and is excellent for covering banks. *C. microphyllus* has narrow, evergreen, dark green leaves and makes a stiffly branched dense bush no more than 2 or 3 ft. high and willing to spread itself over a bank or against a wall. *C. conspicuus decorus* makes a compact mound about 3 ft. high, but often much broader, with neat evergreen leaves and scarlet fruits which are usually untouched by birds. *C. simonsii* is stiffly erect in habit, deciduous and will reach 10 ft. if left to its own devices but can be clipped to form an excellent hedge. It has small rounded leaves. There are many more varieties listed in the nurserymen's catalogues.

All cotoneasters are perfectly hardy, will grow in any reasonable soil and need no pruning, unless this is necessary to keep them in bounds when it may be done in spring. All can be raised from seed sown in spring or from cuttings in a frame in July.

CRATAEGUS (Hawthorn, Thorn, Quick). Hardy deciduous trees. 15 to 20 ft. White, pink or red flowers in May; red, yellow or black berries in autumn and winter. The two common hawthorns, *Crataegus monogyna* and *C. oxyacantha*, are very similar in appearance and much confused. Both are densely branched, spiny trees but it is *C. monogyna* which is commonly used as a hedge plant and *C. oxyacantha* which has produced the most beautiful garden varieties. The latter are well worth planting as ornamental trees of modest size. One, named Paul's Scarlet (or *coccinea plena*), has bright red flowers; the other, named Double Pink (or *rosea flore pleno*), has pink flowers. The Glastonbury Thorn, another variety, is occasionally planted because of its habit of flowering twice, in mid-winter and again in May. Better as a garden tree is the Plum-leaved Thorn, *C. prunifolia*, because of its fine scarlet berries and the wonderful autumn colours of its rather large leaves. Another excellent kind is *C. carrierii* (also known as *C. lavallei*), which has large orange-red berries usually untouched by birds.

Crataegus oxyacantha

All crataegus are perfectly hardy and will grow practically anywhere. If it is necessary to restrict them, they can be pruned in winter. The single-flowered species are best increased from seed sown out of doors in spring, but this is a rather slow process. Double-flowered thorns, and also hybrids such as *C. prunifolia* and *C. carrierii*, are grafted in spring or budded in summer on to seedlings of the common thorn.

CRINUM. Slightly tender bulbs. 3 ft. White or pink flowers from July to August. These are handsome plants with broad strap-like leaves and trumpet-shaped pink or white flowers carried in clusters on stout stems. Unfortunately they are rather too large for the greenhouse and not quite hardy enough to be reliable out of doors except in sunny, sheltered places and in the milder parts where frosts are not severe or prolonged. They usually survive near the sea or planted at the foot of a sunny wall or fence.

Crinum bulbs are very large and should be planted so that their tips just show through the surface. In winter they may be protected with some dry litter. They can be left undisturbed for many years to make clumps of slowly increasing size.

CROCOSMIA. Hardy corm. 2 ft. Orange-red flowers in July. *Crocosmia masonorum* is closely related to the montbretias and looks rather like a very superior montbretia with broad, ribbed, sword-shaped leaves and arching flower stems bearing short spikes of quite large orange-red flowers. It is a handsome plant for warm sunny places and fairly good well-drained soils.

The corms should be planted 2 in. deep in March or April. In many parts of the country they can be left undisturbed for years until overcrowded when they can be lifted, divided and replanted in March. In very cold places it may be wise to lift some plants each October, place them in a frame or greenhouse for the winter in soil but with very little water, and replant out of doors the following April.

CROCUS. Hardy corm. 3 to 4 in. White, yellow, blue, mauve or purple flowers from October to April. In addition to the well-known garden crocuses with relatively large flowers in a wide range of colours and all spring flowering, there are a number of wild crocuses well worth planting, especially in the rock garden. Their flowers are, in general, more fragile and as some flower in autumn or winter they may need the protection of a pane of glass against heavy rain. Typical of these wildings are *Crocus byzantinus*, which produces its violet flowers in autumn; *C. speciosus*, the most popular autumn-flowering crocus with flowers in various shades from white and silvery blue to a fairly deep bluish-purple; *C. imperati*, buff outside, violet within and in bloom by January; *C. vernus*, with pale mauve flowers in March; *C. sieberi* and *C. tomasinianus*, both spring-flowering and available in various shades of lavender and purple, *C. chrysanthus*, one of the loveliest and most easily grown of the spring-flowering species with numerous varieties ranging from white and yellow to deep blue and purple, and the Cloth-of-gold Crocus, *C. susianus*, with golden-yellow flowers in March.

All crocuses like sun, though most will also grow satisfactorily in light shade. The wild kinds like rather gritty well-drained soils but the garden varieties will grow in almost any soil. The autumn-flowering kinds should be planted during July or August, all the others in September or October. They are all increased by separating the clusters of corms.

CYCLAMEN. Hardy and half-hardy tuberous-rooted perennials. 3 to 12 in. White ranging to crimson flowers in November to March and July to September. The cyclamen that most people know is a winter-flowering greenhouse plant but there are also fully hardy kinds, some flowering in spring, some in late summer or autumn.

The greenhouse kind is the Persian Cyclamen, *Cyclamen persicum*. It is grown from seed sown in August in an unheated greenhouse, the seedlings being pricked out and later potted singly in small pots of JIP.1 or equivalent soil. They are then repotted at intervals until, by the following June, they

Crinum powellii

crocus

reach the 5- or 6-in. pots in which they will flower. They should bloom from November to March. For the first 18 months the cyclamen should remain in a cool greenhouse, though artificial heat will be needed in winter to maintain a temperature around 10°C. (50°F.). After flowering, plants can go to a frame without heat and remain until August when they should be repotted and returned to the greenhouse. At all times the bun-shaped tubers should be kept sitting almost on top of the soil.

The hardy cyclamen are also raised from seed but are usually purchased as small tubers. If possible, these should be obtained growing in pots and be planted in rather leafy or peaty soil in a partially shaded place. The tubers should be just covered and should subsequently be left undisturbed for as long as possible. If happy, cyclamen spread by self-sown seedlings so that just a few tubers will, in a few years, develop into a thriving colony.

Good hardy kinds are the Spring Cyclamen, *C. coum*, with crimson flowers from December to March; the European Cyclamen, *C. europaeum*, with crimson flowers from July to September and the Neapolitan Cyclamen, *C. neapolitanum*, with pink or white flowers in August and September. All have much smaller flowers than the Persian Cyclamen which is itself available in double-flowered as well as single-flowered varieties, in a wide range of colours and in small-flowered as well as large-flowered strains.

Cyclamen neapolitanum

CYMBIDIUM. Tender orchid. 2 to 3 ft. Flowers in various shades and mixtures of white, cream, yellow, pink, purple and green and produced for most of the year. This is one of the most popular and easily grown families of orchids. Cymbidiums produce their flowers in graceful arching spikes mainly in winter and spring, though there are kinds in flower for most of the year. The flowers last a long time either on the plant or when cut. The plants make bulbous-like growths above ground and are increased by careful division of the clusters of bulbs (they are correctly called pseudobulbs) when they are repotted in spring. Cymbidiums may be grown in a mixture of three parts of fibrous loam, one part of chopped sphagnum moss, two parts of osmunda fibre and one part of beech or oak leafmould. Pots must be very well provided with crocks for drainage and the pseudobulbs are kept well above the compost. Cymbidiums need a temperature around 10°C. (50°F.) in winter, and in summer will require no artificial heat. Instead they should be permanently shaded and syringed frequently with clear water to maintain a cool moist atmosphere. They need less water in autumn and winter. There are a great many garden varieties differing in colour and size of bloom.

cymbidium

CYPRIPEDIUM (Lady's Slipper, Slipper Orchid). Hardy and tender orchids. 1 to 1½ ft. Green, yellow, brown and white flowers for most of the year. The popular name of these orchids refers to the curious pouched shape of the flower rather like a very broad slipper. Behind this there is a sepal, broad and upstanding, and two lateral petals.

In one of the most popular species, *Cypripedium insigne* (also known as *Pathiopedilum insigne* under which name it will appear in some catalogues) the pouch is a mixture of yellowish-green and brown, the sepal white and green spotted with brownish-purple. It is an easy plant to grow in a compost of two parts of good loam, one part of chopped sphagnum moss and one part of osmunda fibre. Plants should be potted just like any other greenhouse subject and grown in a cool greenhouse, temperature around 7 to 10°C. (45 to 50°F.) in winter, with no artificial heat in summer, at which season they should be shaded from hot sunshine. They should be watered freely in summer, moderately at other times. There are many garden varieties and hybrids, some very magnificent and expensive but many obtainable at quite modest prices. Some kinds require more warmth and are better suited to the intermediate than the cool greenhouse.

In addition there are several hardy lady's slippers which will thrive in cool, leafy or peaty soils and partially shaded positions. The British Lady's Slipper, *Cypripedium calceolus*, is a rare native with yellow and purple

cypripedium

flowers; the Japanese Lady's Slipper, *C. speciosum*, is rose pink and white.

All kinds, both hardy and tender, can be increased by careful division at potting or planting time.

CYTISUS (Broom). Hardy deciduous shrubs. Prostrate to 7 ft. White, pink, yellow or crimson flowers from April to July. The Common Broom, *Cytisus scoparius*, is well known to all gardeners. It has whippy green stems, is 5 ft. or more in height and flowers in May and June. Typically bright yellow it has numerous varieties ranging in colour from cream to crimson. The Warminster Broom, *C. praecox*, is similar in habit, shorter and more compact and produces its pale yellow, rather unpleasantly scented flowers in April and May. The White Portugal Broom, *C. albus*, has smaller white flowers produced on very thin arching stems in May. It often exceeds 6 ft. in height.

Three good brooms for rock gardens, walls or banks are *C. ardoinii*, prostrate, deep yellow, May; *C. beanii*, bushy and 1 ft. high, rich yellow, May, and *C. kewensis*, widely arching and $1\frac{1}{2}$ ft., pale yellow, April to May. The Purple Broom, *C. purpureus*, is also prostrate and excellent for banks as it spreads underground binding soil together. Its pale purple flowers are produced in May.

A very different shrub is the Moroccan Broom, *C. battandieri*, with long flexible stems, silvery leaves and upstanding clusters of yellow flowers in June and July. The flowers have a strong pineapple perfume. This broom can be grown as an open-branched shrub to 8 ft. high or it can be trained against a sunny wall or trellis.

All cytisus like light well-drained soils but there are few soils in which they will not grow. They need sun and are not as a rule very long lived. Cytisus can be pruned lightly as soon as the flowers fade but should never be cut back into the old hard wood which does not produce new growth readily. All are easily raised from seed sown in spring but seedlings of garden varieties and hybrids may vary in colour and habit, so these are usually grown from summer cuttings. *C. purpureus* can be divided in autumn.

For the Etna Broom and the Madeira Broom, see Genista.

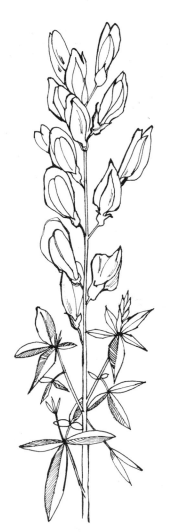

Cytisus canariensis –
see Genista, page 70

DAHLIA. Half-hardy, tuberous-rooted perennials. 1 to 6 ft. Flowers in all colours except true blue from July to October. Though dahlias are tender plants likely to be damaged by the slightest frost, they can be grown quite satisfactorily without a greenhouse or frame because they have tuberous roots which can be stored dry throughout the winter. These roots are lifted in autumn when the foliage has been blackened by frost and, after the stems have been cut off a few inches above the tubers, they are placed in boxes or simply stacked on the floor in any dry, frostproof place. A spare room, cupboard, loft, shed or cellar will serve— but it must be frostproof. It is wise to sprinkle the tubers with flowers of sulphur as a protection against disease. The following spring, between mid-April and early May, the roots are planted out of doors in rather rich, well-cultivated soil and a sunny position. If required, the roots can be carefully divided before being planted.

Alternatively, dahlias can be grown from cuttings. For this purpose the roots are placed in a cool or intermediate greenhouse in early March and are just covered with soil. Shoots will soon appear and are severed when about 3 in. long and inserted as cuttings in a close frame. When rooted they are potted singly in small pots, grown on in the greenhouse for a few weeks and then removed to a frame to be hardened off in time for planting out of doors in late May or early June.

dwarf hybrid dahlias

Hibiscus syriacus Woodbridge is a colourful late-flowering shrub, which produces its gay flowers in September

Kniphofia Royal Standard, one of the aptly named Red-hot
Pokers, is a fine perennial for fairly rich soil

Dahlias can also be grown from seed treated as for half-hardy annuals and sown in March-April in a temperature of 15 to 18°C. (59 to 65°F.), pricked out into boxes or potted individually in JIP.1 or peat potting compost and hardened off for planting out in late May or early June. The shorter bedding varieties are frequently grown in this way.

There are a great many varieties of dahlia, differing in height, and in shape, size and colour of flower. These different types are distinguished by names such as Decorative, with fully double, broad-petalled flowers; Cactus, in which the petals are rolled lengthwise so as to form a spiky flower; Ball-flowered, with globular flowers fashioned rather like a honeycomb, Pompon, similar but with much smaller flowers; Single, with just one row of large petals and a button-like centre; Collarette, similar to the singles but with a collar of short petals often in a contrasting colour around the central disc; Bedding, with flowers of various shapes on plants 2½ ft. or less in height, and so on. Some of these types are only 1 ft. or so in height and suitable for bedding, but most are from 3 to 6 ft. high and must be well staked and tied to prevent breakage of the rather brittle stems. To obtain the finest flowers, buds are restricted to one to each stem, the top bud being retained and side buds removed.

decorative dahlia

DAPHNE. Hardy evergreen and deciduous shrubs. Prostrate to 4 ft. White to purple flowers from February to June. Most daphnes have very fragrant flowers. One of the most popular is the Mezereon, *Daphne mezereum*, which makes a rather stiff bush about 3 ft. high with purple (or sometimes white) flowers clustered along the bare branches in February or March. It is often rather short lived but usually renews itself by self-sown seedlings which will appear around the bush. A much smaller plant is the Garland Flower, *D. cneorum*, a neat little bush only about 1 ft. in height with small evergreen leaves and clusters of pink flowers in spring. This and *D. blagayana*, with creamy-white flowers in early spring on stems that grow flat on the soil, are most suitable for the rock garden. A lovely hybrid daphne named Somerset makes a compact bush 3 ft. high, with abundant pink flowers in May and June. All the foregoing are deciduous.

Daphne odora

By contrast, *D. odora* is evergreen and produces its little clusters of very fragrant purple and white flowers in March and April on bushes 2 to 3 ft. high. The hardiest variety of this, named *marginata*, has a narrow gold margin to each leaf. Another good evergreen is *D. collina*, 1 to 1½ ft. high with purple flowers in April and May.

All these daphnes like sunny places and will grow in most soils. *D. mezereum* is best raised from seed, *D. blagayana* by layering in late spring and the rest by cuttings in July.

DELPHINIUM (Larkspur). Hardy annuals and hardy herbaceous perennials. 2 to 7 ft. Blue, lavender, purple, red, pink and white flowers from June to September. The annual delphiniums are usually known as larkspurs to distinguish them from the perennial kinds. They make slender spikes of flowers, 2 to 3 ft. high, in June, July and August, according to whether the seed is sown in September, March, April or May. Seed can be sown out of doors where the plants are to flower, the seedlings being thinned to 9 or 12 in. The plants thrive best in a sunny open place and are not fussy about soil as long as it is reasonably well drained. Larkspurs make excellent cut flowers as well as being very decorative in the garden and are among the best hardy annuals for autumn (September) sowing.

The hardy perennial kinds fall into main groups: the tall, spire-flowered Elatum varieties and the shorter, branching Belladonna varieties. The former make the boldest display and are magnificent plants for the back of the herbaceous border. Belladonna delphiniums are more graceful and may be used to break up heavier masses of bloom in the garden and for cutting.

All the perennial delphiniums flower in June or July and if the faded flowers are immediately cut off some plants will produce a second crop of bloom in late August or September. Seedlings in their first year usually flower

annual delphinium

in August and September. All like fairly rich but well-drained soils and sunny, open positions. They can be raised from seed sown as soon as ripe in summer or the following spring but seedlings are liable to vary in colour, form and height. For this reason selected varieties are usually increased either by careful division in spring (the best planting time) or by cuttings of firm young shoots cut off close to the crown of the plant in April.

DEUTZIA. Hardy deciduous shrubs. 4 to 8 ft. White to purple flowers from May to July. Deutzias are notable for their elegant sprays of small white, pink or purplish flowers and are easily grown in any reasonably open place and ordinary soil. There are a number of varieties such as Pride of Rochester, double-flowered and white, slightly flushed with purple; Mont Rose, single and purplish-pink; Magician, single, mauve-pink, and Boule de Neige, single and white. All these are quite tall shrubs which will soon reach 6 ft. or more but *Deutzia elegantissima* is much shorter, 4 to 5 ft., with more slender arching stems wreathed in starry lilac-purple flowers in May and early June.

Deutzias can be pruned after flowering if it is desired to restrict their size, the flowering branches being shortened to non-flowering side growths. All can be increased by cuttings in July or autumn.

DIANTHUS (Pink, Sweet William, Carnation). Hardy or tender herbaceous perennials or biennials, hardy rock plants and half-hardy annuals. Prostrate to 5 ft. Most of the flowers are in the white to crimson range and occur between May and August but carnation flowers are produced throughout the year in all colours except blue. The garden pinks are all varieties of dianthus that are suitable for cultivation in the open garden as edgings to beds or borders, or in beds by themselves. They are hardy, free-growing plants with a branching habit and an abundance of single or double flowers on wiry stems in June. They like open, sunny places but are not fussy about soil. All can be raised from cuttings of non-flowering shoots in June and many can also be divided carefully, either in spring or immediately after flowering. Many are very sweetly scented, some with the rich clove perfume associated with carnations. There are numerous varieties and those known as Laced pinks have flowers in two sharply contrasted colours very regularly arranged.

The so-called Allwoodii are hybrids between the garden pinks and carnations. They resemble pinks closely but most have a longer flowering season extending from June to August or September, and there is also a greater range of colours. They are raised from cuttings like the pinks.

In addition to these garden pinks there are many small kinds suitable for planting in rock gardens or on dry walls. Of these three of the best are the Maiden Pink, *Dianthus deltoides*, a trailing plant with masses of small red flowers in July and August; the Cheddar Pink, *D. caesius*, a tufted plant with soft pink flowers in May, and the Tufted Pink, *D. neglectus*, with tight cushions of leaves and almost stemless rose and buff flowers in June. All like sunny places and rather gritty well-drained soils. They can be raised from seed sown in spring or by division of the roots in spring.

The annual pinks or Indian pinks, *D. chinensis* and *D. heddewigii*, are very showy plants flowering in summer from seed sown in a greenhouse, temperature 15 to 18°C. (59 to 65°F.), in February or March. Seedlings are pricked out and hardened off in a frame for planting out of doors in a sunny place in May or early June. The flowers are large, usually with red, crimson or maroon blotches or speckling on a white ground. They grow about 18 in. tall.

Not unlike these are certain garden races of dianthus, such as Delight and Sweet Wivelsfield, the first to be treated as an annual like the Indian Pink, the second as a biennial like the Sweet William.

The dianthus known as Loveliness is also a pink, with fragrant fringed mauve flowers on long slender stems. It is readily raised from seed.

The botanical name of the Sweet Williams is *D. barbatus* and they are listed under this in some catalogues. These charming plants, with big flattish

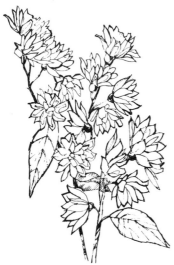
Deutzia Pride of Rochester

Dianthus allwoodii

heads of flowers in June, are usually grown as biennials, though in favourable positions and well-drained soils they will often continue for a number of years. But the usual practice is to sow seed out of doors each May, prick out the seedlings 6 in. apart in a nursery bed of good soil and grow on until October, when the plants are transferred to their flowering quarters. After flowering the plants are destroyed.

Sweet Williams will grow in practically any soil, though they prefer those that are reasonably well drained. There are numerous varieties, differing in height from about 6 to 18 in., and in colour from pink to red. The Auricula-eyed Sweet William has rings of colour on a white base.

All the carnations have been produced from a single wild species, *D. caryophyllus*, but the resultant races are very different. There are two principal classes, the Perpetual-flowering carnation, which is a purely green-house plant, and the Hardy Border carnation, which is primarily an outdoor plant, though it is sometimes grown in unheated greenhouses for the purpose of producing its beautifully formed flowers to perfection. There are great differences both in the cultivation and the appearance of these two classes.

The Perpetual-flowering carnations are rather tall plants, and their flowers, always very double in the varieties cultivated, lack the perfection of form which characterises the best border carnations. They can be made to flower continuously throughout the year and are grown from cuttings of young side-shoots taken between November and March. These cuttings are rooted in sand in a propagating frame within the greenhouse and in a temperature around 15°C. (59°F.). When rooted, the cuttings are potted singly in a good compost, such as JIP.1, in small pots and are moved on gradually into 6- or 7-in. pots in JIP.2 in which they flower. The tops of the shoots are broken out twice, first when the young plants have seven pairs of leaves and a second time when the sideshoots resulting from the first stopping have made about seven pairs of leaves each. The purpose is to encourage the plants to branch more freely. When flower buds appear the small side buds are removed and only the terminal bud on each shoot is permitted to develop into a flower. An average temperature of around 12°C. (55°F.) is required in autumn and winter and as much ventilation as possible should be given consistent with this. It is best to discard plants after their second year or at least after the third year.

Border carnations are much shorter and more spreading in habit and need no stopping of shoots to make them branch. They are grown from layers made from non-flowering shoots. An incision is made in each shoot where it will touch the soil by a sharp knife being drawn slantwise through a joint (the point where the leaves are attached to the stem). This incision is then bent open and the shoot is pegged to the soil and covered with an inch of further soil. If the work is done in July the layers should be well rooted by September or October and can be severed from the parent plant and lifted. If they cannot be replanted straightaway, they are best potted singly in JIP.1 or equivalent soil and kept in a frame or unheated greenhouse until the following spring when they can be planted where they are to flower. Border carnations like good loamy soil but can be grown successfully in a wide variety of soils. The position chosen should be as sunny and open as possible. They only flower in June and July and the flowers are flatter and less ragged than those of perpetual-flowering carnations.

There are a great many varieties in each class of carnation, and those of the border carnations are classified according to colour, for example Selfs, with flowers of one colour throughout; Fancies, with markings of one colour on a different ground colour and Picotees, with a marginal band of colour on each petal contrasting with the colour of the rest of the petal. There is also a classification for scent, Clove carnations having a rather heavy perfume with a suggestion of the aroma of cloves.

DIASCIA (Twinspur). Half-hardy annual. 6 to 9 in. Pink flowers from June to August. *Diascia barberae* is a pretty annual with small salmon-pink flowers of rather unusual shape. They are carried freely on slender stems. Seed should be sown in March-April and germinated in a temperature of 15 to

Dianthus deltoides

Dianthus caesius

Dianthus chinensis

18°C. (59 to 65°F.). Subsequently, seedlings can either be hardened off for planting out of doors in late May or early June in a sheltered sunny place, or they can be potted in JIP.1 or equivalent soil and grown on in a cold or cool greenhouse to make attractive pot plants.

dicentra

DICENTRA (Bleeding Heart). Hardy herbaceous perennials. 15 to 24 in. Pink and white flowers in June and July. These are very elegant hardy herbaceous plants, with fern-like leaves and arching sprays of pendent flowers in early summer. The Bleeding Heart, *Dicentra spectabilis*, grows 2 to 3 ft. high and has quite big pink and white flowers; *D. eximia* and *D. formosa* are bushier in habit, 15 to 18 in. high, with smaller, more numerous pink (or in some varieties white) flowers, and Bountiful is an excellent garden hybrid between them with deeper rose-pink flowers.

All dicentras will thrive in sun or shade, in practically any soil, and the Bleeding Heart also makes an excellent pot plant for the cool or unheated greenhouse. Plants can be increased by division in spring or autumn, the best planting (or potting) time.

DICTAMNUS (Burning Bush). Hardy herbaceous perennials. 3 ft. White or purple flowers in June and July. *Dictamnus albus* is an unusual herbaceous plant with spikes of purple or white flowers in early summer. It gets its popular name, Burning Bush, from the fact that in warm weather it gives off small quantities of an inflammable gas which will ignite if a flame is held close to the plant. It will grow well in full sun or partially shaded positions and almost any soil, and is increased either by seed in spring, or by careful division of the roots in spring or autumn.

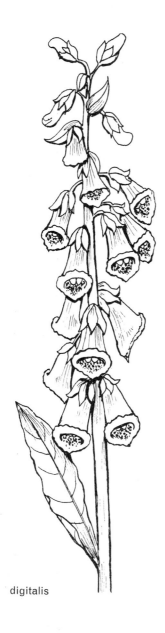

digitalis

DIDISCUS (Blue Lace Flower). Tender or half-hardy annual. 1½ ft. Blue flowers from June to September. *Didiscus caeruleus* is a pretty annual for the cold or cool greenhouse. The very small lavender-blue flowers are carried in feathery heads on 18-in. stems throughout most of the summer. It is easily raised from seed sown in March in a temperature of 15 to 18°C. (59 to 65°F.), the seedlings being potted singly in JIP.1 or equivalent soil. Alternatively, plants can be treated as half-hardy annuals and planted out of doors in early June but the flowers are fragile and should be given a fairly sheltered place.

DIGITALIS (Foxglove). Hardy herbaceous perennials or biennials. 3 to 5 ft. Purple, pink and white flowers from June to July. Digitalis or foxgloves are usually treated as biennials, seed being sown out of doors each May to provide plants which will flower just over a year later. The seedlings are pricked out into a nursery bed, preferably in a shady place, and are transferred in autumn to their flowering quarters. Sometimes plants will continue for several years but usually they die after flowering and producing seed. Once established they will often renew themselves by self-sown seed.

Foxgloves like cool, rather moist soils and partially shaded places but will grow practically anywhere. The Excelsior varieties have large flowers, standing out all round the stems instead of hanging down on one side to form the typical spike of the wild foxglove. Colours range from white and pale pink to crimson, often heavily netted or spotted with one shade on another.

DIMORPHOTHECA (Star of the Veldt). Hardy annuals. 6 to 15 in. White, yellow, apricot to orange flowers from June to August. These are among the most beautiful of daisy-flowered annuals. The flowers, which are quite large, can be had in all shades from pale beige or lemon, through apricot and salmon to orange and also in white. For early flowers in June and July seed should be sown in a greenhouse in March, the seedlings being pricked out and later hardened off for planting out in May. Later flowers in July and August can be obtained by sowing directly out of doors in April or early May where the plants are to flower, and thinning seedlings to 9 in. In either case a sunny position should be chosen, for preference in well-drained soil.

DODECATHEON (American Cowslip, Shooting Star). Hardy herbaceous perennials. 1 to 1½ ft. White to purple flowers in June. Dodecatheon are very pretty, hardy perennials for damp but open places, particularly around pools or at the sides of streams. Despite their common name they are not really at all like cowslips, for the narrow petals are turned sharply back like those of a cyclamen, and they are rosy purple or white. They are, however, carried on bare 12- to 18-in. stems rather in the manner of a cowslip and they appear in early summer. Plenty of peat and gritty sand should be mixed with the soil before planting in spring. The best method of increase is by seed sown in a greenhouse or frame in spring.

doronicum

DORONICUM (Leopard's Bane). Hardy herbaceous perennials. 1 to 3 ft. Yellow flowers in April and May. These are among the earliest flowering hardy herbaceous perennials, the big yellow daisy flowers starting to open in April and being at their best in May. The finest doronicum is named Harpur Crewe and is an improved variety of *Doronicum plantagineum*. It grows 2½ to 3 ft. high. There are also shorter kinds such as *D. caucasicum*, 12 to 18 in., which has a very distinctive variety named Spring Beauty with fully double flowers, and *D. cordatum*, which is only 6 in. high.

All thrive in sun or partial shade and are not in the least fussy about soil. They can be divided in spring or autumn, the two best planting seasons.

DRYAS. Hardy herbaceous perennials. Prostrate. White or pale yellow flowers in May and June. These are mat-forming plants suitable for sunny banks and rock gardens. The most familiar is *Dryas octopetala*, a fairly rare British plant with white flowers that look rather like single roses and are followed by fluffy grey seed heads. *D. drummondii* is similar but with pale yellow flowers. Both are plants requiring very gritty well-drained soil. They grow well on limestone. Increase is by seed sown in gritty soil in a frame in spring or by division in spring.

E

ECCREMOCARPUS (Chilean Glory Flower). Half-hardy climber. Orange or red flowers from July to October. This is a beautiful and unusual climber which can be grown very easily from seed. Growth is slender and the leaves have an elegant ferny appearance, but it is the tubular orange or scarlet flowers produced in long sprays that are really striking. Seed should be sown in a greenhouse or frame, temperature 15 to 18°C. (59 to 65°F.), in spring and seedlings potted singly and hardened off for planting out in late May. The plants should be given a warm, sunny, sheltered place and some good support to climb on, such as a trellis against a south-facing wall. In such a place they will live for years and flower profusely every summer, though they may be killed right back to their fleshy roots each winter.

eccremocarpus

ECHINACEA (Purple Cone Flower). Hardy herbaceous perennial. 3 ft. Purple or white flowers in August and September. The large reddish-purple daisy flowers of echinacea each have a central disk which adds to the striking appearance of the bloom. One of the best varieties is Robert Bloom but there are others differing in the shade of purple and also a white-flowered form. The flowering season is August and September and the plants will grow best in sunny places and fairly good, well-drained but not dry soils. They are best increased by division in spring or autumn.

ECHINOPS (Globe Thistle). Hardy herbaceous perennials. 2 to 5 ft. Blue or white flowers in July and August. Echinops are striking and easily grown hardy plants with small blue flowers crowded into spherical

echinops

heads. The seed head is also globular and has a spiky appearance which makes it almost as decorative as the flower. Heights range from about 2 to 5 ft. and all varieties can be easily raised from seed sown in a frame, or out of doors in March. Good clumps can also be carefully divided in spring or autumn or root cuttings can be taken in winter. Practically any soil and open, sunny position will suit these handsome plants, which, because of their long deep searching roots, are able to survive in quite dry places. Good kinds are *Echinops ritro*, deep blue, 3 ft.; Taplow Blue, pale blue, 5 ft. and Veitch's Dwarf Blue, bright blue, 4 ft.

ECHIUM (Viper's Bugloss). Hardy annuals. 1 ft. Blue, purple or white flowers from June to August. Some of the echiums are grand plants with great rosettes of leaves and tapering spikes of blue flowers, but there are also rather tender plants only occasionally encountered in sheltered gardens in mild parts of the country. Far more generally useful are the garden races derived from a Mediterranean annual named *Echium plantagineum*. These are very easily grown, free flowering, dwarf and compact plants with curling clusters of purple, blue or white flowers all summer. They can be grown from seed sown in spring or early autumn where the plants are to flower, seedlings being thinned out to about 6 in. They will grow practically anywhere but succeed particularly well in hot, sunny places and rather dry, well-drained soils.

ENDYMION (Bluebell). Hardy bulbs. 1 to 1½ ft. Blue, pink or white flowers in May. The Common Bluebell, *Endymion non-scriptus*, is a lovely spring-flowering bulb but it grows so freely in the wild that it is not often planted in gardens. The Spanish Bluebell, *E. hispanicus*, is not a native British plant and as it produces a stiffer and more substantial flower spike than *E. non-scriptus* it is frequently planted. There are pink- and white-flowered forms as well as blue.

All bluebells will grow in almost any soil and in sun or shade. Bulbs should be planted in autumn 4 or 5 in. deep. Plants can be increased by division of the bulb clusters in late summer.

epimedium

EPIMEDIUM (Barrenwort). Hardy perennials. 1 ft. White, yellow or red flowers in April and May. These are useful plants for shady places. They grow only about 1 ft. high, produce their loose sprays of white, pale yellow or reddish flowers in spring and are chiefly remarkable for their attractive foliage which often takes on fine autumn tints at the end of the year. Epimediums are not fussy about soil though they do not like very dry places. All can be increased by division in spring or autumn.

ERANTHIS (Winter Aconite). Hardy herbaceous perennials with tuberous roots. 2 to 3 in. Yellow flowers in February and March. The winter aconites flower very early, carpeting the ground in February and March with their golden flowers which would resemble buttercups were it not for the little ruff of green around each. They are grown from little tubers which are sold dry in the autumn and should be planted as soon as available in August or September. Plant 2 in. deep in reasonably good soil and a cool shady place. Winter aconites will make a pretty carpet beneath deciduous trees or shrubs and can be left undisturbed for years. They can be increased by lifting and dividing the clusters of tubers in August.

EREMURUS (Fox-tail Lily). Hardy herbaceous perennials. 3 to 6 ft. White, yellow, orange or pink flowers in June and July. These beautiful plants carry their flowers in long erect spikes and are among the most distinctive summer-flowering perennials. Unfortunately, they are not the easiest of plants to grow since they make wide-spreading fleshy roots which do not like to be disturbed. They should be planted in September in a sunny sheltered place and fairly rich but well-drained soil. They do well on limestone or chalk though this is not essential for them. In cold localities it is wise to cover the roots in late winter with sand, straw or bracken as the young shoots may be injured by frost as they push through in spring.

Propagation is by careful division in August or September or by seed sown in spring, but seedlings take several years to reach flowering size. The High-down Hybrids, in a variety of colours, are the most satisfactory to grow.

Calluna vulgaris

ERICA (Heather, Heath, Ling). Hardy and half-hardy evergreen shrubs. 6 in. to 8 ft. White to crimson flowers produced throughout the year. The heathers or heaths belong to two distinct genera, *Calluna* and *Erica*, but the differences are of botanical rather than of horticultural significance. All the same it is necessary to know both names since they are frequently used in nurseries and gardens.

There is only one species of calluna, named *Calluna vulgaris*. It is a common wild plant in Britain, often known as Ling, 1 to 2 ft. high and flowering in August and September. The common form is rarely planted in gardens but there are a number of specially selected varieties which are fine garden plants. These include some with double flowers in long narrow spikes such as *alba plena*, white, and H. E. Beale, pink, also varieties with coloured leaves such as Golden Feather and Gold Haze, both yellow, and *serlei rubra*, reddish-purple.

Erica cinerea

There are a number of different species of erica and most of them have numerous varieties. *Erica arborea* is the Tree Heath, which can grow 8 ft. or even more high and has white flowers from March to May. *E. carnea* is a dwarf heath, 6 to 18 in. high according to variety, flowering from December to March and popular not only for its compact habit and good colour range but also because it will grow in soils containing some lime or chalk. Springwood White and Springwood Pink are good and typical varieties. *E. cinerea* is the native Bell Heather, around 9 in. high and flowering from June to September. There are many varieties including some with golden or purplish-red foliage. *E. darleyensis* is heather pink, 18 in. high, flowering from November to April. It will tolerate some lime or chalk, as will *E. mediterranea*, a taller plant, 2 to 4 ft., with white and pink varieties. *E. tetralix*, the Cross-leaved Heath, is 9 to 18 in. high and flowers from June to October and *E. vagans*, the Cornish Heath, has a similar range in height and flowering season. Both have white and pink varieties and *E. vagans* has a fine cerise variety named Mrs D. F. Maxwell.

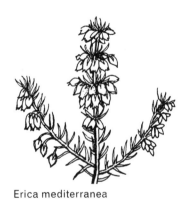

Erica mediterranea

All these hardy heathers thrive in rather sandy or peaty soils but they can be grown successfully in most soils that are not chalky or limy. Varieties of *E. carnea*, *E. darleyensis* and *E. mediterranea* tolerate chalk and lime but are just as well without it. They like open sunny places, are best planted between October and March and can be trimmed with shears after flowering to keep them compact. They are increased by summer cuttings of firm young shoots or by layering.

In addition to these hardy heathers there are some half-hardy kinds which are usually grown as pot plants in cool greenhouses. All are winter flowering. Two of the most popular are *E. gracilis*, rosy-purple or white and *E. hyemalis*, white tipped with pink. They can be grown in JIP.1 without lime and with extra peat. They require no shading, may be stood out of doors or in a frame from June to September and must be watered rather carefully at all times as either excessive wetness or dryness can kill them.

ERIGERON (Fleabane). Hardy herbaceous perennials. 1 to 2 ft. Blue, mauve, pink, orange or crimson flowers from June to August. Erigerons are easily grown hardy plants with flowers very like those of Michaelmas daisies but appearing throughout the summer. Plants are usually about 2 ft. high but there are dwarfer varieties, particularly in the orange shades. Most are very easily grown in almost any soil and reasonably open position, but the orange shades are usually more difficult and should be given specially well-drained soil. A few kinds are not completely hardy but are useful because they will grow in very hot places. Of these, *Erigeron mucronatus* is like a small pink and white daisy, immensely free flowering and capable of colonising sunny walls by self-sown seedlings. *E. glaucus*, the

erigeron

Beach Aster, has much larger pale blue or pink flowers and will grow in almost pure sand. All can be increased by division in spring or autumn.

ERINUS. Hardy rock plant. 2 to 3 in. Purple, carmine, pink or white flowers from April to June. This pretty little plant often spreads rapidly by self-sown seedlings in the crevices of walls and similar stony places. It makes neat rosettes of leaves and the small flowers are carried freely in short spikes. Seed provides a ready means of increase but seedlings tend to revert to the normal purple colour, so selected colour forms must be increased by division, preferably in spring.

ERODIUM (Heron's Bill). Hardy rock plants. Prostrate to 6 in. Pink, yellow or white flowers from May to October. Erodiums are pretty little plants for the rock garden, mostly making small hummocks or spreading carpets of growth. The Corsican Heron's Bill, *Erodium corsicum*, has grey leaves and rose-pink flowers throughout the summer. It is an excellent rock plant, and so is *E. reichardii roseum* with soft green leaves studded with pink flowers from May to October. *E. chrysanthum* is a little taller with divided grey leaves and soft yellow flowers.

All kinds will grow readily in almost any soil and open sunny position. Erodiums can be increased by division in spring or autumn.

erodium

ERYNGIUM (Sea Holly). Hardy herbaceous perennials and biennials. 3 to 4 ft. Blue, purple or white flowers in July and August. These are very distinctive plants with stiff, spiny leaves and teazle-like heads of flowers, usually blue, though in the Giant Sea Holly, *Eryngium giganteum*, the large spiny bracts around the very pale flowers are bone white. This species, however, is very short lived usually behaving as a biennial and so should be renewed from seed annually.

Two of the easiest and most long lived are *E. planum* and *E. tripartitum*, both with thimble-size flower heads in large, branching sprays. There is also a lovely kind known as Violetta with amethyst-violet flowers. All flower in summer and are from 3 to 4 ft. in height. Eryngiums can be planted in spring or autumn and are best raised from seed in spring, though they can also be increased from root cuttings in winter.

All eryngiums like well-drained, sandy soils and often prove rather impermanent in the rich or moist soils of gardens. They are, nevertheless, well worth trying for their very unusual appearance and their excellence as dried cut flowers for winter decoration.

eryngium

ERYTHRONIUM (Dog's-tooth Violet, Trout Lily). Hardy bulbs. 4 to 12 in. Purple, pink, yellow or white flowers in March and April. The nodding flowers of the erythroniums are more like those of cyclamen than of violets. They are delightful little plants for cool shady places in soil containing plenty of leafmould or peat. They will grow well near or even under trees and shrubs provided they do not get starved or become very dry. The bulbs are planted in autumn, 2 in. deep and about 6 in. apart, and the plants can be left undisturbed for years to spread slowly by natural increase of bulbs and possibly also by seedlings. Only when overcrowded need they be lifted, divided and replanted in September.

The most popular kinds are *Erythronium dens-canis*, the Dog's-tooth Violet, with russet and green marbled leaves and pink or purple flowers on 4- to 6-in. stems; *E. revolutum*, the Trout Lily, pink or white flowers on 6- to 12-in. stems, and *E. tuolumnense* as tall as the last and with yellow flowers.

ESCALLONIA. Hardy or slightly tender evergreen or deciduous shrubs. 5 to 8 ft. Pink to crimson and white flowers in June and July. The best kinds of escallonia are all evergreen shrubs with neat shining green leaves and small pink or red flowers carried all along the slender and often arching branches. Not all are fully hardy and some are only seen at their best near the sea or in the milder counties but *Escallonia langleyensis*, with

An effective mixed border which includes shrubs, such as the
hypericum in the foreground, roses and annuals

The graceful flowers of arctotis, often called African daisies

Perennial asters, colourful and hardy border plants

Some of the brilliant Ghent varieties of deciduous azalea

The distinctive Cup-and-saucer Vine, *Cobaea scandens*

The handsome flowers of *Colchicum autumnale*

The evergreen shrub *Ceanothus* Cascade, good for a sunny wall

Dianthus Cocktail, a pretty variety of the garden pink

Striking flower heads of the perennial *Echinops ritro*

The very effective *Buddleia davidii* White Cloud

One of the more unusual clematis, the charming *C. alpina*

Blue Peter, a variety of the lovely *Crocus chrysanthus*

Cytisus scoparius sulphureus, one of the many brooms

Fuchsia, petunia and lobelia attractively grouped in an urn

Prince of Orange, an old variety of the popular fuchsia

This group of bedding plants is a blend of decorative foliage
with flowers such as ageratum, antirrhinum and pelargoniums

soft carmine flowers, will stand a lot of cold and so will the lovely pale pink Apple Blossom. C. F. Ball is rosy-crimson but not so hardy and there are numerous other garden varieties differing a little in habit and the colour of the flowers. In seaside gardens *E. macrantha* is often used as a hedge plant. They can be pruned in July or after flowering and this is the best time to trim escallonias grown as hedges. Escallonias like sunny places but are not in the least fussy about soil. All can be increased by cuttings in July.

eschscholzia

ESCHSCHOLZIA (Californian Poppy). Hardy annuals. 1 ft. Yellow, orange, red, pink or white flowers from June to September. These annuals have a sprawling habit with grey-green ferny leaves and poppy-like flowers produced in profusion throughout the summer. The commonest variety has orange flowers but there are others ranging from ivory white, through pink to crimson.

All eschscholzias can be raised from seed sown in March, April, May or September where the plants are to flower. They delight in well-drained, even rather dry, soils and hot sunny places but can be grown in almost any open position. They often spread rapidly by self-sown seedlings but these tend to revert to the common yellow-flowered type and so it is wise to repurchase seed of special colours annually.

EUONYMUS (Spindle Tree). Hardy evergreen and deciduous shrubs. Prostrate to 8 ft. Red and yellow fruits in autumn in some varieties. The two evergreen kinds commonly grown are the Japanese Euonymus, *Euonymus japonicus*, a tall, well-branched shrub very popular for hedge making near the sea, and the Creeping Euonymus, *E. fortunei* (also known as *E. radicans*), a low-growing shrub which will spread widely if planted on the flat, or grow vertically to a considerable height if planted against a wall. Both have forms with variegated leaves, silver-variegated in *E. fortunei*, usually gold in *E. japonicus*, though there is also a silver form of this. The flowers of these shrubs are insignificant but they are worth planting for their foliage. They can be grown in sun or shade and in almost any soil but *E. japonicus* may be damaged by frost in cold districts or particularly severe winters. All can be increased by cuttings taken in autumn and rooted in a frame. Pruning can be carried out at any time from May to August.

Euonymus europaeus

The deciduous spindle trees are very different in appearance since most produce fine crops of brightly coloured fruits in the autumn. The Common Spindle Tree, *E. europaeus*, and the Broad-leaved Spindle Tree, *E. latifolius*, both have cerise fruits splitting open to reveal orange seeds. Their foliage also turns red and yellow in autumn, but even better in this respect, though far inferior in fruit, is the Winged Spindle Tree, *E. alatus*. All are perfectly hardy and easily grown in almost any soil and open place. They can be increased by seed in spring or by cuttings in summer or autumn. As a rule pruning is unnecessary but overgrown plants can be reduced in size in February or March.

EUPHORBIA (Spurge, Poinsettia). Hardy herbaceous perennials or biennials, tender deciduous shrub. Sprawling to 5 ft. The spurges have yellow, orange or green flower-like bracts from April to July, the poinsettias have scarlet, pink or white bracts from December to March. The hardy euphorbias are grown partly for their decorative foliage and partly for the leafy bracts that surround the rather insignificant flowers. Two of the most striking are *E. griffithii*, 3 to 4 ft., with reddish-orange bracts mainly in April and May and *E. wulfenii*, almost a shrub, 4 ft. high with huge heads of greenish-yellow bracts in early summer. By contrast, *E. myrsinites* is almost prostrate, with greenish-yellow bracts. *E. epithymoides* is 12 to 18 in. high, with lime-yellow bracts. The young shoots of *E. sikkimensis* are red, the bracts pale yellow; *E. lathyrus*, the Caper Spurge, stands bolt upright with leaves splayed out horizontally and has big heads of light green bracts. It is said that moles do not like it. *E. cyparissias* spreads rapidly, is 1 ft. high and has fine heather-like leaves which turn rich yellow in the autumn.

Euphorbia wulfenii

Euphorbia pulcherrima

Most spurges prefer sunny places and well-drained soils but some will grow practically anywhere. They can be readily increased by division in spring except *E. lathyrus* which must be raised from seed—it usually dies after flowering but leaves plenty of self-sown seedlings behind.

The poinsettia is botanically known as *Euphorbia pulcherrima* but in gardens and nurseries is almost invariably listed under its popular name. As is the case with the other euphorbias the flowers are insignificant but they are surrounded by a ring of large coloured leaves or 'bracts' and it is for these that the poinsettia is grown. It is a plant for the intermediate or warm greenhouse, grown in pots in JIP.3 or equivalent rich soil. Though plants can be grown on from year to year, the old plants are often discarded after cuttings have been taken from them in April or May and rooted in a propagator, preferably with bottom heat. Subsequently the rooted cuttings are potted individually and grown on in the greenhouse, shaded from direct sun in summer and watered and fed fairly freely. When in flower poinsettias may be brought into a room for a time, but should not be allowed to get dry or be chilled and should be returned to the greenhouse within a few weeks.

EXACUM. Tender annual or biennial. 9 to 12 in. Lilac blue and yellow flowers from August to December. This is a bushy little annual which makes an excellent pot plant for the cold or cool greenhouse or a sunny window. The lilac-blue flowers, each with a yellow centre, are sweetly scented.

Plants are readily raised from seed sown in March for flowering from October to December or in September for flowering from August to October. A temperature of 15 to 18°C. (59 to 65°F.) will ensure quick germination but thereafter plants can be grown on with considerably less warmth. After the first pricking out in JIP.1, or equivalent soil, pot the seedlings separately in JIP.2 or equivalent and move on as necessary to 4- or 5-in. pots in which they will flower. Water moderately throughout and only shade from strong sunshine from June to September.

Exacum affine

F

FELICIA (Blue Marguerite, Kingfisher Daisy). Half-hardy perennials and annuals. 6 to 18 in. Blue flowers from June to September. *Felicia amelloides*, the Blue Marguerite, is a dainty perennial, 18 in. high, producing a succession of small blue daisies throughout the summer. It is not fully hardy but will survive the winter out of doors in areas where frosts are not severe or prolonged if given a warm sheltered position in well-drained soil. Elsewhere it may be grown as a half-hardy annual, seed being sown in a greenhouse or frame, temperature 15 to 18°C. (59 to 65°F.), in February or March and seedlings hardened off for planting out in late May. Alternatively, it may be grown as a cool greenhouse pot plant, in which case it will need no more than frost protection in winter.

Felicia bergeriana, the Kingfisher Daisy, is a half-hardy annual and is grown from seed in the manner described for *F. amelloides*. It is 6 to 8 in. high and has bright blue yellow-centred flowers.

FORSYTHIA (Golden Bells). Hardy deciduous shrubs. 6 to 10 ft. Yellow flowers in March and April. The abundant yellow flowers of the forsythias appear in March or early April and are among the most brilliant to be seen at that season. One of the finest garden varieties is named *spectabilis* and makes an erect bush up to 10 ft. high, though it can be kept a good deal smaller by cutting out the old flowering stems each spring as soon as the flowers fade. All stems that have not flowered should be retained unpruned. Lynwood has even finer flowers and there are numerous other garden varieties.

Forsythia suspensa makes longer, more arching (or even sprawling) stems

Forsythia suspensa

and can be trained as a wall or fence climber. The flowers are pale yellow. There is an attractive variety of this named *atrocaulis* in which the stems are dark purple and contrast strikingly with the flowers.

Forsythias thrive in practically any soil and sunny or partially shaded position. They can be increased by half-ripe cuttings in summer, hard-wood cuttings in autumn or by layering in late spring.

FRANCOA (Bridal Wreath, Maiden's Wreath). Half-hardy perennials. 2 to 3 ft. White to red flowers in June and July. The francoas make excellent pot plants for cold or cool greenhouses or to be grown in light rooms. The flowers are borne in long narrow curving spikes and are white or pink sometimes spotted with purplish-red. They are almost hardy and where frosts are not severe and prolonged may be grown out of doors. They are not fussy about soil and will grow in full sun or partial shade. In pots they should be grown in JIP.2, or equivalent compost, and should be watered fairly freely from April to September, moderately from October to March. Francoas can be raised from seed but are usually increased by division in March-April, the best time for repotting.

FREESIA. Half-hardy corms. 1½ to 2 ft. Flowers in all colours from November to May and July to August. These lovely flowers, notable for their fragrance, can be grown from seed or from corms. Seed is sown thinly in 5-in. pots in JIS or equivalent seed compost in a cool greenhouse in February or March and the seedlings thinned to 1½ in. apart. They are grown on in a frame or unheated house during the summer and are watered fairly freely. From October they may be given just a little warmth to bring them into flower during November or December. After flowering the plants are gradually allowed to die down until by June they will require no watering. In July or early August the corms are shaken out and repotted, six or seven to a 5-in. pot in JIS or equivalent seed compost. These corms will give flowers a little later than the seedlings, roughly from January to May.

It is also possible to buy specially prepared corms which can be planted out of doors in March or April to flower in July or August. These special corms will not flower again out of doors though they can be lifted and grown on in pots for greenhouse flowering.

In very mild places, where frosts are not severe or prolonged, freesias can be grown permanently out of doors. The hardiest for this purpose is probably the creamy-yellow form of *Freesia refracta*.

The colour range is from white, palest lavender and soft lemon, to deeper shades of blue and yellow and cerise red. All grow about 18 in. tall and carry their clusters of flowers on slender stems which need some support, such as a few thin sticks with soft string looped round them.

FRITILLARIA (Fritillary, Snake's Head, Guinea Flower, Crown Imperial). Hardy bulbs. 1 to 3 ft. White to purple and green, yellow or orange flowers in April or May. One of the best of these distinctive plants for outdoor cultivation is the Snake's Head or Chequered Fritillary, *Fritillaria meleagris*. This is distinctive and elegant, with slender 12- to 18-in. stems terminated in April or May by quite large, pendent, purple and white or purple and mauve flowers. There are also white varieties which may be veined or chequered with green. All are grown from small bulbs which should be planted in autumn, 2 or 3 in. deep, in soil which is fairly moist and rich. The bulbs need not be lifted annually and can often be naturalised in grass that is not mown before July.

The Crown Imperial is also a species of fritillaria, its botanical name being *Fritillaria imperialis*. In some catalogues it is listed under this name. It is a very striking hardy plant with broad strap-shaped leaves and stiff 3-ft. flower spikes terminated by tufts of small leaves and showy hanging clusters of yellow or reddish flowers with a rather unpleasant foxy smell.

The Crown Imperial is grown from large bulbs which should be planted in autumn in any ordinary soil and open sunny place. Cover with about 3 in.

freesia

Fritillaria imperialis

of soil and leave undisturbed for years until overcrowded when the clumps can be lifted in September, divided and immediately replanted.

FUCHSIA. Hardy or half-hardy deciduous shrubs. Prostrate to 5 ft. White, pink, red and purple flowers from June to October. In places where frosts are not severe or prolonged many varieties of fuchsia can be grown out of doors without protection, but other varieties are more tender and are better treated as greenhouse pot plants in winter. Such vigorous varieties as *Fuchsia magellanica riccartonii* and *F.m. gracilis* are often used for hedges in mild places and make fine substantial screens of permanent branches. In slightly colder places these 'hardy' fuchsias may be killed to ground level each winter but shoot up again from the base in spring. Under these conditions they naturally do not make such large plants.

If grown as pot plants, fuchsias may be stood out of doors all summer and need only be brought into a frostproof greenhouse or frame in October. Another way of using them is as summer bedding plants, planted out of doors from June to October and then over-wintered in a frostproof greenhouse or even in a light outhouse or garage.

All fuchsias are very easily grown in practically any soil and sunny or partially shaded positions. They can be trained and pruned to various shapes such as pyramids or standards. All varieties are easily raised from cuttings, which can be rooted at almost any time of the year, spring and early autumn being the favourite seasons. These cuttings should be inserted in sandy soil in a close frame.

Mrs Popple and Margaret, both with red and purple flowers, are two of the most reliable for outdoor cultivation, but there are many others such as Madame Cornelissen, red and white, Chillerton Beauty, pink and violet, and the various forms of *Fuchsia magellanica*. In addition to the large-flowered fuchsias, of which there are many varieties both single and double, there are the very beautiful narrow-tubed varieties derived from the more tender species such as *F. fulgens*, with scarlet flowers and one kind, *F. procumbens*, which is completely prostrate. Its orange and violet flowers are small but they are followed by quite large globular purple fruits.

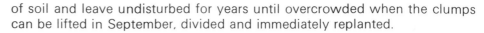

AILLARDIA (Blanket Flower). Hardy herbaceous perennials and half-hardy annuals. 8 to 24 in. Yellow, orange, red or crimson flowers from June to August. There are both perennial and annual kinds of gaillardia but it is the perennials that are most widely grown. All have showy flowers of the daisy type, often yellow with a broad scarlet band, though there are varieties of the perennial gaillardia, such as Wirral Flame and Mandarin, that are mainly reddish-bronze. Most grow about 2 ft. high and are apt to be straggly, so that the support of a few hazel twigs thrust in around the plants in late spring is welcome. There are also dwarf self-supporting varieties. All like sunny places and light well-drained soil, and all make good cut flowers.

The perennial gaillardias can be raised from seed sown in spring but seedlings are likely to vary in colour. For this reason selected forms are increased either by root cuttings in winter or by careful division in spring. The annual gaillardias must be grown each year from seed, which may be sown in a greenhouse or frame in March or out of doors in late April or May, the seedlings being thinned to about 9 in. apart.

GALANTHUS (Snowdrop). Hardy bulbs. 6 to 8 in. White and green flowers from January to March. These lovely early spring-flowering plants are grown from bulbs which should be planted in early autumn 4 in. deep. They will grow in almost any soil and situation, though the Common

Fuchsia magellanica gracilis

gaillardia

Galanthus nivalis

Snowdrop prefers cool, partially shaded positions and is ideal for planting around shrubs or trees. Snowdrops can also be naturalised in grass, provided the grass is not cut until the leaves have died down in June.

There is no kind more beautiful than the Common Snowdrop, *Galanthus nivalis*, but the double-flowered variety of this makes a better display in the mass. There are several other kinds, such as *G. elwesii*, *G. ikariae*, *G. plicatus* and garden varieties of *G. nivalis* such as Atkinsii, S. Arnott and Straffan, which have flowers of superior size. All are white with green markings. *G. elwesii*, *G. ikariae* and *G. plicatus* prefer more open sunny places and are good bulbs for the rock garden.

Snowdrops can be left undisturbed for years, but when they do get over-crowded they can be lifted, divided and replanted in March immediately after flowering.

galega

GALEGA (Goat's Rue). Hardy herbaceous perennials. 4 to 5 ft. Blue, mauve or white flowers from June to August. Though these are rather coarse and rampant perennials, they are nevertheless useful because of the freedom with which they flower and the ease with which they may be grown in practically any soil and place. All make big bushy plants 4 or 5 ft. in height. The pea-type flowers are produced in small clusters from June to August and are bluish-mauve in ·*Galega officinalis*, pale blue in variety *hartlandii* and pinkish-lilac in Lady Wilson. All can be increased by division in spring or autumn.

GALTONIA (Spire Lily, Summer Hyacinth). Hardy bulb. 3 ft. White flowers in July and August. *Galtonia candicans* is a handsome plant with broad strap-shaped leaves and stout 3-ft. flower spikes terminating in long heads of hanging white flowers. It used to be known as *Hyacinthus candicans* and is related to the spring-flowering hyacinths but is so much bigger and looser that there is not much real resemblance. It is fairly hardy and will grow in any reasonably good soil and sunny position and can be left undisturbed until overcrowded. It can then be lifted in March or April, the bulb clusters divided and replanted immediately. Purchased bulbs are also best obtained in spring. They should be spaced about 1 ft. apart and be covered with 3 in. of soil.

gardenia

GARDENIA (Cape Jasmine). Tender evergreen shrub. 2 to 4 ft. White flowers produced throughout the year. Gardenias are grown for their intensely fragrant white flowers which may be single or double. They make excellent pot plants grown in JIP.2, or equivalent soil, or they can be planted in a bed of good soil on the floor of a greenhouse. Gardenias need a fair amount of warmth, either intermediate or warm house conditions, especially if winter flowers are required. Plants should be watered rather freely from April to September, moderately from October to March and will benefit from fairly frequent feeding from May to late August. They should be syringed with water daily in spring and summer as they like a moist atmosphere. Shade should be given from May to September. Propagation is by cuttings of young growth in spring.

GARRYA (Silk Tassel Bush). Hardy evergreen shrub. 6 to 8 ft. Grey-green catkins in January and February. *Garrya elliptica* is a fine hardy evergreen shrub which makes a rounded bush and covers itself in January or February with long, slender greenish-yellow catkins. There are male and female plants and, though both bear catkins, it is in the male form that they are longest and most attractively coloured. The Silk Tassel Bush, as it is appropriately called, is not fussy about soil, but likes a warm, sheltered, sunny position. If desired it may be trained against a sunny wall and will then grow considerably taller. It is increased by cuttings of firm young shoots in July or August, rooted in a propagating frame, preferably with some bottom heat. No pruning is needed but when grown against a wall any badly placed or overcrowded stems can be removed in spring.

garrya

gazania

Genista lydia

Genista hispanica

Gentiana acaulis

GAZANIA (Treasure Flower). Half-hardy herbaceous perennials. Prostrate to 1 ft. Yellow, orange, purple or bronze flowers from June to September. These are showy perennials which are not quite hardy enough to be grown reliably out of doors winter and summer, though they do survive in many seaside gardens. They are trailing in habit and the large single daisy flowers are produced during most of the summer. They may be lemon, orange, purple or bronze, usually with a band of a darker, almost black colour. They like light well-drained soils and hot sunny places and are ideal for planting on dry banks, terrace walls and rock gardens. Gazanias can be raised from seed sown in spring in a cool or intermediate greenhouse, or from cuttings of firm young shoots taken at almost any time from April to October and rooted in a greenhouse or frame.

GENISTA (Broom). Hardy deciduous or evergreen shrubs. 2 to 20 ft. Yellow flowers from April to July. These shrubs are almost inextricably mixed up with cytisus, indeed the plant which most gardeners will first think of as a 'genista', the Fragrant Genista, which is sold in tens of thousands as a pot plant each spring, is really a cytisus which can turn up in catalogues as *Cytisus canariensis, C. fragrans* or *C. racemosus*. It is on the borderline of hardiness and can be grown out of doors only in the mildest parts of the country, when it will make a fine bush of considerable size. But if grown in a 6- or 7-in. pot, it will make a neat plant a couple of feet high, smothered in small, sweetly-scented yellow flowers in spring or early summer. It is an ideal plant for a cool greenhouse since it needs no more than protection from frost. It can be grown in JIP.2 or equivalent soil and should be watered fairly freely from April to September, rather sparingly from October to March. The Porlock Broom is a hybrid from this plant, much like it in appearance but hardier and suitable for planting out of doors in many sunny, sheltered places.

Genista lydia is quite hardy and makes a graceful spreading but rather dwarf bush covered with golden flowers in June. The so-called Spanish Gorse, *G. hispanica*, is another dwarf spreading genista—a dense, spiny plant with golden flowers in May. The Dyer's Greenwood, *G. tinctoria*, is a prostrate shrub very free flowering in June and July and even more effective in its double-flowered variety. It will grow well on top of a terrace wall or on a sunny ledge in the rock garden. At the other end of the scale is the Mount Etna Broom, *G. aetnensis*, which grows 15 or 20 ft. high, has slender hanging branchlets and abundant small yellow flowers in July. The Madeira Broom, *G. virgata*, is also a big but stiffer bush producing its yellow flowers in June and July.

All genistas like sun, warmth and good drainage. They will grow in the poorest of soils and can be raised from seed sown in spring and most can also be increased by cuttings of firm young growth in July and August.

GENTIANA (Gentian). Hardy rock plants or herbaceous perennials. Prostrate to 18 in. Blue, purple, or white flowers from April to November. Almost all the gentians that matter from the garden standpoint are low-growing, spreading plants, suitable for the rock garden. The one notable exception is the Willow-leaved Gentian, *Gentiana asclepiadea*, which makes slender arching stems, 18 in. or so in height, bearing purple or white blooms in June and July. It is a plant for cool, partially shady places. Most of the other kinds like sunny open places in soil containing plenty of peat or leafmould as well as gritty sand to keep it open.

Gentiana acaulis, is typical of the family, making spreading tufts of growth on which the large deep blue flowers sit in spring. The Spring Gentian, *G. verna*, is much smaller, much brighter and purer in colour, and a little more difficult to grow. There are several summer-flowering kinds with clusters of purple flowers such as *G. lagodechiana* and *G. septemfida*, and these are amongst the easiest to grow, thriving in most soils and in almost any reasonably open place. For early autumn there is the lovely Chinese Gentian, *G. sino-ornata*, with sky-blue flowers striped with white. It dis-

70

likes lime and will grow in practically pure peat and sand. *G. macaulayi* is similar in appearance and requirements.

All these gentians can be increased by careful division in spring and most can also be raised from seed sown in a greenhouse or frame in spring.

Gentiana sino-ornata

GERANIUM (Cranesbill). Hardy herbaceous perennials. Prostrate to 3 ft. Blue, purple, magenta or white flowers from May to September. These plants have nothing to do with the popular bedding plants known as geraniums, which are correctly pelargoniums and are described here under that name. The true geraniums are rock or herbaceous plants, quite hardy and easily grown in almost any soil and open position.

Typical of the range of the family are the Bloody Cranesbill, *Geranium sanguineum*, and the Blue Geranium, *G. ibericum*, the first a low-growing spreading plant with magenta flowers, the latter 2 ft. high with bright lavender-blue flowers. Both flower in June and July. *G. sanguineum* has a delightful variety, the Lancastrian Cranesbill, *G. sanguineum lancastriense*, which is even more mat forming and has clear pink flowers. The Meadow Cranesbill, *G. pratense*, is much like *G. ibericum* and it has several good varieties including one with perfectly double lavender-blue flowers and one with white flowers; *G. grandiflorum* is shorter and has large purplish-blue flowers. *G. endressii* will grow anywhere, in sun or semi-shade, is 12 to 18 in. high and has bright pink flowers all the summer. The Dusky Cranesbill, *G. phaeum*, is well named as its flowers are an almost blackish-purple, while in *G. armenum* they are magenta. Both are around 2 ft. in height. *G. macrorrhizum* is a mat-forming plant, excellent as ground cover with aromatic leaves and small pale pink flowers. *G. subcaulescens* has small rosy-carmine flowers on 6- to 8-in. stems and is a good plant for the rock garden. There are many more. All can be increased by division in the spring and autumn.

gerbera

GERBERA (Barberton Daisy). Tender herbaceous perennials. 1 to 1½ ft. Yellow, orange, pink and red flowers from May to August. These graceful plants, with narrow-petalled daisy flowers, are a little too tender to be grown out of doors except where frosts are neither severe nor prolonged, but are ideal as pot plants for the cool greenhouse. They like a gritty, well-drained soil.

Plants can be raised from seed sown in a temperature of 15 to 18°C. (59 to 65°F.) in spring. Later, seedlings should be potted singly in a John Innes type compost containing rather more than the usual quantity of sand. Plants must be watered freely in summer, very sparingly in winter. They like sun, air and just enough artificial heat to exclude frost. Gerberas produce their flowers in summer on 12- to 18-in. stems. The colour range is from pink to flame, with many lovely intermediate shades of apricot and orange.

GEUM (Avens). Hardy herbaceous perennials. 1 to 2 ft. Yellow, orange or red flowers from June to September. These easily grown hardy herbaceous plants have an unusually long flowering season. Typical of the family are Mrs Bradshaw, with semi-double scarlet flowers; Lady Stratheden, yellow, and Fire Opal, coppery orange, all borne on 2-ft. stems from June to September. A smaller plant is *Geum borisii* with single orange-red flowers on 1-ft. stems.

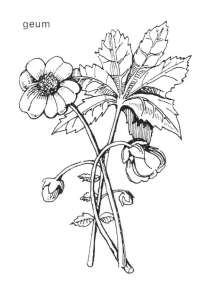
geum

All are quite hardy but like well-drained soils and warm sunny situations. Though geums can be raised from seed sown in spring, there is often some variation in the colour or quality of the flowers of garden varieties, so selected varieties are better increased by division in spring. *G. borisii*, being a species unimproved by hybridization, comes true to type from seed.

GLADIOLUS. Half-hardy corms. 1½ to 4 ft. Flowers in all colours from May to September. These brilliant summer-flowering plants are grown from corms almost all of which must be planted between March and May. They like a sunny open situation and rather rich well-drained

large-flowered gladiolus

soil. Corms should be spaced at least 6 in. apart and be covered with 3 in. of soil. The heavy flower spikes of some of the bigger varieties may require individual staking. About six weeks after flowering the plants should be lifted, the tops cut off about an inch above the new corms, and the old withered corms removed from beneath the new corms. Then the new corms are stored away for the winter in a cool dry frostproof place. A number of small cormlets may be found around the main corms. These can also be stored away and replanted the following spring but they may take a year or so to attain flowering size.

There are a great many varieties differing in size, form and colour of bloom. The Miniatures, Butterfly varieties and the Primulinus varieties have smaller flowers but do not differ in their cultural requirements. The Early-flowering gladioli, which may be listed as *Gladiolus colvillei* or *G. nanus*, must be planted in autumn and since they are too tender to over-winter out of doors except in very mild districts they are usually grown as pot plants in a slightly heated greenhouse. Potted in September or October and grown on in a temperature around 10°C. (50°F.) they will flower the following May or June. After flowering the corms are treated like those of outdoor gladioli. The Byzantine Gladiolus, *G. byzantinus*, with magenta flowers in May and June, is the hardiest of all and can be left out of doors throughout the year except in very cold places.

butterfly gladiolus

GLORIOSA (Glory Lily). Tender bulb. Climbing. Crimson and yellow flowers from July to September. This remarkable plant has handsome light crimson and yellow flowers shaped rather like those of a turk's cap lily. It is, in fact, closely related to the lilies but has slender stems and climbs by tendrils, though not to any great height. It can be grown easily in an intermediate greenhouse in JIP.1 or peat potting compost. Pot in March or April covering bulbs with 2 in. of compost, water rather sparingly at first, freely as growth starts and maintain a rather moist atmosphere by frequent syringing with water. Shade from direct sunshine from June to August inclusive. After flowering gradually reduce the amount of water and keep quite dry from about November to early March when the bulbs can be repotted. Increase is by division of the bulb clusters at potting time.

GLOXINIA. Tender tuberous-rooted plants. 9 to 12 in. Purple, violet, red, pink and white flowers from July to September. These are immensely showy greenhouse plants with velvet-green leaves and large funnel-shaped flowers in rich or brilliant shades of purple, violet, pink and red, sometimes spotted or veined on a white ground. They have tuberous roots which can be stored dry during the winter, with little more than frost protection, but they need a fair amount of warmth once they are started into growth in February or March. It is usual to start the tubers by placing them almost shoulder to shoulder in seed boxes filled with peat or sand, and keeping them in a temperature of 18°C. (65°F.). Pot them singly in JIP.1 or equivalent soil in 3-in. pots as soon as they start to make leaves. Thereafter they are grown on in a similar temperature and are moved on into 5- or 6-in. pots for flowering in summer. Little artificial heat is likely to be required from May onwards as gloxinias thrive in cool or intermediate house temperatures. They must be watered freely and be shaded from strong sunshine. In autumn they are gradually dried off and may be tapped out of their pots and be packed close together on the greenhouse staging, but should not be shaken clear of soil till they are restarted into growth.

GODETIA. Hardy annuals. 8 to 24 in. Mauve, pink to crimson and white flowers from June to August. Godetias are easily grown in practically any soil and sunny or shady position. There are two main types: the tall godetias with spikes of flowers about 2 ft. high, and the dwarf or azalea-flowered varieties which make bushier plants from 8 to 12 in. high. Both types are grown from seed sown in March, April, May or September where the plants are to flower. Seedlings should be thinned to 6 or 9 in.

primulinus gladiolus

GYPSOPHILA. Hardy herbaceous perennials or rock plants, and hardy annuals. Prostrate to 3 ft. White or pink flowers from May to September. Three gypsophilas are valuable garden plants, one an annual, one a hardy herbaceous plant and one a rock plant.

The Annual Gypsophila, *Gypsophila elegans*, is a thin-stemmed, sprawling plant producing loose sprays of fairly large white or pink flowers from June to September. Seed may be sown in March, April, May or September where the plants are to flower, seedlings being thinned to 6 in.

The perennial kind, *G. paniculata*, is a taller, more branching plant, making a bush of slender but stiff stems to a height and breadth of 3 ft. The flowers, produced in July and August, are small, single white in the common variety, double white in Bristol Fairy and double pink in Flamingo. Rosy Veil is pink and semi-sprawling in habit. All have long tap roots which should be disturbed as little as possible. They will grow in any reasonably well-drained soil and sunny place, but prefer chalky soils. Single-flowered kinds can be raised from seed, but the doubles are either grafted on roots of single-flowered seedlings or are raised from cuttings of non-flowering shoots in summer.

The Creeping Gypsophila, *G. repens*, is a slender trailing perennial with small white or pale pink flowers similar to those of *G. paniculata* but produced in late spring and early summer. It likes well-drained soil and a sunny place and looks most attractive planted in a rock garden or on a dry wall. It can be raised from seed sown in spring.

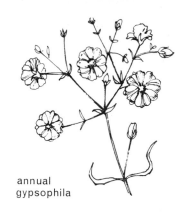

annual
gypsophila

H

AMAMELIS (Witch-hazel). Hardy deciduous shrubs. 8 to 12 ft. Yellow or orange flowers from November to February. These winter-flowering shrubs have remarkable flowers with narrow, twisted, yellow or coppery-orange petals often with a pleasant fragrance. Some varieties start to flower in November and others continue until February. The best is the Chinese Witch-hazel, *Hamamelis mollis*, which is sweetly scented, deep yellow in the common form and pale yellow in the variety *pallida*.

All are quite hardy and easily grown in any reasonably rich soil and in full sun or partial shade. They make big, open bushes and do not normally require pruning, but if they grow too large they can be reduced in size after flowering. Increase may be by layering in spring or detaching rooted suckers in autumn.

hamamelis

HEBE (Veronica). Hardy or slightly tender evergreen flowering shrubs. 2 to 12 ft. White, pink, red, crimson, purple and blue flowers from July to October. These handsome shrubs, still listed as veronica in many nursery catalogues, are valuable both for their foliage and their flowers, which are produced in spikes and often continue well into the autumn. One of the hardiest is *Hebe brachysiphon*, a neat 5-ft. bush with box-like leaves and white flowers in July. Most showy are the many garden hybrids such as Autumn Glory, purplish-blue, and Simon Delaux, red, which thrive best in mild coastal districts or places where frosts are not severe or prolonged. The Willow-leaved Veronica, *H. salicifolia*, has long, narrow spikes of white flowers and may be anything from 5 to 10 ft. high. Midsummer Beauty is rather similar but lavender blue. *H. andersonii variegata* has pale lavender flowers and cream-variegated leaves and *H. armstrongii* is grown for its tiny coppery-coloured leaves.

All these can be increased by cuttings in summer or early autumn. They like sun and warmth but are not fussy about soil. If overgrown they can be pruned in spring.

helenium

HELENIUM. Hardy herbaceous perennials. 3 to 6 ft. Yellow or bronzy-crimson flowers in July and August. Heleniums are easily grown plants thriving in practically any soil and reasonably open situation. They flower in July and August, the colour range of their daisy-like flowers being from yellow to wallflower red. Good varieties are Madame Canivat, yellow and bronze, 3 to 4 ft.; Moerheim Beauty, wallflower red, 4 ft., and Riverton Gem, yellow splashed with bronze red, 5 to 6 ft. All can be increased by division in spring or autumn.

HELIANTHEMUM (Sun Rose). Hardy evergreen rock plants. 9 to 12 in. White, yellow, orange, copper, pink to crimson flowers in May and June. These are bushy, sprawling plants admirable for planting on sunny rock gardens or dry walls. The flowers do not last long but are constantly replaced, so that a plant will remain highly decorative throughout May and June. In fact, helianthemums are amongst the most vividly coloured of all rock plants.

Most varieties have single flowers but a few, such as Jubilee, yellow, and Fireball, crimson, are double. All can be increased by cuttings in July in a propagating frame and seed may also be sown in spring but seedlings are likely to vary greatly in colour and quality of flower. Plants can be kept more compact and bushy by being lightly clipped with shears each July after flowering, but care must be taken not to cut back into any of the hard old wood.

helianthemum

HELIANTHUS (Sunflower). Hardy herbaceous perennials and annuals. 2 to 8 ft. Yellow or crimson flowers from July to October. There are both annual and perennial sunflowers, almost all perfectly hardy and easily grown in almost any soil and reasonably open place. The perennial kinds are excellent plants for the middle or back of the border.

Most spectacular of the annuals is the Giant Sunflower, *Helianthus annuus*, with 7- or 8-ft. stems carrying huge flowers largely composed of a central pad-like brownish-purple disk which later produces a crop of large seeds, often used for poultry feeding. The disk is surrounded by a fringe of yellow petals. The whole plant is too clumsy to be really beautiful but can be striking in the right place. The seeds should be sown in pairs in March or April where plants are to flower and later the seedlings should be thinned to one at each position. There are also smaller annual sunflowers from 3 to 4 ft. in height, with flowers from pale to deep yellow and in shades of bronze and crimson or in mixtures of these colours. All are grown from seed sown out of doors in March, April or September, the seedlings being thinned to at least a foot apart.

Of the perennials the best are Loddon Gold, 5 ft. high with large double golden-yellow flowers; *maximus*, 4 ft. high with single yellow flowers, and Monarch, 6 to 7 ft. high with very large deep yellow flowers, each with a black centre. All flower in early autumn. Monarch is the only one that needs any special care, as in cold, wet places the roots may die in winter. Under these conditions it is best to lift some roots each autumn and place them in a frame until the following spring. All will grow in any reasonably good well-drained soil and can be easily increased by division in spring or autumn. As they grow fast it usually pays to lift and divide the roots every second or third year.

helianthus

HELICHRYSUM. Hardy or half-hardy evergreen shrubs and half-hardy annuals. 1 to 3 ft. White, yellow, orange, pink to crimson flowers from June to September. The plant which most people know under this name is *Helichrysum bracteatum*, a showy half-hardy annual with 'everlasting' flowers—flowers composed of rather chaffy petals which can easily be dried and used for winter decoration. For this purpose the flowers are cut just before they are fully open and are suspended head downward in a cool, airy shed or room for a few weeks to dry.

The annual helichrysum is grown from seed sown in a greenhouse, temperature 15 to 18°C. (59 to 65°F.), in March or April, the seedlings being pricked out and later hardened off for planting out of doors 9 in. apart in May or early June. Alternatively, seed can be sown out of doors in late April or early May where plants are to flower. Plants grow 1½ to 2½ ft. in height and like a sunny place and a well-drained soil. There is a good colour range from yellow to dark red.

There are several grey-leaved helichrysums which are bushy plants ranging from about 1 to 3 ft. in height. All are near the borderline of tenderness and are plants for sheltered sunny places in particularly well-drained soil. They can be raised from cuttings in summer or early autumn. Among the best are *H. bellidioides*, only 3 in. high with white everlasting flowers, and *H. splendidum*, usually listed as *H. trilineatum*, 1½ to 3 ft. high with silver-grey leaves and yellow flowers in July.

heliopsis

HELIOPSIS. Hardy herbaceous perennials. 4 to 5 ft. Yellow flowers in July and August. Heliopsis are hardy herbaceous plants closely resembling sunflowers but without the tendency to become invasive, which makes some sunflowers a nuisance. Most kinds are about 5 ft. high and produce their single or double, deep yellow flowers in July and August. One of the finest is the Zinnia-flowered Heliopsis, *Heliopsis scabra zinniaeflora*. All are easily grown in practically any soil and open place and can be increased by division in spring or autumn.

HELIOTROPIUM (Heliotrope, Cherry Pie). Half-hardy perennials. 1½ to 2 ft. Purple flowers from June to August. This is a favourite plant used for summer bedding or as a greenhouse pot plant and often known as Cherry Pie. It is famous for the perfume of its lavender-purple flowers, though some forms have far less of this than others. Heliotrope can be grown from seed or cuttings. Seed is sown in a greenhouse, temperature 15 to 18°C. (59 to 65°F.), in February or March, the seedlings being pricked off or potted singly in JIP.1, or equivalent soil, and subsequently hardened off for planting out of doors in early June. Cuttings are prepared from firm young shoots in spring or early summer, and are rooted in a propagating frame with bottom heat. Heliotropes like a sunny place and a fairly good soil. If grown in a greenhouse throughout the year they do best in intermediate house conditions in winter but will survive in a cool house if necessary.

heliotrope

HELIPTERUM (Rhodanthe). Half-hardy annuals. 1 ft. Pink or white flowers from July to September. These are 'everlasting' flowers with chaffy petals which dry easily if cut and handled in exactly the same way as *Helichrysum bracteatum*. Cultivation is also the same as for that plant. The colour range of *Helipterum manglesii*, the kind usually grown, is more restricted than that of the helichrysum and the flowers are smaller, but they are decorative and freely produced.

HELLEBORUS (Hellebore, Christmas Rose, Lenten Rose). Hardy herbaceous perennials. 9 to 24 in. White to maroon or green flowers from November to April. This is the family to which belong both the Christmas Rose and the Lenten Rose as well as several other handsome herbaceous perennials. The Christmas Rose, *Helleborus niger*, has white flowers on stiff 12-in. stems in November, December or January. The Lenten Rose, *H. orientalis*, has white, pale pink to deep maroon flowers on 18-in. stems in March and April. The Corsican Hellebore, *H. corsicus*, has handsome foliage and pale green flowers in big clusters on 2-ft. stems in February and March. All the hellebores can be grown in any reasonably good soil and most enjoy cool, partially shady places but the Corsican Hellebore thrives in full sun.

All can be raised from seed sown in spring though this is often very slow in germinating. Plants can be divided but hellebores do not like disturbance and may take several years to settle down again.

Helleborus orientalis

hemerocallis

HEMEROCALLIS (Day Lily). Hardy herbaceous perennials. 2 to 4 ft. Yellow, orange, pink to mahogany-crimson flowers in July and August. These are easily grown hardy perennials with lily-like flowers which individually only last for a day but are produced in succession throughout July and August. The flowers are borne on stems 2 to 4 ft. high and the colour range is from pale yellow through orange to an intense mahogany crimson. All will grow in practically any soil and sunny or partially shaded position and can be increased by division in spring or autumn.

HESPERIS (Sweet Rocket). Hardy herbaceous perennial or biennial. 2 to 3 ft. White or purple flowers in June. This old-fashioned plant with the common name of Sweet Rocket has loose spikes of single or double flowers which are sweetly scented. It will grow freely in most soils in sun or partial shade and, though normally short lived, the single-flowered forms usually reproduce themselves by self-sown seedlings. Unfortunately, the more beautiful double-flowered varieties do not produce any seed and must be increased by division in spring. It is not nearly so easy to maintain stocks in this way and in consequence double varieties are scarce.

heuchera

HEUCHERA (Alum Root, Coral Bells). Hardy herbaceous perennials. 15 to 24 in. White, pink or red flowers in July and August. Heucheras are tufted perennials with rounded leaves and elegant sprays of small white, pink or red flowers in July and August. They are excellent plants for the front row of the border and are useful cut flowers as well.

There are numerous varieties differing mainly in colour, or a mixed strain, such as the Bressingham Hybrids, will give all the heuchera colours. All are about 2 ft. high except *Heuchera tiarelloides* which is not much over 1 ft. Heucheras are not fussy about soil, will grow in sun or partial shade and are best increased by division in spring or autumn.

HIBISCUS. Hardy deciduous shrubs, tender shrubs and hardy annuals. 18 in. to 12 ft. Flowers of all colours from June to October. There are a number of different species of hibiscus quite different in their cultural requirements and the purpose they serve in the garden. *Hibiscus syriacus* is one of the finest late-flowering shrubs, producing its white, pink, carmine or blue mallow-like flowers in September. There are both single- and double-flowered varieties. It makes a rather stiff bush, eventually reaching a height of 12 ft., though it can be kept smaller by pruning in February. It likes a warm sunny position but is not fussy about soil. Increase is by autumn cuttings.

The Annual Hibiscus, *H. trionum*, is raised from seed sown in a greenhouse, temperature 15 to 18°C. (59 to 65°F.), in February or March, seedlings being pricked out and hardened off for planting out 9 in. apart in a sunny place in May. The plant grows 18 in. high and produces its yellow and maroon flowers in summer followed by inflated seed vessels rather like little Chinese lanterns. They can be used very attractively in flower arrangements.

The Rose Mallow, *H. rosa-sinensis*, is a tender shrub with flamboyant scarlet, pink, yellow or buff flowers in summer. It will succeed under intermediate or warm house conditions but otherwise can be grown without difficulty provided it can be given a fair amount of room. It should be watered freely from April to September, moderately from October to March and can be increased by cuttings of firm young growth in spring or summer in a propagator.

Hibiscus rosa-sinensis

HIPPEASTRUM (Amaryllis, Barbados Lily). Half-hardy and tender bulbs. 1 to 2 ft. White, pink to crimson flowers from November to June. These showy bulbous-rooted plants are sometimes known as amaryllis, a name that really belongs to the Belladonna Lily. The Barbados Lily, *Hippeastrum equestre*, has very large funnel-shaped flowers, usually crimson or scarlet, though there are also pink and white varieties. The flowers are carried on straight stiff stems, 2 ft. high, between March and June and the strap-shaped leaves appear after the flowers.

Plants must be grown in a greenhouse throughout. In winter they are rested and need little water and a temperature around 7 to 10°C. (45 to 50°F.). From February to April plants are started into growth by being given more water and a temperature of 15 to 18°C. (59 to 65°F.). Alternatively, specially prepared bulbs can be purchased in September, potted straight away and grown on in a warm greenhouse or warm, well-lighted room to flower by Christmas or even earlier.

Another species, *H. pratense*, often listed as *Habranthus pratensis*, is nearly hardy and can be grown out of doors, where frosts are unlikely to be either severe or prolonged, if planted in a very sheltered sunny place, as at the foot of a wall facing south. The scarlet flowers are produced in May or June on 1-ft. stems.

HOSTA (Plantain Lily). Hardy herbaceous perennials. 1½ to 3 ft. White or mauve flowers from July to September. Though some hostas have quite attractive flowers, these plants are grown principally for their large and handsome leaves. These are broad and grey-blue in *Hosta sieboldiana;* narrow and shining green in *H. lancifolia;* wavy, light green with a central band of white in *H. undulata;* wavy, dark green edged with white in *H. crispula,* and yellow margined with green in *H. fortunei albopicta.* There are numerous others but names tend to be confused and it is wise to select the kinds one likes while they are in leaf. One of the most handsome in flower is *H. sieboldiana,* which has tubular white flowers in August.

Hostas will thrive in sun or shade in practically any soil, but are seen at their best in fairly rich, slightly moist soils. They can be increased by division in spring or autumn.

hosta

HOYA (Wax Flower). Tender climbers or trailers. White, pink and purple flowers from July to September. The popular name Wax Flower is appropriate as the pendent clusters of small star-shaped flowers do look as if fashioned in wax. Two species are commonly grown, *Hoya carnosa,* a twiner with white or flesh-pink flowers each with a little purple eye, and *H. bella,* a much smaller plant with arching or trailing stems with white and purple flowers. Both are heavily scented.

Hoya carnosa will thrive in cool or intermediate house conditions and should be allowed to twine around a pillar, up a trellis or on wires. *H. bella* prefers the warmer atmosphere of the intermediate house and can be grown in pots or hanging baskets without needing any support. Both should be grown in JIP.1, or equivalent soil, should be watered freely from April to September, moderately from October to March and should be shaded from direct sunshine in summer. They can be increased by cuttings taken in spring or summer and rooted in a propagating case preferably with bottom heat.

HYACINTHUS (Hyacinth). Hardy bulbs. 1 to 1½ ft. Flowers in all colours from December to May. These popular spring-flowering bulbs are usually seen in pots or bowls indoors or under glass but can equally well be grown in beds out of doors. Bulbs should be obtained in August or September for pot or bowl culture, October or November for planting out of doors. If in drained pots, ordinary JIP.1 or equivalent compost may be used; if in bowls without drainage holes, special bulb fibre containing charcoal and crushed oyster shell must be used. In either case the bulbs may be placed almost shoulder to shoulder and should be almost, but not quite, covered. Pots and bowls should then be put in a cool place for at least eight weeks for the bulbs to make roots. After this they may be brought into a living room or greenhouse either with or without artificial heat according to the time at which flowers are required. After flowering bulbs can be planted out of doors.

When grown in the garden, bulbs should be spaced 8 in. apart and be

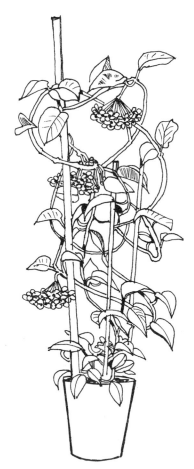

Hoya carnosa

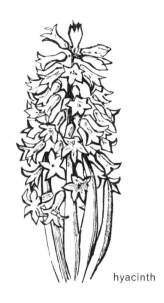
hyacinth

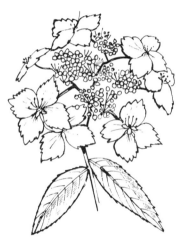
Hydrangea petiolaris

covered with 2 in. of soil. They like fairly rich but porous soil and a sunny place. Bonemeal can be applied at 4 oz. to the sq. yd. prior to planting. After flowering leave the foliage to die down, then lift the bulbs and store them in a dry, cool place until planting time.

HYDRANGEA. Hardy or slightly tender deciduous shrubs and climbers. 3 to 6 ft. White, blue, pink to purple flowers from July to September. These very handsome summer-flowering shrubs are mostly too tender for really cold gardens, though they do excellently where frosts are neither severe nor prolonged. One of the hardiest is *Hydrangea paniculata*, which produces its large cone-shaped clusters of cream-white flowers in late summer. Unlike other kinds, it can be pruned hard back each March if the finest flower heads are required. This will restrict height to about 3 ft. whereas unpruned plants may eventually reach 6 ft. Also hardy in most places is *H. arborescens grandiflora*, a rather broad shrub, 3 or 4 ft. high, with light green leaves and globular heads of creamy-white flowers in July and August.

The coloured hydrangeas are derived from *H. macrophylla* and either have globular heads of flowers or else flat heads in which all the central flowers are small and bead-like with an encircling ring of the typical broad flat flowers. The latter type are known as Lacecaps. Colours range from white to crimson and purple, but colour is affected by the soil. In an acid soil the pink or red varieties become blue or purple and the reverse effect occurs in an alkaline (chalky) soil though these effects can be modified by chemical treatment. Blueing powders are available for increasing the blue or purple colour and must be used according to manufacturers' instructions. A similar result can be obtained by watering every week, from the time growth starts until the flowers are fully open, with 2 gallons to each plant of a solution made by dissolving $\frac{1}{4}$ oz. of iron sulphate and $\frac{1}{4}$ oz. of aluminium sulphate in each gallon of water. It is wise to confine any chemical treatment to varieties that do 'blue' readily, for example, Generale Vicomtesse de Vibraye, Garten-Baudirektor Kuhnert and Maréchal Foch.

All these hydrangeas succeed in sun or partial shade. They like plenty of moisture, need no pruning beyond the removal of faded flower trusses each March (except for *H. paniculata* as explained above) and are readily increased by cuttings in summer.

Hydrangeas also make excellent pot or tub plants for the greenhouse, heated or unheated. They must be freely watered while in growth but otherwise need no special care. If rather acid loam and plenty of peat are used, the flowers of coloured varieties will come blue or purple.

In addition to the above, one species, *H. petiolaris*, is a vigorous climber. It will cling to walls, tree trunks or similar supports with aerial roots like an ivy, can grow up to a considerable height and produce flat clusters of white lacecap flowers in June and July. It is one of the hardier kinds.

HYPERICUM (St John's Wort, Rose of Sharon). Hardy deciduous or evergreen shrubs and rock plants. 6 in. to 5 ft. Yellow flowers from June to September. The shrubby hypericums, of which there are many, are useful because of their usually long flowering season and the ease with which they will grow in any reasonably good soil and in sun or partial shade. From a garden standpoint many are much alike with saucer-shaped golden-yellow flowers produced on freely-branched bushes 3 to 5 ft. high. The variety Hidcote is one of the best because of the good size of its flowers and the fact that in a mild winter it can be almost evergreen. *Hypericum moserianum* is much shorter, usually under 2 ft., with smaller flowers very freely produced; it has a variety, *tricolor*, with leaves attractively variegated with pink and cream.

The Rose of Sharon, *H. calycinum*, is a trailing evergreen suitable for covering banks or carpeting the ground wherever weeds are to be smothered. It has a particular liking for chalk and will grow well in shade or in hot dry places. The large golden-yellow flowers appear throughout the summer.

Of the rock-garden kinds four of the best are *H. olympicum*, 1 ft. high with pale yellow flowers; *H. repens*, with thin wiry stems and deep yellow flowers; *H. coris*, which in appearance is intermediate between the previous two and *H. fragile*, 6 in. high, with pale gold flowers.

All these hypericums thrive in any ordinary soil and open, sunny position. Most kinds can be increased by seed in spring and the Rose of Sharon can also be divided in autumn.

IBERIS (Candytuft). Hardy annuals and hardy herbaceous perennials. 3 to 18 in. White, pink or purple flowers from May to August. There are both annual and perennial kinds, the annuals are usually listed as candytuft and the perennials as iberis, which is the botanical name for this entire group of plants. The annual kinds have either flattish heads of white, pink or purple flowers or, in the Rocket Candytuft, *Iberis amara*, spikes of white flowers in summer. They are easily grown from seed sown in March, April, May or September where the plants are to flower, the seedlings being thinned to 4 to 6 in. and the plants discarded after flowering. They like a sunny place and almost any soil.

The perennial kinds are equally accommodating and are fine plants for a sunny rock garden or dry wall, growing 9 to 15 in. high and having evergreen foliage. They can also be grown from seed, though seedlings are unlikely to flower before their second year. Alternatively, cuttings can be rooted in a frame in summer. Most have white heads of flowers in May and June, one of the best varieties being named Snowflake, but the Gibraltar Candytuft, *I. gibraltarica*, has pale lilac-purple flowers. It is not so hardy as most and should be given a specially sunny place in well-drained soil. The lowest growing kind is *I. saxatilis*, often not exceeding 3 in. in height.

annual iberis

IMPATIENS (Balsam, Busy Lizzie). Hardy and half-hardy annuals and half-hardy perennials. 6 in. to 6 ft. White, pink, red or purple flowers produced all year. The Balsam, *Impatiens balsamina*, is a half-hardy annual grown from seed sown in an intermediate or warm greenhouse in March, April or May. The seedlings are potted on, first into 3-in. pots, then to 5-in. and, if necessary, eventually to 8- or 9-in. pots. They are watered freely and will produce their long spikes of pink, scarlet, crimson or white double flowers from June to September. Balsams are commonly grown as pot plants but may also be planted out in summer as bedding plants in warm, sunny places.

There are two species of Busy Lizzie, *I. wallerana* (formerly *holstii*) and *I. sultani*, but they are so much alike and have been so frequently hybridised to produce improved garden varieties that there is no need to distinguish between them. They are half-hardy perennials frequently grown as half-hardy annuals and they make freely-branched plants varying in height from 6 to 18 in. The flowers are single, white, pink, scarlet or purple and are very freely produced in summer if the plants are grown as half-hardy annuals and planted out of doors in May or early June. If they are grown as pot plants in a cool or intermediate greenhouse the flowers are produced more or less throughout the year.

impatiens

Busy Lizzies can be grown from cuttings which will root in a propagator at any time in spring or summer. However, they are so easily raised from seed that this is the method usually adopted. Cultivation is then the same as for the Balsam but plants will thrive in full sun or partial shade.

A third species sometimes grown is *I. roylei*, a hardy annual with pink or purple flowers from July to September. It makes a big branching plant 5 or 6 ft. high and likes damp places though it can be grown in ordinary beds

Incarvillea delavayi

provided they do not become very dry. It spreads readily by self-sown seedlings and has become naturalised by stream-sides and canals in many parts of the country.

INCARVILLEA. Hardy herbaceous perennials. 1½ to 2 ft. Pink or carmine flowers from May to June. These remarkable plants have showy trumpet flowers rather like those of a gloxinia in shape. They are quite hardy, and the tuberous roots should be planted in a sunny place in rather rich but well-drained soil. In addition to the usual rosy-red varieties, of which *Incarvillea delavayi* is typical, there is a lovely soft pink variety named Bees' Pink. All can be increased by careful division in spring.

IPOMOEA (Morning Glory). Half-hardy annuals and perennials. Climbing. Blue, purple, pink and white flowers from July to September. These are vigorous twining plants of which one of the loveliest varieties is Heavenly Blue, with broadly funnel-shaped, sky-blue flowers produced from July to September. Flying Saucers is similar but blue and white. Both are half-hardy perennials but are almost invariably grown as half-hardy annuals and discarded after flowering. They can be grown as greenhouse pot plants trained around three or four slender bamboo canes, or they can be planted out of doors in early June in a warm sunny spot. In either case seed is sown two to a pot in a greenhouse or frame, temperature 15 to 18°C. (59 to 65°F.), in February or March. There are also pink- and red-flowered morning glories, probably of hybrid origin, which should be grown as half-hardy annuals in exactly the same way as Heavenly Blue and Flying Saucers.

By contrast, *I. learii* is a true perennial, though too tender to be grown out of doors in Britain. It is a very vigorous twiner with purplish-blue flowers all summer and is best grown in frostproof greenhouses or conservatories planted in a bed of good soil and trained to wires below the rafters. It can be grown from seed. Some species have been renamed Pharbitis.

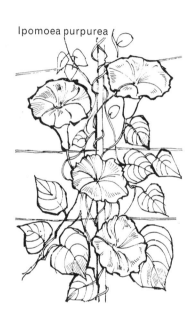

Ipomoea purpurea

IRIS. Hardy herbaceous perennials and bulbs. 4 in. to 4 ft. Flowers of all colours from November to July. The popular June-flowering or Bearded Irises are herbaceous perennials with fleshy root-like stems (rhizomes) which lie flat on the surface of the ground. They have a wide colour range and in height vary from about 9 in. to 4 ft. All are hardy and easily grown in almost any soil and sunny place, though they like a chalky soil best provided it is not starved. All can be increased by division in spring, summer (immediately after flowering) or autumn.

There are also dwarf irises, of rather similar general appearance and habit, such as the Crimean Iris, *Iris chamaeiris*, which flowers in May, is 1 ft. or less in height and suitable for the front of the border or the rock garden. Flowers are white, yellow, lavender or purple.

The Siberian Iris, *I. sibirica*, flowers in June and makes big clumps of narrow grassy leaves and slender flower stems, bearing blue, purple or white flowers in June. It will grow anywhere, but likes best a place near the edge of water. Plants can be divided in spring or autumn. The Swamp Iris, *I. laevigata*, and the Japanese Iris, *I. kaempferi*, are, even more, water lovers, the former likes to be planted actually in water 2 or 3 in. deep, the Japanese Iris in the boggy ground around pools. Both grow about 3 ft. high and produce their showy purple or violet flowers, often splashed with white, in June and July. Increase is by division in spring.

The Algerian Iris, *I. unguicularis*, makes large leafy clumps in which the pale blue flowers are sometimes partially hidden, but it is a very useful plant as it flowers in winter from about November to March. It likes warm, sunny places and usually flowers most freely in well-drained soil. It can be increased by division in spring.

Also for early flowering there are several bulbous irises, of which the two best are the Violet-scented Iris, *I. reticulata*, with violet-purple flowers on 6-in. stems in February or March and the nearly allied but shorter and paler blue *I. histrioides*, which flowers in January. Both are best suited to the rock

Iris kaempferi

Many herbaceous plants flower in late summer and autumn and
are especially useful in adding colour to the garden then

The rather uncommon and delightful *Geranium psilostemon*

Helenium Mahogany, a lovely variety growing to 2½-ft.

The colourful everlasting flowers of helichrysum

Baby Blue-eyes, the apt common name for *Nemophila menziesii*

Passiflora caerulea, a good climber for warmer areas

Platycodon, a perennial commonly called Balloon Flower

Scabiosa caucasica, a hardy perennial for a sunny place

Spring Beauty, a good variety of the bulb *Scilla sibirica*

Vinca minor, particularly fine evergreen ground cover

Ligularia, a useful plant for
the wild or poolside garden

A distinctive herbaceous
perennial—*Lythrum salicaria*

Malope, a pretty and easily
grown hardy annual

The daisy-like pyrethrums,
long-flowering perennials

A touch of gaiety with striped
petunias and trailing lobelias

King's Ransom, a hybrid tea rose
of medium height

Plants, such as petunias, tagetes and pelargoniums,
can be massed in window boxes to give a riot of colour

garden in a sunny, sheltered place and rather gritty soil, or they can be grown in pots or pans in the unheated greenhouse. *I. danfordiae*, which is 4 in. high and has yellow flowers in March, requires similar treatment but should be fed each autumn with bonemeal as the bulbs are apt to decline in size and then do not flower.

The Spanish Iris, *I. xiphium*, and the English Iris, *I. xiphioides*, are also bulbous rooted but they are far taller, flower in early summer and make excellent cut flowers. They are available in a range of colours from white, through cream and pale mauve to deep yellow, bronze and violet. The rather similar blue *I. tingitana* is more tender and usually forced under glass as an early cut flower. Bulbs of all these should be planted or potted 3 or 4 in. deep in September and bulb clusters can be separated into single bulbs at the same time and replanted.

IXIA. Half-hardy bulbs. 1½ ft. Red, crimson, orange, yellow and white flowers in May and June. Ixias are graceful but not very hardy bulbs which can either be planted out of doors in a very sheltered, sunny place, or can be grown as pot plants in an unheated or slightly heated greenhouse. Bulbs should be planted or potted 2 or 3 in. deep in October. They like well-drained soils but should be watered fairly freely while they are making their leaves and slender 18-in. flower stems, which are terminated in June by spikes of starry flowers in a wide range of brilliant and sometimes unusual colours. After flowering, water for pot plants should be gradually reduced so that growth may die down. Increase is by division of the clusters of bulbs in July when leaves wither.

IXIOLIRION. Half-hardy bulbs. 1 to 1½ ft. Mauve or blue flowers in May and June. These are attractive small bulbs for a very sunny, sheltered border or rock garden. They have clusters of small trumpet-shaped flowers in various shades of blue, some much more attractive than others. Treatment is the same as for ixias.

ixia

J ASMINUM (Jasmine). Hardy deciduous climbers or shrubs and tender evergreen climbers. White or yellow flowers in November to February or June to August.** These plants may be listed in catalogues under either their common name of jasmine or the botanical name *Jasminum*. Though there are shrubby kinds such as *Jasminum revolutum*, a bushy plant, 5 to 6 ft. high, with yellow flowers in early summer, it is the climbing jasmines that are most useful. The two most popular are the Winter Jasmine, *J. nudiflorum*, a rather stiff plant with drooping green stems carrying buttercup-yellow flowers in mid-winter, and the Common Jasmine or Jessamine, *J. officinale*, a rampant, twining plant with slender stems bearing sprays of white fragrant flowers throughout the summer. Both will grow in almost any soil. *J. officinale* likes sun and warmth and is excellent on a fence, trellis or arbour. *J. nudiflorum* will grow in sun or shade and is happiest against a wall. It can be allowed to grow without support, in which case it will sprawl about covering a good deal of ground, but more usually it is grown against a wall or fence, its slender stems tied to trellis, wires or other convenient supports.

Jasminum
nudiflorum

Two more tender jasmines worth cultivation in places where frosts are neither severe nor persistent, or elsewhere in cool greenhouses, are *J. polyanthum* and *J. mesnyi* (*primulinum*). The first resembles the Common Jasmine but has more numerous, intensely fragrant white flowers in late spring and summer. *J. mesnyi* resembles the Winter Jasmine, but has larger, semi-double yellow flowers in spring.

None of these jasmine requires any regular pruning but if they need to be restricted they can be shortened or thinned in spring. All are readily increased by layering in late spring.

K

Kalanchoe blossfeldiana

KALANCHOË. Tender succulents. 8 to 12 in. Pink to crimson and white flowers produced all year. The kalanchoës make excellent pot plants for a cool greenhouse and can also be grown successfully in a sunny window. The most popular kind is *Kalanchoë blossfeldiana*, with clusters of small scarlet flowers which may be produced at almost any time of the year. This and other kinds should be grown in JIP.1, or equivalent soil, and should be watered fairly freely from April to September, rather sparingly for the rest of the year though the soil should never be kept quite dry. Kalanchoës are usually increased by cuttings in late spring, but can also be raised from seed sown in a temperature of 15 to 18°C. (59 to 65°F.) in March or April.

KALMIA (Calico Bush, Sheep Laurel). Hardy evergreen shrubs. 3 to 8 ft. Pink and white flowers in June. These evergreen shrubs produce in early summer clusters of pink and white or rosy-red flowers that are like tiny Chinese lanterns. The kind commonly grown, the Broad-leaved Kalmia, *Kalmia latifolia*, also known as the Calico Bush, makes quite a big bush, 6 or 8 ft. high, but there is also a dwarf kind, the Narrow-leaved Kalmia, *K. angustifolia*, also known as Sheep Laurel, which is anything from 1 to 3 ft.

All kalmias like rather moist peaty soil but will grow in most soils that contain no lime or chalk. They will grow in sun or partial shade and can be increased by layering in May or June.

kerria

KERRIA (Batchelor's Buttons). Hardy deciduous shrub or climber. 4 to 8 ft. Yellow flowers in April and May. There is only one species of kerria but it has both single- and double-flowered varieties and they differ markedly in habit. It is the double-flowered variety, *Kerria japonica pleniflora*, that is called Batchelor's Buttons. The flowers are like little golden pompons and are very freely produced in April and May. Growth is long and rather sprawling, and really looks its best when trained against a wall or fence, though the kerria will make a big loose bush in the open. By contrast, the single-flowered variety has much shorter stems, 4 to 6 ft. high, and is usually allowed to make a thicket of growth without support.

Both spread freely by suckers and will grow anywhere in sun or shade. The older stems can be cut out each year when the flowers fade. Rooted offsets or suckers detached in autumn provide the easiest method of propagation.

kniphofia

KNIPHOFIA (Red-hot Poker, Torch Lily). Hardy herbaceous perennials. 2 to 5 ft. Red, orange, yellow or white flowers from June to October. The Common Red-hot Poker, *Kniphofia uvaria*, really does produce flower spikes that justify the name, scarlet at the top and yellow below, carried in July or August on stiff stems 3 to 4 ft. high. There are, however, many other kinds in which the resemblance to a poker is less marked; one, named Maid of Orleans, actually has creamy-white flowers, and another, *K. galpinii*, has slender spikes of orange flowers. There is a fine kind named Royal Standard which is yellow tipped with red and only 3 ft. high, and many more varying in height and the colour of their flowers.

All like fairly rich soils, well drained in winter but with plenty of water while the flower spikes are developing. They should be given a sunny place and a few kinds may need a little protection in winter, which can usually be given by tying their evergreen leaves together to form a kind of tent over the crowns of the plants, the most frost-sensitive part. Kniphofias can all be increased by division in spring or autumn and can also be raised from seed, though seedlings, except those from species, are likely to vary in habit and colour. Seed is best germinated in spring in a cool greenhouse or frame but seedlings can be grown on out of doors.

KOLKWITZIA (Beauty Bush). Hardy deciduous shrub. 6 to 8 ft. Pink flowers in June. This very attractive shrub has flowers very much like those of a weigela but smaller, soft pink with a yellow throat and, as a rule, very freely produced. It is completely hardy and not at all fussy about soil but it will flower most freely in a sunny place. Pruning is not necessary but if bushes get too large the old flowering stems can be cut out as soon as the flowers fade. Propagation is by cuttings in summer or autumn.

laburnum

L

LABURNUM. Hardy deciduous trees. 15 to 20 ft. Yellow flowers from May to June. These favourite May- or June-flowering trees can be grown almost anywhere, in heavy soil or light, sun or shade, though they will flower best in an open place. They make open, branching trees, 15 to 20 ft. in height and not as a rule very long lived, though they can easily be renewed from seed sown in spring. However, seed saved from hybrids such as *Laburnum vossii* and *L. watereri* may vary slightly in habit and flower quality. No regular pruning is required but if the trees get too big branches can be shortened or removed in winter.

One of the finest kinds is *L. vossii*, as the yellow flower trails are of extra length; *L. watereri* is very similar and so is the Scotch Laburnum, *L. alpinum*, which is a little later in flower and has a sweet scent. The Common Laburnum, *L. anagyroides*, is a little earlier flowering and has markedly shorter, scentless flower trails. It is adviseable to remember that the seeds are poisonous and, since they are usually produced in large numbers, the laburnum is not a good tree for a garden in which young children play.

lachenalia

LACHENALIA (Cape Cowslip). Tender bulbs. 8 to 12 in. Yellow or orange flowers from January to May. These make excellent pot or basket plants for cool greenhouses. The leaves are strap shaped and the tubular flowers are carried in loose spikes. Bulbs should be potted in August, September or October, about five in each 4- or 5-in. pot in JIP.2 or equivalent soil and covered to a depth of 1 to 2 in. They should be watered rather sparingly at first, fairly freely as growth starts, but after flowering watering should be gradually decreased until the bulbs can be left quite dry from June until August when they can be shaken out and repotted. Increase is by separation of the bulb clusters at potting time.

LAMIUM (Dead Nettle). Hardy herbaceous perennials. 6 to 12 in. Purple flowers from March to October. The Red Dead Nettle is a pretty but troublesome weed not grown as a garden plant, but the Variegated Dead Nettle, *Lamium maculatum*, has dark green leaves with a broad stripe of white down the middle and is an excellent carpeting plant for the front of the border or for rough banks and rock gardens. There is also a golden-leaved variety which spreads more slowly. Both will grow anywhere though the colour of the golden variety is best developed in a sunny place. They can be increased by division at practically any time of the year.

lantana

LANTANA. Half-hardy perennials. 2 to 3 ft. Yellow, pink or red flowers from May to October. Lantanas were once popular for summer bedding along with pelargoniums, begonias and fuchsias and also as pot

Lathyrus odoratus

Lathyrus latifolius

Lavandula spica

plants for cool greenhouses. For some reason they have become unfashionable, but this neglect is undeserved as they are showy plants with clusters of small verbena-like flowers produced over a very long season. Some of the colours, too, are unusual including combinations of yellow or orange with coppery red.

Lantanas like a warm sunny position and well-drained soils. They are easily raised either from seed sown in a temperature of 15 to 18°C. (59 to 65°F.) in March or by cuttings of firm young growth taken in July and August and inserted in sandy soil in a propagating frame.

LATHYRUS (Sweet Pea, Everlasting Pea). Hardy annuals or hardy herbaceous perennials. 1 to 7 ft. or climbing. White, pink to crimson, and pale blue to purple flowers from May to September. *Lathyrus odoratus* is the botanical name of the Sweet Pea though it is seldom used in catalogues. Sweet peas are popular annuals which can be treated in several different ways. To obtain the finest flowers seed is sown in early September in small pots in a frame, the seedlings being kept in this until the following April when they are planted out in deeply worked, well-manured ground and an open sunny place. They are spaced 1 ft. apart, usually in a double row 1 ft. wide, with a 4- or 5-ft. alleyway between this and the next double row. Each plant is given a tall bamboo cane and is restricted to one stem only, which is regularly tied to the cane. All side growths and tendrils are removed. When the plant reaches the top of the cane it is untied, lowered, laid along the row for several feet and then tied to the bottom of another cane which it can continue to ascend. This is known as the cordon system.

The natural system is to allow the plants to grow unchecked and climb into brushy hazel branches stuck into the ground, as for training culinary peas, or up netting, tripods of canes or any other convenient supports. The seed can either be sown in pots or boxes in a frame or greenhouse in January or February or directly into the open ground in March or April, and in the former instance the seedlings are planted out about 6 in. apart in April or May.

There are a great many varieties and new ones are added to the list every year. Cupid sweet peas are dwarf varieties growing only about 1 ft. high and needing little or no support, and there are varieties of intermediate height as well as the normal varieties which can climb to 6 or 7 ft.

The Everlasting Pea, *Lathyrus latifolius*, is a perennial closely resembling the Sweet Pea in many respects, though the flowers are individually smaller, are more closely packed in the spike and are only available in rose pink and white. The plant climbs much like a Sweet Pea and dies down to ground level in autumn, springing up again from the base in spring. It is very easily grown in almost any soil and sunny position and is readily increased by seed sown in spring out of doors or in a frame.

Another less vigorous climber is *L. grandiflorus*. It has flowers larger individually and a much deeper magenta-purple but they are only carried two or three on a stem, for which reason this plant is sometimes called the Two-flowered Pea. It can be grown in the same way as the Everlasting Pea and enjoys a warm, sunny place.

Very different to these is *L. vernus*, the Spring Bitter-vetch, which is frequently grown under its old name *Orobus vernus*. This is a bushy plant, about 1 ft. high, with slender stems and sprays of small purple or pink and white flowers in April and May. It needs a sunny place and well-drained soil and is raised from seed.

LAVANDULA (Lavender). Hardy evergreen shrubs. 1 to 3½ ft. Lavender, purple or white flowers from July to September. There are several varieties of the Old-English Lavender, *Lavandula spica*, varying in height and colour. Hidcote is particularly dwarf, only 1 to 1½ ft. high, with deep purple flowers. At the other extreme is the giant Grappenhall, nearly 4 ft. high and rather pale lavender blue in colour. Twickel Purple is intermediate in height and colour. *Alba* has white flowers and *rosea* lilac-pink flowers.

All lavenders like well-drained soils and sunny places. They thrive on chalky soils. It is a good practice to trim them over lightly with shears as soon as the flowers fade. They are not, as a rule, very long lived, but can be increased by cuttings in a frame in August or out of doors in autumn.

Very distinct from these and not quite so hardy is the French Lavender, *L. stoechas*, which makes a neat bush about 12 in. high and carries its deep blue-purple flowers in compact clusters throughout the summer.

lavatera

lavatera

LAVATERA (Annual Mallow, Tree Mallow). Hardy annuals and hardy deciduous shrubs. 3 to 7 ft. Pink flowers from June to September. The kind most commonly seen in gardens is the Annual Mallow, *Lavatera trimestris*, which makes a bushy plant 3 to 4 ft. high, covered with large rose-pink flowers throughout the summer. It is very easily grown from seed sown out of doors in March, April, May or September where the plants are to flower. Seedlings should be thinned to 12 in. This plant will grow in almost any soil and open sunny place.

The Tree Mallow, *L. olbia*, is much bigger, 6 or 7 ft. high, making an open not much branched bush with soft pink flowers throughout the later summer. Though perennial, it is not very hardy and does best in light well-drained soils and mild places, particularly near the coast. It is useful because of its very rapid growth, and it can be raised easily from seed sown in a frame or greenhouse in spring or by cuttings in July. The stems are often considerably damaged by frost in winter and should be cut back to sound growth in April.

LAYIA (Tidy-tips). Hardy annual. 1 to 1½ ft. Yellow and white flowers from June to August. The only kind grown is *Layia elegans* and it is known as Tidy-tips because the yellow petals of its neatly formed daisy flowers are tipped with white. It is grown from seed sown out of doors between March and early May where the plants are to flower. Seedlings should be thinned to about 6 in. It likes a sunny place in reasonably good, well-drained soil.

LEONTOPODIUM (Edelweiss). Hardy herbaceous perennial. 9 in. White flowers in June and July. The Edelweiss, *Leontopodium alpinum*, is a rock plant with star-shaped flower heads densely clad in white down and with narrow grey leaves. It is grown more for sentiment and because of the many legends attached to it than for its beauty. It should be given an open, sunny place in well-drained soil and in winter will benefit from the protection of a pane of glass supported a few inches above it to ward off rain. Propagation is by division in spring.

Leucojum aestivum

LEPTOSIPHON. Hardy annuals. 3 to 6 in. Yellow, orange, pink, red or purple flowers from June to September. The annuals commonly grown as leptosiphon in gardens and so listed in most catalogues are, in fact, hybrids of plants correctly known as gilia. They are admirable annuals for rock gardens or for sowing in the chinks between paving slabs since they are only a few inches high and, though small in flower, bloom with such freedom that they make a very gay display. Sow thinly in March, April or early May where the plants are to flower and do not thin the seedlings.

LEPTOSYNE. Hardy annuals. 1 to 1½ ft. Yellow flowers from June to August. These are members of the daisy family and the kind commonly grown, *Leptosyne stillmanii*, produces bright lemon-yellow daisy flowers on 12- to 18-in. stems for a long period in summer. It is attractive in the border and useful as a cut flower. It is easily grown from seed sown in March or April out of doors where the plants are to flower, seedlings being thinned to 6 or 8 in. Leptosyne likes a sunny place and reasonably well-drained soil.

Leucojum autumnale

LEUCOJUM (Snowflake). Hardy bulbs. 6 to 18 in. White, green or pink flowers from February to May and in September. These are bulbous plants which look rather like large snowdrops but have more bell-shaped flowers. The three kinds commonly grown are the Spring Snowflake,

lewisia

Leycesteria formosa

liatris

Leucojum vernum, with white green-tipped flowers on 6-in. stems in March and April; the Summer Snowflake, *L. aestivum*, with larger but similarly coloured flowers on 18-in. stems in April and May and the Autumn Snowflake, *L. autumnale*, with small, white, pink-tinted flowers on 6-in. stems in October.

All like much the same conditions as snowdrops, and the Spring and Summer Snowflakes should be planted in autumn. The Autumn Snowflake should be planted in July or early August. Propagation is by division of the bulb clusters at planting time but the less frequently the bulbs are disturbed the better.

LEWISIA. Hardy rock plants. 3 to 12 in. Pink or apricot flowers in May and June. These very beautiful plants make rosettes of fleshy leaves from which the flower stems grow bearing clusters of star-shaped flowers in many lovely shades of pink, salmon and apricot. They like to grow on their sides in sunny crevices between stones in a dry wall or rock garden but they need plenty of good soil behind into which to root and do not like being starved or completely dried out. Yet in winter they must have good drainage and some kinds appreciate a little shelter. The best way to grow them is to prepare a mixture of good lime-free soil, sharp sand and peat in the proportions of 2:1:1 with a little well-rotted manure or compost added in, and place plenty of this in and behind the crevices in which the plants are to grow. They can be increased by careful division in spring or by seed.

LEYCESTERIA (Himalayan Honeysuckle). Hardy deciduous shrub. 6 to 7 ft. Maroon and white flowers from July to September. A shrub of very rapid growth that makes long green stems terminated in late summer by small trails of pendent maroon and white flowers followed by dark purple berries. This is not a showy plant but it is distinctive in habit and flower and it will grow practically anywhere in sun or shade. The rather soft stems are often considerably damaged by frost in winter but this is of small account as the finest effect is obtained by cutting out all the older stems each March and retaining only the best of the younger growth after removal of any damaged portions. Leycesteria can be increased by detaching rooted stems in autumn or winter.

LIATRIS (Blazing Star, Gay Feather). Hardy herbaceous perennials. 1½ to 3 ft. Reddish-purple flowers in July and August. Liatris are hardy herbaceous perennials of unusual appearance and considerable beauty. The rather fluffy looking reddish-purple flowers are borne on stiff, narrow spikes in July and August and the flowers start to open from the top of the spike downwards. There are several kinds which do not vary much except in height, which may be anything from 1½ to 3 ft. One of the best is named Kobald and is about 2 ft. high.

All thrive best in sunny places and soils containing plenty of humus so that they do not dry out rapidly in hot weather. The tuberous roots should be planted so that they are just covered with soil. Increase is by careful division in spring, which is also the best planting season.

LIGULARIA (Giant Ragwort). Hardy herbaceous perennials. 3 to 4 ft. Yellow flowers in July and August. These are rather coarse plants but useful in the wild garden or beside pools and streams. The best is *Ligularia clivorum* (or *dentata*) a plant often listed as *Senecio clivorum*. It has large heart-shaped leaves and heads of big orange-yellow daisy flowers. It is not fussy about soil, will grow in sun or semi-shade and can be increased by division in spring or autumn.

LILIUM (Lily). Hardy and half-hardy bulbs. 2 to 7 ft. White, yellow, orange, pink to crimson flowers from April to September. A great many plants which are popularly called lilies, such as African Lily, Arum Lily and Belladonna Lily, are not really lilies at all, but there are in addition so many true lilies that it is difficult to give any brief account of them. All have bulbous roots and all can be planted in autumn, though some experts prefer to move them in early spring when they are already growing. This is really only practicable when plants are being moved from one part of the garden to another, as dry bulbs are usually only offered for sale in autumn and winter.

Lilium candidum

From the cultural standpoint lilies may be divided into hardy and slightly tender varieties. The hardy lilies can all be grown out of doors, but the slightly tender varieties are better treated as cold or cool greenhouse plants except in the mildest parts of the country. The most important of these greenhouse kinds is the Easter Lily, *Lilium longiflorum*, with long white trumpet flowers in spring. The bulbs should be planted low down in 9- or 10-in. pots, one in a pot, in JIP.1 or peat compost without lime or chalk, and should be repotted each year in October.

The hardy lilies should almost all be planted so that the bulbs are covered with about twice their own depth of soil, for example, a 2-in.-deep bulb will need a 6-in.-deep hole. One notable exception to this is the popular white Madonna Lily, *L. candidum*, which should be barely covered with soil, and will, after a while, work itself out so that the top of the bulb is exposed. This lily is also exceptional in that it is best planted in August though it can be moved later. The Nankeen Lily, *L. testaceum*, also likes shallow planting.

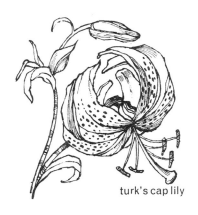

turk's cap lily

Most lilies like to have their flowers and leaves in the sun but their roots in the shade. This can be arranged by planting them among low-growing shrubs or leafy plants such as evergreen azaleas or peonies. Many will also thrive in the dappled shade provided by trees fairly widely spaced as in thin woodland. The majority of lilies like deep soils containing plenty of leafmould or peat and few like really chalky soils though there are exceptions to this, notably the Scarlet Turk's Cap Lily, *L. chalcedonicum*, and the Martagon Lily, *L. martagon*.

One of the easiest of all lilies to grow is the Regal Lily, *L. regale*, with broad white trumpets on 4-ft. stems in July. Others that can be grown in most gardens are the Orange Lily, *L. croceum*, with clusters of large upward-pointing orange or yellow flowers on 2- to 3-ft. stems in June; the Tiger Lily, *L. tigrinum*, with hanging clusters of orange, maroon-spotted flowers on 5-ft. stems in August; *L. henryi*, similar in habit but taller and with orange or apricot flowers; the Martagon or Old Turk's Cap Lily, *L. martagon*, which bears 20 to 30 dull purple or waxy white flowers on 4-ft. stems, and the Panther Lily, *L. pardalinum*, also with turk's cap flowers, reddish-orange spotted with maroon on 5-ft. stems. The Golden-rayed Lily of Japan, *L. auratum*, is a giant of 6 to 7 ft., with wide white trumpets spotted with gold and sometimes flushed with pink. It needs a peaty soil and is not one of the easiest to keep going for many years. The very graceful lily with white, crimson-spotted, hanging flowers in September, which is a favourite in florists' shops, is usually simply called Speciosum (which means handsome) from its botanical name *L. speciosum*. It can be grown out of doors in a sheltered place, but is more often grown as a greenhouse plant like the Easter Lily.

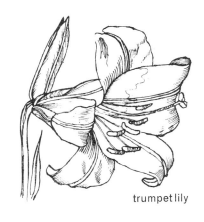

trumpet lily

There are also a great number of hybrid lilies such as the Mid-century Hybrids, Aurelian Hybrids, Olympic Hybrids, Golden Clarion Strain, Pink Perfection Strain, etc., which will be found described in catalogues.

All lilies can be increased by division of the bulb clusters at planting time. A few, and notably *L. regale* and the Formosan Lily, *L. formosanum*, can be raised easily from seed sown in a frame or cool greenhouse in spring. Some lilies, such as *L. tigrinum* and *L. henryi*, make tiny bulbs up the flowering stems where the leaves join them and these bulbils can be detached in late summer and planted separately. Some lilies can also be increased by detaching individual bulb scales in autumn and placing these in boxes filled with sand and peat.

LIMNANTHES (Meadow Foam). Hardy annual. 6 in. Yellow and white flowers from May to July. This is a pretty little annual valued for its early flowering and much sought after by bees. It makes a low mound of pale green ferny leaves studded with saucer-shaped flowers, pale yellow at the centre white around the edge. It is also known as Meadow Foam.

upright-flowering lily

limnanthes

limonium

It is very easily grown from seed sown thinly in March, April or September where the plants are to flower, seedlings being thinned to about 6 in. It is not fussy about soil, prefers open places and is excellent for rock gardens or the edges of beds.

LIMONIUM (Sea Lavender, Statice). Hardy herbaceous perennials and half-hardy or tender annuals. 1½ to 2 ft. Blue, lavender, pink, white and yellow flowers from July to September. These have sprays of small flowers prized because they can be dried for winter decoration. The flowers of the annual statices, *Limonium sinuatum* and *L. bonduellii*, are larger than those of the perennials and together give a range of blue, pink, white and yellow. Seed should be sown in a temperature of 15 to 18°C. (59 to 65°F.) in February or March, the seedlings being pricked out and hardened off for planting out in May or early June, 9 in. apart in rows 18 in. apart in good soil and a sunny place. The flowers should be cut with long stems just before they are fully open in July or August, and suspended head downwards in a cool, airy shed or room to dry. The Candelabra Statice, *L. suworowii*, is a tender annual with narrow pink spikes in a candelabra-like formation. It is usually grown as a cool greenhouse pot plant from seed treated as for the other annual kinds.

Best of the perennial kinds is the Broad-leaved Statice, *L. latifolium*, with tiny lavender flowers in big spreading sprays in August. It is an excellent border plant thriving in well-drained soils and sunny places and its flowers can be cut and dried in the same way as those of the annual kinds. It is increased by root cuttings in winter or by seed in spring.

LINARIA (Toadflax). Hardy annuals, rock plants and hardy herbaceous perennials. Prostrate to 4 ft. Flowers of all colours from May to September. One of the prettiest and most useful of these is the Annual Toadflax, *Linaria maroccana*, with slender 12-in. spikes of flowers, rather like tiny antirrhinums, in a variety of colours in summer. It is quite hardy and can be grown from seed sown in March or April where the plants are to flower. It likes sun, is not fussy about soil and seedlings should be thinned to about 6 in.

The Alpine Toadflax, *L. alpina*, is rather like a miniature version of this, 6 in. high with lilac and orange or shrimp-pink flowers. It is readily raised from seed but is a perennial, so it is not necessary to raise it afresh each year. Seed should be germinated in spring in a frame or greenhouse and the seedlings transferred to particularly gritty, well-drained soil in a sunny rock garden or dry wall.

The Purple Toadflax, *L. purpurea*, has the merit that it will grow practically anywhere, but it seeds itself about so freely that it can become a nuisance. It is a perennial with slender spikes of purple or pinkish flowers, 3 to 4 ft. high, throughout the summer.

The Ivy-leaved Toadflax, sometimes known as Kenilworth Ivy, used to be botanically named *Linaria cymbalaria* but this has now been changed to *Cymbalaria muralis*. It may be found under any of these names and is a pretty trailing plant which will grow in walls with little or no soil. Typically bluish-lilac there are varieties with deeper purple or pale pink flowers. Similar in character but with larger blue-violet flowers is *L. pallida*, and *L. aequitriloba* is smaller, more compact and excellent for growing in the crevices between paving slabs. Both these have also been renamed cymbalaria. All are hardy perennials easily grown in almost any soil and in sun or shade and readily propagated by division at almost any time of the year.

LINUM (Flax). Hardy annuals, hardy herbaceous perennials and rock plants. Red, blue, yellow or white flowers from June to September. There are a number of species of flax differing considerably in habit but all with rather similar funnel-shaped flowers composed of fragile overlapping petals. Two of the most popular are the Annual Flax,

Lilium regale, which produces its spectacular trumpets on 4-ft. stems in July, is one of the easiest lilies to grow

Grape hyacinths add vivid colour to the other spring-flowering
bulbs. This species, *Muscari armeniacum*, is fragrant

Linum grandiflorum, with scarlet flowers on 1-ft. high stems, and the perennial kind, *L. perenne*, with pale blue flowers on 18-in. stems. The Narbonne Flax, *L. narbonense*, is very like *L. perenne* but perhaps a shade darker in colour. In addition there are *L. flavum*, about 9 in. in height and with more compact clusters of bright yellow flowers, and the so-called Tree Flax, *L. arboreum*, a tiny shrub of 9 to 12 in., otherwise very much like *L. flavum*. Gemmel's Hybrid is much like the Tree Flax and a particularly fine plant. Yet another kind is *L. salsoloides* with slender spreading stems and white flowers with a fine network of purplish veins which gives them a pearly appearance.

All flaxes like sunny places and well-drained soils. They can be grown in rock gardens or dry walls and *L. grandiflorum*, *L. perenne* and *L. narbonense* are also suitable for borders. Seed of the Annual Flax should be sown in March, April, May and September where the plants are to flower, the seedlings being thinned to 9 in. The perennial kinds can also be raised from seed sown in a frame or greenhouse in spring but there will be no need to renew seedlings annually. Gemmel's Hybrid should be increased by summer cuttings as it is variable in colour and flower quality if raised from seed.

Linum grandiflorum

LITHOSPERMUM (Gromwell). Hardy herbaceous perennials and shrubs. Prostrate or trailing. Blue flowers in May and June. One of the loveliest of pure blue flowers for the sunny rock garden, rock bank or dry wall is *Lithospermum diffusum*, still often listed in gardens and nursery catalogues under its old name *L. prostratum*. It is a prostrate ever-green shrub with narrow leaves and flowers individually quite small, but so blue and produced so freely in May and June that there are few plants to equal it for beauty at its season. The two finest varieties are Heavenly Blue and Grace Ward. All need a lime-free and well-drained soil but otherwise are not in the least difficult to grow.

Linum flavum

By contrast, the Blue (or Purple) Gromwell, *L. purpureo-caeruleum*, is a rare British plant which favours chalky or limestone soils. It is less neat in habit and more herbaceous than *L. diffusum* and the flowers are not such a fine blue, in fact they start by being reddish-purple but change to bright blue as they age.

All the lithospermums can be increased by cuttings rooted in a frame in July or August.

Lithospermum prostratum

LOBELIA. Hardy and half-hardy herbaceous perennials. 6 in. to 3 ft. Blue, purple, pink to crimson or white flowers from May to September. Everyone knows the blue Bedding Lobelia, *Lobelia erinus*, one of the most popular summer-flowering plants and a favourite for edging beds, either by itself or in company with white alyssum. But the Scarlet Lobelia, *L. fulgens*, with slender 3-ft. spikes of scarlet flowers in late summer, is much less familiar, and *L. syphilitica*, which has slender light blue spikes and *L. vedrariensis*, with purple flowers, are even less known.

The Bedding Lobelia and also the Trailing Lobelia, *L. tenuior*, which resembles it except in its trailing habit, are strictly speaking half-hardy perennials but are almost invariably treated as half-hardy annuals. They are then raised from seed sown in a temperature of 15 to 18°C. (59 to 65°F.) in February or March, seedlings being pricked out and hardened off for planting out, or, in the case of the Trailing Lobelia, planting in hanging baskets and window-boxes, in May. They will grow practically anywhere and should be spaced 6 in. apart.

The scarlet and the other tall blue- or purple-flowered kinds are also perennials and sufficiently hardy to be grown out of doors in places where the soil is unlikely to be more than surface frozen in the winter. Elsewhere, it is a wise precaution to lift some plants each autumn and over-winter them in a frame or cool greenhouse. They thrive in good rich soil well supplied with water in summer but by no means waterlogged in winter. They are increased by division in spring, the best planting season.

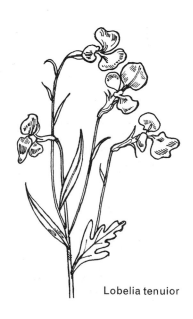
Lobelia tenuior

LONICERA (Honeysuckle, Woodbine). Hardy deciduous or ever-green climbers and shrubs. 5 to 20 ft. Yellow, orange, red or crimson flowers from June to September and November to March. The Common Honeysuckle, or Woodbine is botanically named *Lonicera peri-clymenum*, and is often listed as such in catalogues. It is a vigorous twining plant that needs no introduction as its fragrant flowers in summer are familiar to all, but there are many other climbing honeysuckles not so well known, and several shrubby ones, of which the most popular is the Box-leaved Honey-suckle, *L. nitida*, an excellent hedge plant.

The two finest scented climbing honeysuckles are the Early Dutch and Late Dutch, both varieties of *L. periclymenum* with flowers of superior size and colour. The first flowers in May and June, the second in July and August. The Japanese Honeysuckle, *L. japonica*, is a nearly evergreen climber, but even better is its variegated variety, *aureo-reticulata*, with leaves netted with yellow. All these plants will grow in practically any soil and situation. The Chinese Honeysuckle, *L. tragophylla*, with unusually large deep yellow unscented flowers, should have a rather rich, moist soil and a shaded position, and the Trumpet Honeysuckle, *L. sempervirens*, a nearly evergreen climber with fine scarlet flowers, needs a sunny sheltered wall as it is not very hardy. Yet another fine honeysuckle requiring shelter and shade is *L. tellmanniana*. It has orange-yellow scentless flowers in June and July. All these climbing honeysuckles are readily increased by layering at practically any time.

The Box-leaved Honeysuckle has neat, rounded evergreen leaves and makes a good hedge up to about 5 ft. It can be clipped really severely and kept to a very narrow hedge. It will grow anywhere and can be increased by cuttings in a frame in autumn.

In addition, there are some shrubby deciduous or semi-evergreen honey-suckles of which the best are *L. fragrantissima* and *L. standishii*. Both flower in winter and the creamy-white flowers are rather inconspicuous but fragrant. They will grow in any reasonably good soil, in sun or partial shade and attain a height of 5 to 6 ft.

LUNARIA (Honesty). Hardy biennials. 2 ft. Purple or white flowers from May to June. The botanical name of Honesty is *Lunaria annua*, which would seem to imply that it is an annual though in fact it is a biennial which must be sown one year to flower the next. Though the purple, or occasionally white, flowers are quite attractive, Honesty is grown primarily for its decorative seed pods which are like oval disks of parchment. They will last for months (even years) and are much used in winter flower arrangements. There is also a variety with white-variegated leaves.

Honesty is easily grown in any reasonably good soil and sunny or partially shady position. Seed should be sown out of doors in May or early June and seedlings pricked out 6 in. apart to grow on for transference to flowering quarters in the autumn. Alternatively, seedlings can be thinned out to about 9 in. and left to grow where they were sown. Honesty often renews itself by self-sown seedlings if all the seed vessels are not cut off.

LUPINUS (Lupin). Hardy herbaceous perennials, hardy annuals and deciduous shrubs. 1½ to 6 ft. Flowers in all colours from May to September. Three quite distinct types of lupin are grown in gardens: the Herbaceous Lupin, *Lupinus polyphyllus*, the Tree Lupin, *L. arboreus*, and the Annual Lupin, *L. hartwegii*, but the first is by far the most popular. It is a magnificent plant, very varied in colour and producing its robust, 2- to 4-ft. spikes of flowers in June. It dislikes lime, but will grow well in almost any other kind of soil, particularly those that are sandy or well drained, and in a reasonably open situation. It is not a long-lived plant but can be renewed cheaply from seed sown in a frame in March or out of doors in May. Seedlings vary in colour and flower shape, so specially desirable forms should be increased by cuttings of firm young shoots in April inserted in a frame. The finest forms are the Russell lupins.

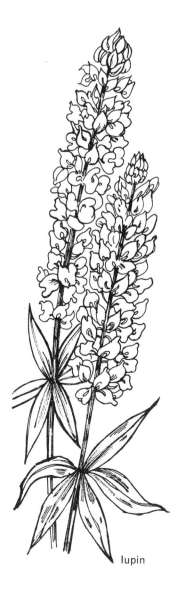

lupin

The Tree Lupin is a much bigger, bushier plant usually 4 or 5 ft. high though occasionally considerably more. It also has smaller spikes of flowers, produced in June, and the colour range is confined to yellow and white. It delights in well-drained sandy soils and does well near the sea. It is easily raised from seed or cuttings in spring or early summer. Though a shrub it is seldom long lived. In cold districts stems may be damaged in winter and these should be cut back to healthy new growth in spring.

The Annual Lupin is grown from seed sown out of doors in March, April, May or September, the seedlings being thinned to at least 1 ft. apart. There are numerous colours, but the flower spikes are not very large and the plants tend to be coarse and leafy.

LYCHNIS (Maltese Cross, Jerusalem Cross, Campion). Hardy herbaceous perennials. 1 to 3 ft. Pink to carmine flowers from June to August. The three most popular kinds are the Maltese or Jerusalem Cross, *Lychnis chalcedonica*, a plant with flattish heads of scarlet flowers on 3-ft. stems in July and August; the Rose Campion, *L. coronaria*, a more branching plant with grey leaves and magenta flowers in June and July, and *L. viscaria*, a shorter plant usually grown in its double-flowered form which is a vivid carmine.

All like well-drained soils and sunny places but are otherwise very easy to grow. All can be increased by careful division in spring and also, with the exception of the double-flowered form of *L. viscaria*, by seed in spring.

Lychnis chalcedonica

LYSIMACHIA (Loosestrife, Creeping Jenny). Hardy herbaceous perennials. Prostrate to 3 ft. Yellow flowers from June to August. There are several loosestrifes with spikes of yellow flowers in June and July, the most familiar being *Lysimachia vulgaris*, and the most graceful the Whorled Loosestrife, *L. verticillata*. All are about 3 ft. high. These and other similar kinds will grow in almost any soil and situation. A plant that needs a little more care and should be given a sunny place in well-drained soil is *L. clethroides*, with short, curling white flower spikes in August. Quite different from all these is the Creeping Jenny, *L. nummularia*, a prostrate plant with buttercup-yellow flowers in early summer. It likes damp places but will grow anywhere. All can be increased by division in spring or autumn, the best planting times. The Purple Loosestrife is described under Lythrum.

LYTHRUM (Purple Loosestrife). Hardy herbaceous perennials. 2 to 4 ft. Magenta or pink flowers from June to August. The purple loosestrifes grown in gardens have been derived from two species, *Lythrum salicaria*, a British wild plant which in some forms can reach 4 ft. in height, and *L. virgatum*, which is usually shorter and has more slender flower spikes. Good varieties are Robert, magenta, 4 ft.; Lady Sackville, rose pink, 4 ft., and The Rocket, rose pink, 2 ft. All will grow in almost any soil, including those that are rather damp, prefer open places and can be increased by division in spring or autumn.

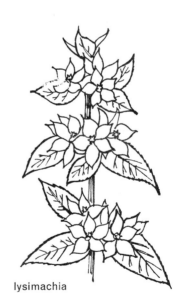
lysimachia

MAGNOLIA. Evergreen and deciduous shrubs and trees. 6 to 30 ft. White, pink or purple flowers from March to September. Most magnolias are deciduous but there are a few evergreen kinds of which the best for general planting is *Magnolia grandiflora*, a large tree with shining laurel-like leaves of considerable size and big white fragrant flowers produced in August and September. It is sufficiently hardy to be grown fully in the open in places where frosts are neither severe nor very prolonged.

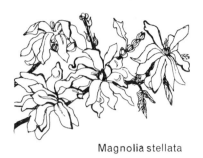

Magnolia stellata

In colder places it can often be grown successfully trained against a sunny wall, but it needs plenty of room.

The deciduous magnolias can be roughly divided into spring- and summer-flowering kinds. The spring magnolias all have erect flowers shaped a little like tulips, whereas many of the best of the summer-flowering kinds have hanging saucer-shaped flowers, each with a central boss of crimson stamens. Among the best of the spring kinds are the Star Magnolia, *M. stellata*, the first to open, a big bush rather than a tree, with white or pale pink flowers; the Yulan, *M. denudata*, white, to 20 ft.; the group of hybrid magnolias named Soulangeana with large flowers varying in colour from white to quite a deep rosy-purple; the Willow-leaved Magnolia, *M. salicifolia*, and very similar *M. kobus*, both medium-size trees with quite small but very numerous white flowers.

Best of the summer-flowering kinds are the Chinese Magnolia, *M. sinensis*, the Highdown Magnolia, *M. highdownensis*, and *M. sieboldii*, all with white and crimson intensely fragrant flowers and 12 to 25 ft. high but wide spreading.

There are also larger tree magnolias such as *M. campbellii*, white flushed with pink, its variety *mollicomata*, deeper pink and the hybrid *veitchii*, white flushed pink, but though these grow rapidly it may be 10 to 20 years before they start to bloom.

All magnolias like deep, loamy soils and, though many will put up with lime, most kinds are better without it. The spring-flowering kinds do best in sun, the summer-flowering kinds do not object to a little shade. None requires any pruning. All can be increased by layering in May or June or by seed sown in a frame or greenhouse in spring—a slow process.

MAHONIA. Hardy evergreen shrubs. 1 to 10 ft. Yellow flowers from November to May. Mahonias have holly-like leaves and produce their clusters or sprays of yellow flowers in winter or spring to be followed in many cases by crops of small purple berries. Two of the best are *Mahonia aquifolium*, which grows 3 or 4 ft. high and flowers from March to May, and *M. japonica*, which produces its slender spikes of pale yellow flowers in clusters like wheel spokes from January to March. They are sweetly scented. The former will grow practically anywhere in sun or shade, but *M. japonica* likes a fairly sheltered position with protection from cold winds. So does the beautiful hybrid Charity, which is considerably taller than *M. japonica*, up to 10 ft., flowers earlier, from November to February, and carries its deeper yellow flowers in more erect clusters.

mahonia

All mahonias can be increased by autumn cuttings and some can also be divided in autumn or winter.

MALCOLMIA (Virginian Stock). Hardy annual. 6 in. White, pink, red or lilac flowers from June to September. *Malcolmia maritima* is the botanical name of the pretty little Virginian Stock and it may be listed under either name in catalogues. The flowers have rather the appearance of confetti and as they appear very quickly after sowing this is an excellent plant for a child's garden. All that is necessary is to sprinkle seed very thinly in March, April, May or September where the plants are to flower.

MALOPE. Hardy annual. 2½ to 3 ft. Magenta flowers from June to September. This easily-grown hardy annual is not unlike lavatera but it has more intensely magenta flowers. It makes a big, leafy plant and flowers all the summer. Seed should be sown in March, April, May or September where the plants are to flower, seedlings being thinned to 12 in. Malope likes a sunny place and will grow in practically any soil.

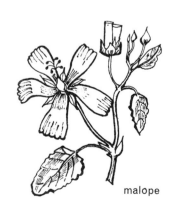

malope

MALUS (Crab Apple). Hardy deciduous trees. 15 to 25 ft. White, pink or red flowers in April to May. A number of crab apples are very handsome flowering trees of moderate size. Some, such as the Crimson Crab, *Malus lemoinei*, the Purple Crab, *M. purpurea*, and the Japanese

Crab, *M. floribunda*, are grown principally for their flowers; others such as John Downie, Dartmouth Crab, Golden Hornet and the Siberian Crab, *M. baccata*, are grown mainly for their abundant and highly coloured fruits.

Crab apples are hardy, easily grown trees thriving in almost any soil and liking best an open, sunny position. Most will eventually reach a height of 20 to 25 ft. if left to their own devices, but *M. floribunda* seldom exceeds 15 ft. and is somewhat weeping in habit. All can be kept smaller by a little thinning and shortening of long branches in winter. Many can be raised from seed sown in spring, but this is a slow process and seedlings may vary considerably from their parents. The usual method of increase is by budding in summer on to apple stocks.

MATRICARIA (Scentless Mayweed, Feverfew). Hardy annuals or perennials. 8 to 18 in. White or yellow flowers from June to September. It is convenient to consider under this name plants which may turn up in catalogues (perhaps correctly) under different names. All have finely divided leaves and some are grown primarily as foliage plants, others for their small ball-shaped yellow or white flowers. Though some may be short-lived perennials they are almost always grown as hardy or half-hardy annuals. Golden Ball and Snowball are typical varieties grown primarily for their flowers and may be listed as matricaria or as *Chrysanthemum parthenium*. *Aureum* is grown for its golden leaves and may be listed as matricaria, *Chrysanthemum parthenium* or as *Pyrethrum aureum*.

All should be grown from seed either sown in a cool greenhouse or frame in March and April, in which case seedlings are pricked out and hardened off for planting out of doors about 8 in. apart in May; or seed can be sown out of doors in April and May where the plants are to grow and the seedlings thinned to 8 in. When grown as foliage plants they can be pinched or clipped occasionally to keep them neat.

MATTHIOLA (Stocks). Hardy and half-hardy annuals and hardy (or nearly so) biennials. 1 to 3 ft. White, pink, red, crimson, purple or mauve flowers from March to September. The most popular kind, the Ten-week stock, is a half-hardy annual from 1 to 3 ft. high, grown from seed sown in a moderately-heated greenhouse, temperature 13 to 15°C. (56 to 59°F.), in March. Seedlings are pricked out and grown on with plenty of light and ventilation for eventual hardening off and planting out in late May or early June. A second sowing can be made in late June to give plants to flower in pots in the greenhouse in winter. There are many colours. All are fragrant.

Ten-week Stock

Brompton stocks are 2 to 3 ft. high with a less extensive colour range, and they are grown as biennials, seed being sown out of doors or in a frame late in June to give plants which can be placed in their final beds in October or March to flower the following May or June. They need a sunny, sheltered place in well-drained soil and are not fully hardy in cold places and heavy, poorly drained soils.

East Lothian stocks are intermediate between the other two types. Sown in a greenhouse in February, they will flower in August; sown in August and over-wintered in a frame, they can be planted out in April to flower in June or July.

All stocks like fairly rich but well-drained soils. It is the double-flowered forms that are most highly prized, and in one strain of Ten-week stock, known as Hanson's, the double-flowered seedlings can be recognised by their leaf colour which is a paler green than in those that will produce single flowers. As this difference tends to disappear if the plants are grown in too warm a place it is desirable to keep the seedlings at 9 to 10°C. (49 to 50°F.) for 7 to 10 days prior to pricking out when the dark green seedlings should be discarded.

The Night-scented stock is a much less showy plant, with small single purplish flowers which are intensely fragrant after dark. It is a hardy annual and can be sown in March, April or May where the plants are to grow.

Night-scented Stock

Meconopsis betonicifolia

MECONOPSIS (Blue Poppy, Himalayan Poppy, Welsh Poppy). Hardy biennials and perennials. 6 in. to 5 ft. White, yellow, blue, violet, pink or rose flowers from June to August. The most popular of these is the Himalayan Blue Poppy, *Meconopsis betonicifolia*, a plant of exceptional beauty, which in its best forms has sky-blue flowers carried in summer on 3-ft. stems. Inferior strains may have purplish- or amethyst-coloured flowers. Plants are readily raised from seed sown in a frame or cool greenhouse in sandy peat in spring. The seedlings must be planted out in a partially shaded place in deep, well-drained but not dry soil, containing plenty of leafmould or peat. They will flower in their second year and may prove somewhat impermanent thereafter, particularly if they get too dry in summer or too wet in winter.

There are other interesting kinds requiring similar treatment, notably the Chinese Yellow Poppy, *M. integrifolia*, 3 ft. high with large primrose-yellow flowers, and the Nepal Poppy, *M. napaulensis*, a taller plant with blue, purple, pink or deep rose flowers and handsome leaves clothed in tawny hairs. Both these species usually die after flowering, so seed should be sown every year.

The Welsh Poppy, *M. cambrica*, really is a hardy herbaceous perennial and is about 1 ft. in height with yellow poppy flowers in summer. It revels in cool, partially shaded places, is not fussy about soil, and can be grown from seed sown thinly in spring where the plants are to grow. Once in the garden it will probably spread itself widely with self-sown seed. It grows wild in some parts of the British Isles.

mesembryanthemum

MESEMBRYANTHEMUM (Hottentot Fig, Ice Plant, Livingstone Daisy). Half-hardy annuals and perennials. Creeping to 1 ft. Magenta, pink, orange, yellow or white flowers from June to September. Most of the plants commonly known as mesembryanthemum in gardens have been reclassified by botanists and so may appear in up-to-date catalogues under their new names such as dorotheanthus and lampranthus. All are succulent plants which can be grown out of doors in winter only in places where frosts are light and of short duration. They delight in sun and warmth, will thrive in the sandiest of soils and have flowers which bear a superficial resemblance to those of daisies, though they are quite unrelated. Colours are varied and often extremely brilliant as in *Mesembryanthemum roseum*, which is a vivid rose pink; *M. spectabilis*, which has magenta flowers; *M. brownii*, tangerine and *M. aurantiacum* with larger reddish-orange flowers. All these may be listed as species of *Lampranthus*. These and many other fine kinds are perennials and can be increased by cuttings in summer of early autumn, but there are also a few annuals of which the most popular is the Livingstone Daisy, *M. criniflorum*, a prostrate plant with flowers in a variety of colours including apricot, pink and red. Seed should be sown in March, April or May in a temperature of 15 to 18°C. (59 to 65°F.), the seedlings being pricked out and later hardened off for planting out of doors in a sunny place in late May or June. Its new name is *Dorotheanthus bellidiflorus*.

The perennial plant known as the Ice Plant for its small glistening grey-white leaves is usually called *M. crystallinum* in gardens but is now correctly a species of *Cryophytum*.

All kinds can be grown in a greenhouse with frost protection in winter and without heat in summer, or may be planted out in late May and, with the exception of annual kinds, be returned to a greenhouse in early October.

Mimulus luteus

MIMULUS (Musk, Monkey Musk, Monkey Flower). Hardy herbaceous perennials. 6 to 24 in. Yellow, orange, red or pink flowers from May to September. The old-fashioned Musk, *Mimulus moschatus*, which was grown for its characteristic odour, no longer produces this, no one knows why. It is still occasionally cultivated for its small yellow flowers produced on a more or less prostrate plant, but other kinds of mimulus are more decorative. Of these one of the most popular kinds is *M. cupreus*, 6 to

9 in. high, with showy yellow or coppery-orange flowers spotted with crimson. There are also varieties and hybrids of it, some with entirely scarlet or crimson flowers. *M. luteus*, the Monkey Musk, or Monkey Flower, is not unlike *M. cupreus* in flower but taller, to 18 in., and earlier in flower. Both these are grown as herbaceous perennials in sun or partial shade and have a special liking for moist places.

Very similar to *M. luteus* and probably derived from it is *M. variegatus*. This has larger flowers varying in the amount of red spotting or blotching on the yellow ground colour. Though also perennial this monkey flower is usually grown as a half-hardy annual, seed being sown in March or April in a slightly heated greenhouse and seedlings pricked out and hardened off for planting out of doors in May or early June.

monarda

MOLUCELLA (Bells of Ireland, Shell Flower). Half-hardy annual. 2 ft. Green flowers from July to September. This plant is a great favourite with flower arrangers. It is grown not so much for its small white scented flowers as for the apple-green funnel-shaped calyx which surrounds each of them. As the flowers are borne in whorls one above the other in quite a tall spike the effect is striking and very different from that of any other flower. It is grown from seed sown in a moderately heated greenhouse in March or early April or out of doors in late April or early May. Seedlings raised under glass are pricked out and hardened off for planting out of doors, 9 in. apart, in May or June and seedlings from outdoor sowings should be thinned to a similar distance. Molucella needs rather rich but well-drained soil and a sunny position. Some flower arrangers prefer to grow it throughout in a greenhouse rather than plant it outside.

MONARDA (Bergamot, Oswega Tea, Bee Balm). Hardy herbaceous perennials. 2 to 3 ft. Scarlet, pink, mauve, purple and white flowers in July and August. These are rather leafy plants with clusters of scarlet, pink, mauve, purple or white flowers in July and August and aromatic foliage. All will thrive in practically any soil that is not very dry and they like a reasonably open position. They are readily increased by division in spring and autumn. Three of the best varieties are Cambridge Scarlet, Croftway Pink and Blue Stocking, purple.

MONTBRETIA. Hardy corms. 2 to 3 ft. Yellow, orange or coppery-red flowers from August to September. These are very easily grown hardy perennials which make clusters of small corms. By separating these and planting them singly about 2 in. deep in spring, they can be increased very rapidly. The orange, yellow or coppery-red flowers are produced in slender 2- to 3-ft. spikes in August and September. Montbretias like sun and warmth and will thrive in the poorest of soils, though to see some of the newer large-flowered varieties at their best, they should be given a reasonably good but well-drained soil. These large-flowered varieties, such as Emily McKenzie and His Majesty, are not so hardy as the common montbretia and, except in mild or sheltered places, should be put in a frame from October to April.

muscari

MUSCARI (Grape Hyacinth). Hardy bulbs. 4 to 8 in. Blue or white flowers in April and May. Muscari are spring-flowering bulbs with little spikes of blue flowers like miniature hyacinths. They are easily grown in almost any soil and fairly open position. Bulbs should be planted 2 to 3 in. deep in autumn, and need only be lifted again when the clusters are so overcrowded that flowering begins to suffer. One of the finest varieties is Heavenly Blue. There is also a beautiful kind with much larger but almost prostrate spikes which have a plumed appearance, for which reason it has been called the Feather Hyacinth, *Muscari comosum plumosum*. Another desirable kind is *M. tubergenianum* in which the flowers at the top of the 8-in. spikes are light blue and those at the bottom are dark blue. There are also white-flowered varieties. All can be increased by separating the bulb clusters in late summer.

myosotis

MYOSOTIS (Forget-me-not). Hardy herbaceous perennials or biennials. 6 to 12 in. Blue or pink flowers from March to June. In addition to the Common Forget-me-not, which is used for spring bedding or as a carpet plant beneath trees and shrubs, there are various other kinds, such as the Alpine Forget-me-not, *Myosotis alpestris*, which is shorter and more compact, and the Water Forget-me-not, *M. scorpioides*, which is looser in habit and has a yellow eye to the small blue flowers. Both these are grown as perennials and increased by division after flowering, whereas the Common Forget-me-not is usually grown as a biennial, seed being sown each year in June or July to give plants which can be transferred to their flowering beds in October or November.

The Common Forget-me-not is available in blue- and pink-flowered varieties and will grow in practically any soil, *M. alpestris* prefers a rather gritty, well-drained soil and *M. scorpioides* is happiest beside a pool or stream.

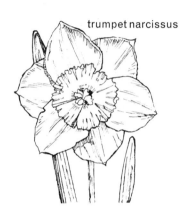

trumpet narcissus

N

NARCISSUS (Daffodil, Lent Lily). Hardy bulbs. 4 to 24 in. White, yellow, orange, red or pink flowers from February to May. There are hundreds of varieties of narcissus, most of them hybrids raised specially for garden use, and for convenience they are classified according to the shape and colouring of their flowers. Typically the narcissus flower is composed of two parts, the cup or corona in the centre and the perianth segments that back it. When the cup is longer than these perianth segments the variety is called a Trumpet-flowered daffodil (or narcissus since the terms are synonymous). Shorter cups are divided according to size into large cups and small cups. There are also varieties with clusters of flowers instead of only one flower to each stem and others with double flowers and with split cups. In most of these groups there are varieties in many different combinations of white, cream, yellow, orange and red, pink and green, descriptions of which will be found in bulb catalogues. Heights of these garden varieties vary from about 9 to 24 in., but in addition there are smaller kinds, some of them wild species such as the Cyclamen-flowered Narcissus, *Narcissus cyclamineus*, and the Hoop-petticoat Daffodil, *N. bulbocodium*.

Narcissus cyclamineus

All narcissi like fairly rich, loamy soils, though they will grow tolerably well in almost any soil. They like sun but do not object to shade provided it is not too dense. Bulbs should be planted between August and November—the earlier in that period the better—and should be covered with their own depth of soil. They can be lifted and the bulb clusters divided in July but it is not desirable to lift them every year as they make a better display when well established. They do well planted in grass provided this is not cut until the narcissus leaves have died down in June. Increase is usually by the natural increase of the bulb clusters which can be split up when the bulbs are lifted. Narcissi can also be grown from seed though it is some years before they flower and seedlings from garden varieties are likely to differ considerably from their parents. Species, however, come true to type from seed and often spread by self-sown seedlings.

Daffodils of all kinds can also be grown in pots or containers in greenhouses, either unheated or moderately heated, or in windows and window-boxes. For this purpose they should be potted (or planted) early in August or the first half of September, if possible, in JIP.2 or equivalent compost. For 8 to 10 weeks after potting they should be kept in a cool, shady (or even completely dark) place to form roots after which they can be brought into a warmer place to hurry them along into flower. Water should be given rather sparingly at first, freely as growth starts but after flowering should be gradually decreased so that by about June they can be quite dry. They can then be removed from

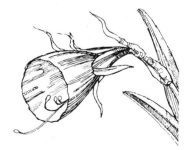

Narcissus bulbocodium

their pots and kept until August or September for planting out of doors but should not be forced a second time.

The larger the bulbs the better both for outdoor planting and for pots as they will produce finer and more numerous flowers. Very small bulbs may not flower at all for a year or so until they have increased sufficiently in size. Failure to flower may also be caused by planting too deeply or in too shady a place.

NEMESIA. Half-hardy annuals. 8 to 12 in. Flowers in all colours from June to September. Nemesia are pretty annuals producing flowers in a wide range of colours throughout the summer. The range is from white, pale yellow and mauve to orange, blue, pink and red. The plants are not fully hardy, so seed should be sown in a greenhouse, temperature 15 to 18°C. (59 to 65°F.), in March or April, seedlings being pricked out and hardened off for planting out of doors, 6 in. apart, in May or early June. They like a sunny place and a rather rich soil, though they will grow almost anywhere.

nemesia

NEMOPHILA (Baby Blue-eyes). Hardy annual. 6 in. Blue flowers from June to August. This attractive hardy annual with clear blue white-eyed flowers is easily grown in practically any soil and sunny place, from seed sown in March, April, May or September where the plants are to flower. Seedlings should be thinned to 4 in.

nemophila

NEPETA (Catmint). Hardy herbaceous perennials 1 to 2 ft. Lavender flowers from May to September. The Common Catmint, *Nepeta faassenii*, is a fine hardy herbaceous perennial for the front of a bed or border. The slender spikes of lavender-blue flowers are produced throughout the summer and the foliage is pleasantly aromatic. It grows about 15 in. high, but Six Hills Giant is taller, about 2 ft., and has rather larger flowers.

All catmints prefer well-drained soils and sunny places, though they will grow almost anywhere. They can be cut back to within a few inches of the ground each March. Propagation is by division in spring which is also the best planting time.

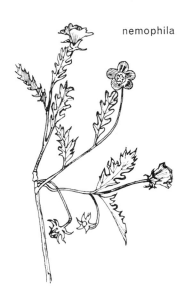

NERINE (Guernsey Lily). Hardy and half-hardy bulbs. 1 to 1½ ft. Pink, red or purple flowers in September and October. Nerines all produce their flowers in rounded clusters on bare stems in early autumn, the leaves appearing later. The colour range is from pink to scarlet with some curious shades of puce or pale purple as well. Bulbs of the greenhouse varieties should be potted in August, the bulbs only about three parts buried in JIP.1 or equivalent compost. They should be watered fairly freely from then until May, but kept almost dry through June and July, during which months they may, with advantage, be placed on a shelf near the greenhouse glass. They require only enough artificial heat to keep out the frost.

Nerine bowdenii and its larger flowered form, Fenwick's Variety, both pink flowered, are sufficiently hardy to be grown out of doors where frosts are neither severe nor prolonged, but for safety should be placed near the foot of a south-facing wall. Plant the bulbs in July, only just covering them with soil. In time they will probably show their 'noses' through the soil, which is their natural habit, and may require some protection in winter with straw, bracken or cloches. Propagation is usually by division of the bulb clusters in August, but plants can be raised from seed though it may be some years before they flower. Good ripening of the bulbs by sun warmth in summer is essential for regular flower production.

nerine

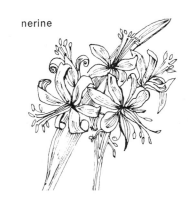

NICOTIANA (Sweet Scented Tobacco, Jasmine Tobacco). Half-hardy annuals. 1 to 3 ft. White, cream, pink, carmine or lime-green flowers from June to September. The smoker's tobacco is not an ornamental plant but the Sweet Scented or Jasmine Tobaccos, derived from *Nicotiana affinis* (or *alata*) and *N. sanderae*, are popular summer-flowering annuals. There are numerous garden varieties with white, cream, lime-green,

nicotiana

nigella

Oenothera biennis

pink or carmine flowers. Heights vary from 1 to 3 ft., some varieties have scented flowers and some keep their flowers open all day, whereas others only open in the evening.

All are raised from seed sown in a warm greenhouse, temperature 15 to 18°C. (59 to 65°F.), in February or March, the seedlings being pricked out into boxes and later hardened off for planting out in May or early June. All these tobaccos will grow in any reasonable soil and in full sun or partial shade.

NIGELLA (Love-in-a-mist). Hardy annuals. 1 to 2½ ft. Blue, pink, purple or white flowers from June to September. These are pretty annuals with fine ferny foliage and cornflower-like flowers surrounded by a ruff of green filaments. Originally blue or white, the colour range has been extended to include various shades of pink or purple. One of the finest varieties is Miss Jekyll, with flowers of deeper blue than the common forms. Persian Jewels Mixed contains all the different colours.

All are raised from seed sown out of doors in March, April May or September where the plants are to flower. Seedlings should be thinned to about 9 in. Love-in-a-mist likes a well-drained soil and sunny position.

NYMPHAEA (Water-lily). Hardy water plants. Floating leaves and flowers. White, yellow, pink to crimson flowers from July to September. Though they appear to float on the surface of pools, water-lilies in fact root, like any terrestrial plant, into soil. There should either be a depth of several inches of good loamy soil in the bottom of the pool or each water-lily should be planted in a basket or box filled with soil and sunk in the pool. Most water-lilies grow best in water 12 to 18 in. deep. A few, such as the White Water-lily, *Nymphaea alba*, like water 2 to 3 ft. deep. By contrast, the Pygmy Water-lily, *N. tetragona*, with white flowers, and its variety Helvola, with pale yellow flowers, do not need more than 5 in. of water and will grow with even less.

Some of the best garden kinds are hybrids such as James Brydon, red, Escarboucle, crimson, and Rose Arey, pink. All should be planted in April or May and may be increased by careful division of their fleshy roots at the same season. They are best left undisturbed for several years until they become overcrowded.

OENOTHERA (Evening Primrose, Sundrop). Hardy herbaceous perennials and biennials. Trailing. Prostrate to 3 ft. Yellow, pink or white flowers from June to September. The Common Evening Primrose, *Oenothera biennis*, is a British plant which should be admitted only to the wilder parts of the garden as it is apt to make itself a nuisance, particularly in rather light, sandy soils. It has pale primrose flowers, individually short-lived, but produced in succession in summer. It is a biennial which must be raised anew each year from seed sown out of doors in May or June, but once established in congenial surroundings it usually maintains itself by self-sown seedlings.

Better as a garden plant is the Sundrop, *O. fruticosa*. This is a perennial, 1½ to 2 ft. high, bearing a profusion of bright yellow flowers in July and August. *O. tetragona* is similar and so is the garden variety Fireworks which has the added attraction of coppery-red flower buds. All these like sun and good drainage and can be increased by division in spring.

Several dwarf kinds are usually grown in the rock garden in full sun and rather light, sandy soil. The best are the Creeping Evening Primrose, *O. missouriensis*, a sprawling plant with greyish leaves and large yellow flowers in August and September, and the Dandelion-leaved Sundrop, *O. acaulis*, which makes a big rosette of leaves rather like a dandelion on which sit the stemless flowers, white at first, changing to pink. *O. missouriensis* is a good perennial which can be increased by division in spring but *O. acaulis*, though it will live for some years in very well-drained soil, is unreliable and better treated as a biennial to be renewed from seed sown each spring or early summer, the plants being discarded after they have flowered.

OLEARIA (Daisy Bush). Hardy or slightly tender evergreen shrubs. 4 to 10 ft. White flowers from May to August. The name is an apt one as the Common Daisy Bush, *Olearia haastii*, is a shapely evergreen shrub, 4 to 6 ft. high with neat rounded leaves and masses of small white daisy flowers in July and August. It will grow almost anywhere and is a particularly good town shrub. A little more exacting is the Tasmanian Daisy Bush, *O. gunniana*, 4 to 5 ft. high, with greyish toothed leaves and even more numerous flowers. It is not very hardy and should be given a particularly warm and sheltered spot. *O. scilloniensis*, which is very similar in appearance, appears to be hardier but it, too, can be killed in cold districts or hard winters. So can the very much larger *O. macrodonta*, sometimes known as New Zealand Holly since it grows wild in New Zealand and has holly-like leaves. It has clusters of white flowers in June and July and can reach a height of 8 or 10 ft. It grows well near the sea and in such places is often planted as a hedge or windbreak.

Omphalodes cappadocica

OMPHALODES (Blue-eyed Mary, Creeping Forget-me-not, Navel-wort). Hardy herbaceous perennials and rock plants. 6 to 12 in. Blue flowers from February to September. These pretty perennials bear some resemblance to forget-me-nots. One of the easiest to grow is the Spring Navel-wort or Creeping Forget-me-not, *Omphalodes verna*, a sprawling, rather coarse-leaved plant with loose sprays of small blue flowers from February to May. It will grow practically anywhere and is a useful front-line plant for the border. *O. cappadocica* is equally accommodating and attractive, about 9 in. high with clusters of bright blue flowers in May and June. The Alpine Navel-wort, *O. lucilliae*, is much neater, no more than 6 in. high, with blue-grey leaves and sky-blue flowers produced in succession all summer. It needs good drainage and a sunny spot, as on a ledge in the rock garden. All can be increased by division in spring.

Onosma tauricum

ONOSMA. Hardy rock plants. 6 to 9 in. Yellow flowers from April to August. These are excellent plants for a sunny rock garden or wall. They have greyish-green leaves and yellow tubular flowers which hang downwards on the curling stems. They enjoy well-drained soil and warm places and can be increased by seed or by summer cuttings. The two kinds usually seen are *Onosma echioides* and *O. tauricum* and they are much alike.

ORNITHOGALUM (Star of Bethlehem, Chincherinchee). Hardy bulbs. 1 to 1½ ft. White flowers from April to August. The Star of Bethlehem, *Ornithogalum umbellatum*, is about 1 ft. high and carries loose sprays of white flowers in April and May. It is perfectly hardy, and is a useful plant for odd corners as it will grow practically anywhere. More exacting is the Chincherinchee, *O. thyrsoides*, with much closer spikes of white flowers which because of their chaffy texture will last indefinitely when cut. It is about 18 in. high and should be grown like a gladiolus, bulbs being planted in fairly rich soil in spring, watered freely in summer and lifted in autumn for dry storage in a frostproof place until planting time. Both kinds can be increased by division of the bulb clusters in autumn or by growing on the tiny bulbs.

Ornithogalum umbellatum

OSMANTHUS. Hardy evergreen shrubs. 6 to 8 ft. White flowers from March to April and September to October. These useful shrubs have suffered from name changing which can make it difficult to find them in catalogues. The most popular kind which gardeners have long known as *Osmanthus delavayi* is now listed in some catalogues as *Siphonosmanthus*

Oxalis adenophylla

delavayi. It makes a big bush of dense habit, with small dark green leaves and tiny white intensely fragrant flowers in March and April. It will grow in full sun or partial shade, is not fussy about soil and does not require pruning though if it does get too big it can be cut back after flowering. *O. heterophyllus* is even bigger and in time can grow to almost tree-like proportions. Its leaves are exceedingly like those of a holly and the other names used for it, *O. aquifolium* and *O. ilicifolius*, describe this. It is, in fact, grown more as a foliage shrub than for its small scented white flowers in autumn and there are varieties with yellow and creamy-white variegated leaves. Cultural requirements are similar to those of *O. delavayi*. All kinds of osmanthus can be increased by summer cuttings.

OXALIS (Wood Sorrel). Hardy or slightly tender rock plants. 3 to 8 in. White or pink flowers from May to September. Oxalis are sun-loving plants for the rock garden or, in the case of *Oxalis rubra* (sometimes wrongly called *O. rosea*) as an edging to beds. The two best rock-garden kinds are the Falkland Island Oxalis, *O. enneaphylla*, and the Chilean Oxalis, *O. adenophylla*, rather similar plants with clustered flowers in summer, white in the first, pink-flushed in the second, sitting close down on the tufted blue-grey leaves. They need the best possible drainage in rather light soil. By contrast *O. rubra* will grow in any warm sunny place and does not mind how poor the soil is. Its bright rose flowers in loose sprays are produced all the summer. It can be easily increased by division in spring and in favourable places can become almost a weed. *O. enneaphylla* can also be carefully divided, but *O. adenophylla* can be increased only by seed.

Paeonia officinalis

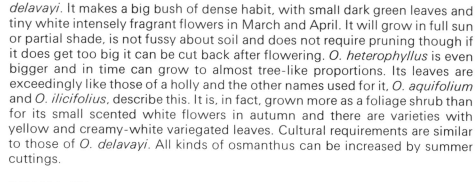

AEONIA (Peony). Hardy herbaceous perennials and hardy deciduous shrubs. 2 to 6 ft. White, yellow, apricot, pink to crimson flowers in May and June. There are both herbaceous and shrubby peonies, the latter somewhat misleadingly known as Tree peonies. They are rather more difficult to grow than the herbaceous kinds, needing deep rich loamy soils, preferably with some additional leafmould or peat. Herbaceous peonies will grow in almost any soil, though they prefer a fairly rich one.

The Common Peony, *Paeonia officinalis*, has crimson, pink or white flowers usually very full and double. The Chinese Peony, *P. albiflora*, has a more varied colour range, with many delicate shades of pink and salmon, as well as rich crimsons and vivid scarlets. The flowers also vary more in form, from single through semi-doubles of all .kinds, to full doubles, and all are fragrant. *P. obovata* has single white flowers; *P. mlokosewitschii* is a beautiful Russian species with soft green leaves and large single yellow flowers. *P. lobata* has deep red single flowers which are scarlet in the variety Sunshine. All these herbaceous peonies flower in May or June and are about 3 ft. high.

The Tree Peony, *P. suffruticosa*, makes a rather soft-stemmed bush up to 6 ft. high and has very large flowers, single or fully double, in many rich colours or combinations of colours. *P. lutea*, is a Chinese tree peony, a species which makes a large bush, 6 ft. high, with rather small single yellow flowers which can be partly hidden by the leaves. Its variety *ludlowii* is superior in this respect and has larger flowers. Both grow rapidly from seed and often spread by self-sown seedlings. *P. delavayi* is almost equally vigorous and easy to grow and has dusky-crimson single flowers.

Planting time for the herbaceous and shrubby kinds is in spring or autumn. Herbaceous peonies can be carefully divided but tree peonies should be layered in spring or early summer or increased by seed sown in spring, but seedlings of garden varieties may differ in colour and flower form from their parents and are usually inferior.

Paeonia albiflora

PAPAVER (Poppy). Hardy annuals, biennials, herbaceous perennials and rock plants. 6 in. to 3 ft. White, yellow, orange, pink, red, crimson, purple or mauve flowers from May to September. All poppies like sunny places and fairly well-drained soils. Best of the true herbaceous perennials is the Oriental Poppy, *Papaver orientale*, well known in its scarlet form but also with pink, purplish and white varieties. The flowers are very large and produced in June on 3-ft. stems. These poppies can be increased by seed sown out of doors in May, by careful division in spring or by root cuttings in winter.

The most popular annual poppies are the Shirley Poppy, *P. rhoeas*, and the Carnation or Peony Poppy, *P. somniferum*, the first a rather slender plant with a wonderful and delicate colour range, the second robust, grey leaved, with big flowers often very double and in rather rich colours. Both are readily grown from seed sown out of doors in March, April, May or September where the plants are to flower, the seedlings being thinned to at least 9 in.

The lovely Iceland Poppy, *P. nudicaule*, is really a perennial but is short-lived and is usually grown either as an annual or biennial. In the first case seed is sown in a cool greenhouse in February or March and seedlings are planted out in May to flower in late summer; in the second they are sown in a frame in June and planted out in late summer to flower the following June. The colour range is mainly in yellow and orange, but with some pink and white as well.

Papaver alpinum is rather like the Iceland Poppy but reduced to about 6 in. in height with flowers to scale. It needs to be grown in gritty or stony soil as it requires quick drainage. It must also have an open, sunny place. It can be grown from seed treated in the same way as the Iceland Poppy and, under congenial conditions, will perpetuate itself by self-sown seedlings. It is not, as a rule, long lived though it is a perennial.

The Himalayan Poppy and Welsh Poppy are species of Meconopsis and are described under that name.

Papaver rhoeas

PASSIFLORA (Passion Flower). Tender climbing plants. Blue, purple, rose-red or white flowers from June to September. This genus includes several highly distinctive climbers with flowers of curious formation—in one kind said to bear the instruments of the Crucifixion. The only one which is at all reliable out of doors, and then only in sunny, sheltered places, is the Blue Passion Flower, *Passiflora caerulea*, a very vigorous plant which will attach itself to any suitable support by tendrils. It can be grown against a south wall and will flower in late summer. The flowers are blue or purple and there is a pure white variety named Constance Elliott. *P. allardii* is very similar to the Blue Passion Flower but the blue is stronger. It can be grown out of doors in the mildest parts of the country but is more commonly grown in a cool greenhouse trained on wires under the rafters. This treatment also suits *P. antioquiensis*, a very handsome species with large, pendent rose-red flowers. All kinds can be raised from seed or by summer cuttings or layers.

Other passion flowers should be grown in sunny, frostproof greenhouses, preferably planted in a border of good soil.

passiflora

PELARGONIUM (Geranium). Half-hardy perennials. Trailing to 2 ft. Pink, red, purple, mauve or white flowers from May to October. These are the plants commonly, though erroneously, called geraniums. There are four principal groups: Zonal-leaved pelargoniums, bushy plants with scarlet, pink or white flowers produced continuously over a very long season, and popular both for summer bedding and as pot plants; Ivy-leaved pelargoniums, which are sprawling in habit, usually pink-flowered, though there are red and mauve varieties, summer flowering and useful in hanging baskets, tubs, or trained as small climbers; Regal pelargoniums, similar to the Zonals in habit but with much larger flowers often blotched with one colour or another, mainly produced in May and June, though some will flower later, and grown primarily as greenhouse pot plants; finally, the Scented-leaved pelargoniums, usually with insignificant flowers but with leaves that are strongly aromatic when brushed or bruised.

pelargonium

zonal-leaved pelargonium

There are varieties of the Zonal-leaved type with elaborately variegated leaves in which rings, or zones, of yellow, green, red and silver may appear in varying combinations. These also make good bedding plants.

Pelargoniums like sun and warmth and all need complete protection from frost. All are easily raised from cuttings of firm young shoots taken in spring or late summer. They are not fussy about soil but when grown in pots a not too rich compost such as JIP.1 or its equivalent should be used. Too much feeding encourages strong growth at the expense of flowers. When grown out of doors pelargoniums should be given a sunny place. They revel in warmth and will withstand dry conditions better than many plants. Because of their susceptibility to frost, pelargoniums should not be planted out of doors until late May and should be returned to the greenhouse by early October, except in the mildest parts of the country. All can be cut back in autumn so that they take less room in the greenhouse during the winter and Regal pelargoniums are often pruned earlier in August when the main flush of flowers is over.

Pelargoniums can also be raised from seed sown in a temperature of 15 to 18°C. (59 to 65°F.) in February or March, seedlings being potted singly in small pots and moved on as necessary to larger ones or planted out of doors in June. First-year seedlings sometimes make a lot of growth but produce few flowers, however in subsequent years they will bloom normally.

penstemon

PENSTEMON. Hardy or slightly tender perennials and rock plants. 3 to 24 in. Pink, red, purple, lavender, mauve, blue or white flowers from April to September. The showiest kinds are the Gloxinia-flowered penstemons, *Penstemon gloxinioides*, with 2-ft. spikes of tubular flowers produced all the summer. The colour range is from white and palest pink to deep red, with some incursions into mauve and purple. These penstemons are very easily grown in almost any soil and sunny position but they are not completely hardy and may be killed by severe or prolonged frost. For this reason it is wise to over-winter some plants in a frame or greenhouse or to strike cuttings in a frame each August or September. These can be planted out the following April or May. Some varieties, such as Garnet, Evelyn and Myddleton Gem, are hardier than others.

In addition there are several smaller-flowered kinds worth growing in the rock garden or at the front of a sunny bed, notably *P. heterophyllus*, about 15 in. high and best represented in its sky-blue variety True Blue, *P. scouleri*, 9 in. high with lilac-blue flowers in May and June, and *P. rupicola*, one of the smallest of all, no more than 3 in. high with ruby-red flowers in June and July.

All penstemons can be increased by cuttings of firm young shoots (non-flowering) in summer and also by seed sown in a greenhouse or frame in spring. Seedlings of *P. gloxinioides* may not come true to colour.

PERNETTYA. Hardy evergreen shrub. 3 to 4 ft. White flowers in May and June; white, pink, red or purple berries from September to December. This evergreen shrub with small leaves and a suckering habit of growth is remarkable for the large round berries it produces in a variety of unusual colours including pink, purple, white and near black as well as red and crimson. It does best in rather moist, peaty soils, though there are few lime-free soils in which it cannot be grown. Pernettya prefers a sunny position, and is most easily increased by detaching rooted suckers in autumn but it can also be raised from seed sown in a frame in spring. It is best to plant several varieties or colour forms together not only for the enhanced effect but also because the flowers are cross pollinated and set better crops of berries.

perovskia

PEROVSKIA. Hardy deciduous shrub. 3 to 4 ft. Lavender flowers in August and September. The name is frequently spelled perowskia. This is a shrub that looks a little like an overgrown and rather leggy lavender. Its long thin spikes of lavender flowers are produced in late summer above the neat grey foliage. Perovskia likes a warm, sunny spot and a particularly well-drained soil. It resents root disturbance and should be purchased as a pot plant so that it can be put in without root breakage. Oddly enough the best method of increase is by root cuttings in winter and these should be inserted singly, one in each small pot. It is best pruned to within a foot of ground level in March.

PETUNIA. Half-hardy annuals. 1 to 1½ ft. Flowers, which are in most colours except strong yellow and orange, from June to September. Petunias have very showy funnel-shaped or double flowers which are produced all the summer. They like sun and warmth but are not fussy about soil. They are raised from seed sown in a greenhouse, temperature 15 to 18°C. (59 to 65°F.), in February or March, seedlings being pricked out and hardened off for planting out in late May or early June.

Petunias are excellent for filling beds, for associating in groups with other summer-flowering plants and for planting in pots, tubs, window-boxes and other containers in JIP.1 or equivalent soil. There are a great many varieties, some with very large flowers and known as Grandiflora petunias, others with smaller flowers and known as Multiflora petunias.

PHACELIA. Hardy annuals. 6 to 8 in. Blue flowers from June to August. These are pretty annuals of which the best is *Phacelia campanularia*, a low-growing plant with intensely blue flowers which really do look rather like those of a campanula, which is what '*campanularia*' means. It likes sun and a well-drained soil and is grown from seed sown in March or April where the plants are to flower in summer. Seedlings should be thinned to about 6 in.

annual phacelia

PHILADELPHUS (Mock Orange, Syringa). Hardy deciduous shrubs. 3 to 15 ft. White and purple flowers in June and July. The mock oranges mostly have white flowers though in some varieties they are blotched with purple and many are extremely fragrant. Some, such as Belle Etoile, Beauclerk and Sybille, are single, others, such as Virginal and Enchantment, are double. Most are vigorous shrubs 8 ft. or more in height, but there are smaller kinds, Sybille seldom exceeds 4 ft. and *Philadelphus microphyllus* is only about 3 ft. One of the tallest is *P. intectus* which can reach 15 ft. and has slightly fragrant single white flowers. It is often listed as *P. grandiflorus*. The popular name Mock Orange aptly describes the flowers of some kinds of philadelphus but Syringa, also commonly used for them, is misleading as it is the botanical name of the lilacs to which mock oranges are unrelated and bear no resemblance.

All philadelphus are very easily grown in almost any soil and, for preference, sunny place. They can be pruned immediately after flowering, the old flowering stems being cut out but all young shoots and non-flowering stems retained. Propagation is by cuttings in autumn.

Philadelphus Virginal

PHLOMIS (Jerusalem Sage). Hardy evergreen shrubs. 3 ft. Yellow flowers in June and July. These are rather soft shrubby plants with grey sage-like leaves and clusters of yellow hooded flowers. They are plants which love sun, warmth and good drainage and may be damaged by frost in winter but usually grow away all right the following spring. In any case they are all the better for being trimmed back a little each April to keep them from becoming straggly. They are easily raised from cuttings in July or August. The kind most usually seen is *Phlomis fruticosa* but there are others such as *P. chrysophylla*, which is similar but has a yellowish tinge to its leaves.

PHLOX. Hardy herbaceous perennials and half-hardy annuals. Prostrate to 4 ft. White, pink, red, crimson, purple and mauve flowers from May to September. One of the most popular of summer-flowering plants is the herbaceous phlox, *Phlox paniculata*, which flowers from July to September and has produced a great many varieties ranging in height from 1 to 4 ft. and in colour from white, palest pink and mauve to vivid scarlet, crimson and deep purple. The phlox have the additional merit of a sweet honey-like fragrance. They are easily grown in sun or shade and almost any soil, and can be increased by division in spring or autumn or by root cuttings taken at any time during the winter.

annual phlox

The Moss Phlox, or Moss Pink, *P. subulata*, is a dwarf mat-forming plant for the rock garden or dry wall. It has narrow leaves and mauve, pink or white flowers in May. All varieties are as easy to grow as the herbaceous phlox but they prefer sunny places. *P. douglasii* is similar but less vigorous.

The Annual Phlox, *P. drummondii*, is also a sun lover, a beautiful sprawling plant with vividly coloured pink, scarlet, purple or white flowers all summer. It is grown from seed sown in a frame or greenhouse, temperature 15 to 18°C. (59 to 65°F.), in February or March, seedlings being pricked out and hardened off for planting out in late May or early June.

PHYGELIUS (Cape Fuchsia, Cape Figwort). Evergreen semi-shrubby perennials. 3 ft. or more. Orange-red flowers from July to October. There is a curious upsidedown look about the curved orange flowers of *Phygelius capensis*, the species of Cape Figwort most usually grown, and they appear in late summer and early autumn. This species grows about 4 ft. high and will go much higher if placed against a wall. Another kind occasionally seen is *P. aequalis*, a shorter plant with duller salmon-orange flowers. Both kinds like a warm sunny spot but will grow in most soils provided they are reasonably well drained. Increase is by division in spring.

physalis

PHYSALIS (Bladder Cherry, Cape Gooseberry, Chinese Lantern). Hardy herbaceous perennials. 1½ to 2 ft. White flowers in summer followed by inflated orange fruits. There are several different kinds of physalis but they do not differ greatly and all require the same treatment. They spread by underground roots and are readily increased by division in spring. They like sunny places and well-drained soils and are apt to die in winter if at all waterlogged. The flowers are white and not particularly effective but they are followed by orange-red or scarlet cherry-like fruits each enclosed in an inflated orange lantern-shaped structure formed by the outer segments of the flower folding over the ripening fruits. Because of their dry papery texture these 'lanterns' will retain their colour for months and are popular for Christmas decorations.

Physostegia virginiana

PHYSOSTEGIA (Obedient Plant). Hardy herbaceous perennial. 1½ to 3 ft. Pink or white flowers from August to October. *Physostegia virginiana*, the wild plant from which the garden varieties have been developed, has narrow pink flower spikes too small and indeterminate in colour to be effective. These faults are completely rectified in such varieties as Vivid, rose-pink, 2 ft. high and *alba*, white, 3 ft. high, both excellent late summer- and autumn-flowering perennials. They will grow in most reasonably good soils in sun or partial shade and can be increased by division in the spring. As they spread fairly rapidly and in so doing tend to starve themselves out it is desirable to lift and divide them every two or three years.

PHYTEUMA (Rampion). Hardy rock plants. 2 to 4 in. Purple flowers in July. These are plants of very distinctive appearance producing compact clusters of flowers that are like tiny blue or purple flasks, each ending in a thin neck. One of the finest is the Tufted Rampion, *Phyteuma comosum*, a squat plant with larger flowers than is usual among rampions. It likes sun and good drainage, a deep fairly rich soil and protection from slugs. It can be increased by division or seed in spring.

pieris

PIERIS. Hardy evergreen shrubs. 4 to 8 ft. White flowers from March to May. These handsome evergreen shrubs are related to the rhododendrons and thrive in the same kind of good loamy or peaty lime-free soils that suit them. The little urn-shaped white flowers are freely produced in sprays or clusters and have a slight resemblance to lily of the valley. In some kinds, notably *Pieris forrestii* Wakehurst and the hybrid known as Forest Flame, the young shoots and leaves are coppery red or creamy white and even more effective than the flowers. Other good kinds are *P. floribunda*, one of the shortest, often not much over 4 ft. in height;

The abundant, richly-coloured flowers of the polyanthus, *Primula elatior*, make a splendid display in spring

Dwarf annuals such as mesembryanthemum, lobelia and iberis
provide a brilliant show of flowers throughout the summer

P. japonica, which has a variety with leaves variegated with creamy white, and *P. taiwanensis*, which resembles the last but holds its flowers more erect. All can be increased by summer cuttings and also by seed. No regular pruning is required but if overgrown they can be reduced after flowering.

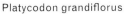
Platycodon grandiflorus

PLATYCODON (Balloon Flower). Hardy herbaceous perennial. 9 to 18 in. Blue or white flowers in July and August. The popular name of this hardy herbaceous plant refers to the flower buds which look like little inflated balloons. They expand to a bell-shaped flower like that of a campanula. The Balloon Flower, *Platycodon grandiflorus*, is typically campanula blue and about 18 in. high but it has a good white variety named *album* and a dwarf blue-flowered variety *mariesii*, about 9 in. high. All like a sunny place and a fairly rich but reasonably well-drained soil and can be increased by division in the spring.

PLEIONE. Hardy or slightly tender terrestrial orchids. 4 to 6 in. Pale pink to purple flowers in April and May. These delightful little orchids can be grown out of doors in mild, sheltered places and in leafy or peaty, well-drained soil, but are more usually grown in pots or pans in a greenhouse which need only be heated in the coldest weather. They enjoy a mixture of loam, peat and sand as in John Innes seed compost but without lime or superphosphate which are better replaced by bonemeal at a rate of 4 oz. to each bushel of the soil mixture. This orchid, like many others, produces bulb-like structures above soil level and these should be planted to about half their depth in April or May. Water fairly freely from April to September then reduce the amount and keep almost dry from November to March. Out of doors cover with cloches in autumn and winter. Grow in a partially shaded place or, under glass, shade from April to September. Repot about every two years and increase by division when repotting.

pleione

PLUMBAGO (Leadwort). Half-hardy climber. Blue flowers from July to October. The small shrubby or herbaceous leadworts that flower so attractively in gardens in late summer and autumn are species of Ceratostigma, under which name they will be found in nursery catalogues and are described in this book.

Here we are concerned with the Climbing or Cape Leadwort, *Plumbago capensis*, a beautiful plant with clusters of pale blue phlox-like flowers produced all summer. It is only half-hardy and though it can be grown out of doors from June to September it must be given the protection of a frost-proof greenhouse in winter. Alternatively, it can be grown as a permanent greenhouse plant either planted in a border of reasonably good soil or in pots or tubs filled with JIP.2 or equivalent compost. It likes a sunny place and should be watered fairly freely from April to September, moderately from October to March. The rather weak stems have no natural means of support and must be tied to stakes, wires or trellis. Growths made the previous year can be shortened considerably in February. Plumbago can be increased by summer cuttings of non-flowering shoots or by seed sown in a greenhouse in spring.

POLEMONIUM (Jacob's Ladder). Hardy herbaceous perennial. 1½ ft. Blue or white flowers in May and June. *Polemonium caeruleum* gets its popular name from the laddered appearance of its rather ferny leaves. The light blue or white flowers are borne on 18-in. spikes in early summer. Jacob's Ladder will thrive in sun or shade and almost any soil and it is completely hardy. It can be increased by division in spring or autumn or by seed in spring and often spreads freely by self-sown seedlings.

POLIANTHES (Tuberose). Half-hardy tuberous-rooted perennials. 2 to 2½ ft. White flowers from June to September. The heavily-scented flowers of the Tuberose, *Polianthes tuberosa*, are produced in

polianthes

spikes and may be either single or double. In very warm sheltered places the Tuberose can be grown out of doors in summer after having been started into growth in spring in a greenhouse. More usually it is treated purely as a pot plant to be grown in a cool or intermediate greenhouse. In October or November the tubers are potted singly in 5-in. pots in JIP.1 or equivalent compost, and are then kept in a cool house until a few weeks before flowers are required. Then they are brought into a temperature of about 18°C. (65°F.). They should be watered rather sparingly at first, freely as flower spikes begin to develop and should not be shaded at any time. The tubers seldom prove satisfactory a second year and are usually discarded after flowering.

Polygonatum multiflorum

POLYGONATUM (Solomon's Seal). Hardy herbaceous perennials. 2 to 3 ft. White flowers from May to June. These graceful herbaceous plants have the great merit that they will grow in quite densely shaded places as well as in more open situations. The creamy-white tubular flowers hang from the arching 2- to 3-ft. high stems in May and June. The two kinds usually seen are *Polygonatum officinale*, and *P. multiflorum*, a rather bigger and more striking plant and therefore the popular favourite. Both can be increased by division of the roots in spring or autumn. They are not fussy about soil.

POLYGONUM (Knotweed). Half-hardy annuals, hardy herbaceous plants, rock plants and climbers. Prostrate to 20 ft. White, pink to crimson flowers from June to October. There are several knotweeds which should never be admitted to gardens because of their habit of running far and wide underground, but there are others which are useful and beautiful plants. One of the smallest is *Polygonum vaccinifolium*, a trailing plant for rock garden or dry wall with tiny spikes of pink flowers in August and September. *P. affine* makes more compact carpets of growth and has stouter 6- to 8-in. spikes of deep pink or carmine flowers and is an excellent plant for the rock garden or the front of a border. At the other extreme is the Russian Vine, *P. baldschuanicum*, one of the most vigorous of all hardy twiners, a plant that in a year or so will climb to the top of a considerable tree or cover a large outbuilding, smothering it in late summer beneath a cloud of tiny white or pinkish flowers. In between are several excellent herbaceous plants, such as the Red Bistort, *P. bistorta superbum*, with spikes of red flowers on 2-ft. stems, or the Bell-flowered Knotweed, *P. campanulatum*, with loose sprays of white or blush-pink flowers which individually look like those of a bell heather. They last from July to October.

Polygonum affine

There is also an annual species, *P. capitatum*, a prostrate plant with green and bronze leaves and tight clusters of soft pink flowers from June to August. It is only half-hardy so seed should be sown under glass in a temperature of 15 to 18°C. (59 to 65°F.) in March or April and seedlings pricked out and hardened off for planting out of doors in May or June. It likes a sunny place and is not fussy about soil. Seedlings should be spaced about 6 in. apart.

All these knotweeds are easily grown. The rock-garden kinds like sun and good drainage, *P. campanulatum* needs plenty of moisture in summer. With the exception of *P. capitatum*, most can be increased by division in spring or autumn but *P. baldschuanicum* is rather difficult to increase and should be layered in May or June.

PONTEDERIA (Pickerel Weed). Hardy aquatic. 2 ft. Blue flowers from July to September. This is one of the few blue-flowered plants to grow at the edge of a pool. It has broad lance-shaped leaves and spikes of purplish-blue flowers which remain decorative for a long time. *Pontederia cordata* likes to grow in water 2 to 3 in. deep and should either be planted in loamy soil on the margin of the pool or be grown in a pot or plastic basket filled with soil and sunk in position. It can be increased by division in April or May which is also the best planting season.

pontederia

PORTULACA. Half-hardy annuals. 6 in. Pink to crimson, yellow and white flowers from July to September. These are trailing, succulent plants for the hottest and sunniest positions in the garden. They have very showy single or double flowers in a good range of colours and are raised from seed sown in a greenhouse, temperature 15 to 18°C. (59 to 65°F.), in March or April. Seedlings must be pricked out and hardened off for planting out in late May or June 6 to 8 in. apart. They can be used as a groundwork in beds, on banks, in rock gardens or on the top of dry walls built with a good core of soil.

potentilla

POTENTILLA (Cinquefoil). Hardy herbaceous perennials, rock plants and hardy deciduous shrubs. Prostrate to 4 ft. White, yellow, orange, red or crimson flowers from April to September. The herbaceous potentillas are all rather sprawling plants, sometimes too leafy for the flowers they produce, but Gibson's Scarlet is a really showy variety, 12 in. high with brilliant red single flowers during most of the summer. Other good kinds are Monsieur Rouillard, semi-double, crimson and orange and William Rollisson, orange-red, both about 18 in. high. They enjoy warm sunny places and well-drained soils and can be increased by division in the spring.

The rock garden kinds can also be a little too invasive. *Potentilla alba* can soon make wide carpets of greyish-green leaves studded with small white flowers in summer and is useful as ground cover. *P. tonguei*, a creeping plant with orange flowers, is better for the rock garden and *P. verna* has bright yellow flowers, mainly in spring with a few to follow in summer. All are sun lovers like the border kinds and can be increased by division.

Most useful of all are the shrubby varieties derived from *P. arbuscula* and *P. fruticosa*. There are a great many of these, all much alike in habit. They make dense dome-shaped bushes 2 to 4 ft. high, flowering continuously from June to September. Typical kinds are Elizabeth, canary yellow; Katherine Dykes, primrose; Tangerine, orange; *vilmoriniana*, silvery leaves and cream flowers and Farrer's White, white, but there are many more All like sunny places and well-drained soils and are improved by annual pruning in spring. Two methods are possible, either to thin out some of the older stems, which results in a larger bush, or to cut everything back to within a few inches of the ground, which gives finer flowers. Propagation is by summer cuttings.

PRIMULA (Auricula, Cowslip, Polyanthus, Primrose). Hardy herbaceous perennials, rock plants and half-hardy perennials usually grown as annuals. 3 in. to 3 ft. Flowers in all colours and produced at all times of the year. The polyanthus is a variety of primula, botanically known as *Primula elatior* and very closely allied to the common British wild primrose, *P. vulgaris*, from which it differs only in having a cluster of several flowers on each stem. Intensive breeding has been carried out to increase the size of the flowers and the colour range. Many of these improved strains are very beautiful though probably not quite as robust in constitution as some of the older and smaller-flowered strains. Though perennials, both *P. elatior*, *P. vulgaris* and their many garden varieties are often grown as biennials, seed being sown in a cool greenhouse or frame any time between March and July. Seedlings are then pricked out into boxes in JIP.1 or equivalent soil and when large enough they are planted out of doors, 3 to 4 in. apart in rows 1 ft., apart in a reserve bed of good rich soil in a partly shaded place. Here they can grow on until it is time to remove them in autumn or early spring to the beds in which they will flower. After flowering they can be left undisturbed, or be lifted, split up and replanted in a reserve bed. Alternatively, they may be discarded.

The garden auriculas are derived from a primula named *P. auricula*. They have been highly developed in gardens, many varieties having been produced with flowers of exquisite shape and very regular clearly defined colourings. These beauties are usually grown as pot plants in frames or

Primula auricula

Primula juliae

Primula vulgaris

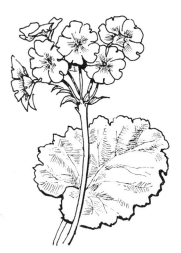
Primula obconica

unheated greenhouses so that their flowers are not spoiled by the weather. Nevertheless, auriculas are perfectly hardy plants and the alpine varieties can be grown out of doors in any reasonably good soil and open position. They relish chalk or limestone, like good drainage and are suitable plants for the rock garden or to edge a bed. Auriculas can be increased by division in spring or autumn or by seed sown in a frame or greenhouse in spring.

In addition to the wild British primrose, the polyanthus and the auricula, there are a number of other hardy primroses which are excellent garden plants. The Caucasian Primrose, *P. juliae*, is a mat-forming plant with almost stemless carmine flowers that has a whole race of hybrids with the British primrose, all pink or magenta in colour. Wanda is the best known.

The Drumstick Primrose, *P. denticulata*, has mauve, purple, pink, rose or white flowers in an almost spherical head in spring and will grow anywhere, though it has a preference for rather damp spots. So has *P. rosea*, a brilliant little rose-pink spring flower for the waterside, only 4 or 5 in. high.

The Candelabra primroses, *P. japonica*, *P. pulverulenta*, *P. helodoxa*, etc., are also plants for damp places. They will thrive along the sides of drainage ditches in leafy or peaty soils and are also at home in the woodland. Their pink, magenta, yellow or white flowers are produced in candelabra-like sprays 2 ft. high. The Tibetan Primrose, *P. florindae*, will actually grow in shallow water, though it is better in the bog garden. The same is true of the Sikkim Primrose, *P. sikkimensis*. Both have big heads of nodding yellow flowers like giant cowslips.

For much dryer places, such as sunny ledges in the rock garden in good loamy soil with some grit and peat for better drainage, there are the Alpine Primrose, *P. marginata*, with heads of lavender-blue flowers in spring and *P. edgeworthii*, lavender flowered in March.

All these hardy primroses can be increased by careful division in spring, also by seed sown as soon as ripe or in spring. Many kinds will spread themselves by self-sown seed.

There are also the three popular races of greenhouse primrose, the Chinese Primrose, *P. sinensis;* the rather similar but slightly taller primrose which has obstinately refused to acquire any other name than *P. obconica*, and the Fairy Primrose, *P. malacoides*, which is small-flowered and far more graceful. The colour range of *P. sinensis* and *P. obconica* is fairly wide, including pinks, reds and blues. That of *P. malacoides* is more limited, mainly pink to red. All are grown from seed sown under glass between April and June (rather late in this period for *P. malacoides* which grows quickly), seedlings being pricked out and later potted singly into small pots in JIP.2 or equivalent compost. They are moved in early autumn to the 4- or 5-in. pots in which they will flower between November and February. They need a light airy greenhouse and a temperature between 7 to 13°C. (45 to 55°F.). All three are strictly perennials but they generally deteriorate after flowering and are so readily raised from seed that they are usually renewed annually in this way. However, it is sometimes worthwhile to retain a few plants of *P. obconica* as they will go on flowering intermittently for months. This primula more than any other is liable to cause a skin rash in those allergic to it.

Finally there is *P. kewensis*, a hybrid with green leaves powdered with grey meal and candelabra heads of bright yellow flowers from November to March. This can be grown from seed like the other greenhouse kinds, but is considerably hardier and also more reliably perennial so is often retained for several years.

PRUNELLA (Self-heal). Hardy herbaceous perennials. 6 to 9 in. Violet, purple, pink or white flowers from June to September. These easily grown plants are useful as ground cover, for edging borders or naturalising in thin woodland. They will grow in most soils in sun or partial shade and are readily increased by division in spring or autumn. All have short spikes of flowers which differ in colour according to variety. Loveliness, pale violet, Pink Loveliness, pink and *alba*, white, are typical.

PRUNUS (Almond, Cherry, Peach, Plum). Hardy deciduous trees and shrubs. 5 to 25 ft. White or pink flowers from November to May. Some of the most magnificent of the decorative trees and shrubs are to be found in this genus. Almonds are among the loveliest of early spring-flowering trees. The Common Almond, *Prunus amygdalis*, makes a tree up to 25 ft. high, but can be kept smaller by a little thinning and shortening of long branches in winter. Its pink blossom appears in March or early April. There is also a hybrid between almond and peach, usually sold as *P. pollardii*, which has deeper pink flowers. Both this and the Common Almond like chalky soils but will grow in practically any soil and open sunny position.

almond

The ornamental cherries are also spectacular early-flowering trees, and one, the autumn-flowering form of the Rosebud Cherry, *P. subhirtella autumnalis*, will actually start to flower in November. It has smaller flowers than most, white or shell pink, but they are produced in great numbers. There is an exceptionally beautiful weeping form of this cherry, *P. subhirtella pendula rosea*, sometimes called the Weeping Spring Cherry since it flowers in March and April.

It is, however, the large-flowered Japanese cherries mainly derived from *P. serrulata* and flowering in April or early May that make the greatest display. All produce their flowers in fine clusters, some being fully double, as in the popular rose-pink Pink Perfection or pink Fugenzo, some single, as in pure white Tai-haku or Yoshino. There is even a pale greenish-yellow variety named Ukon. The Japanese cherries also vary greatly in habit, some being of shuttlecock form such as Kanzan; others widely spreading— Shirofugen and Shirotae; weeping—Cheal's Weeping, or narrowly erect— Amanogawa.

cherry blossom

Many cherries add autumn foliage colour to their other beauties, Sargent's Cherry, *P. sargentii*, being a notable example. The Tibetan Cherry, *P. serrula tibetica*, is grown for its highly polished bark. The Bird Cherry, *P. padus*, is a larger tree with graceful trails of small white flowers in May. Many more will be found in nursery catalogues.

All these cherries are hardy and easily grown in almost any soil and position and they have a liking for chalk. Propagation is by budding on to seedling cherry stocks in summer. No regular pruning is required but diseased or damaged branches should be removed immediately after flowering and wounds painted with Stockholm tar or a tree wound dressing to prevent infection by bacterial canker, a disease to which cherries are very susceptible.

The ornamental peaches, all varieties of *P. persica*, are small trees bearing profuse crops of fine double flowers in April. The most popular is Clara Meyer which is rose pink. Iceberg is pure white and Russell's Red a deep carmine. All these peaches like fairly rich, well-drained soils and sunny places. They are liable to be damaged by cold winds and are not as robust as plums or cherries. In exposed places a disease known as leaf-curl, which causes a curling and reddening of the leaf margins, can be troublesome. It can be controlled by spraying in February and March with lime sulphur or some other good fungicide. Ornamental peaches need no regular pruning and are increased by budding in summer, usually on to plum stocks.

peach

Several very fine trees are varieties of the Cherry Plum or Myrobalan, *P. cerasifera*. One of the most popular of these is the Purple-leaved Plum, *P. pissardii*, with deep purple foliage and small pale pink flowers which are white when fully open. Trailblazer is similar but has larger leaves and sometimes produces good crops of cherry plums which can be used to make jam. *Nigra* has deeper pink flowers and darker purple young foliage. Even better in flower is *P. blireana*, with double rose-pink flowers and coppery-purple leaves. It seldom exceeds 15 ft. in height. Still shorter is the Purple-leafed Sloe, *P. spinosa purpurea*, which is more a shrub than a tree, densely branched and spiny, around 10 ft. high with purple leaves and small white flowers in March or early April. One of the smallest of all is *P. cistena* which looks much like *P. pissardii* but is only 5 to 6 ft. high. It makes an excellent hedge as also do the various varieties of sloe.

All the plums will thrive in practically any soil and reasonably open place and are increased by budding in summer on to special plum stocks. No regular pruning is required.

pulmonaria

PULMONARIA (Lungwort, Jerusalem Cowslip, Spotted Dog, Bethlehem Sage). Hardy herbaceous perennials. 9 to 12 in. Blue, purple or red flowers from March to April. These are herbaceous perennials making low clumps of foliage, often handsomely spotted with pale green or silvery white and producing their clusters of blue, purple or red flowers on 9-in. stems in March and April. One of the best for flowers is Munstead Blue, a good variety of *Pulmonaria angustifolia*, but the Bethlehem Sage, *P. saccharata*, has the most handsomely spotted leaves.

All the pulmonarias are very easily grown in almost any soil and sunny or shady places. All can be increased by division in spring or autumn.

PULSATILLA (Pasque Flower). Hardy herbaceous perennials or rock plants. 9 in. Mauve, purple or pink flowers in April and May. The Pasque Flower, *Pulsatilla vulgaris*, is sometimes listed under its old name *Anemone pulsatilla*. It is a rare British wild plant found on chalk downs and this gives a clue to its cultivation in the garden as it likes chalky or limy soils and open sunny places. It has deeply-divided leaves covered in silken hairs as are the flower stems carrying the anemone-like flowers, which are followed by tousled silken seed heads. *P. vernalis* is even more hairy, a little shorter and a plant for the rock garden in specially well-drained soil, rather than for the front of the border which suits *P. vulgaris* well. Both can be increased by seed sown in a frame or greenhouse in spring or by careful division in spring.

pulsatilla

PUSCHKINIA. Hardy bulb. 6 in. Blue flowers in March. *Puschkinia scilloides* is a most attractive little bulb, very like a scilla as its name implies but with spikes of pale blue flowers. It likes sunny places, is very suitable for the rock garden and the bulbs should be planted 2 in. deep in August or September. It can be increased by division in August but bulbs can be left undisturbed for years.

PYRACANTHA (Firethorn). Hardy evergreen shrubs. 6 to 8 ft. White flowers in June followed by red or yellow berries from September to February. These evergreen shrubs are frequently trained as climbers against walls, though they can equally well be grown as bushes in the open. All have clustered white flowers about mid-summer followed by berries, usually red though there are yellow-berried kinds. The most popular of all is *Pyracantha coccinea lalandei* which has extra large berries of a particularly brilliant orange-scarlet. *P. atalantioides* has crimson berries and also a variety, *aurea*, with yellow berries, but perhaps even better as a yellow-fruited shrub is the form of *P. rogersiana* named *flava*. *P. rogersiana* itself has orange-red fruits smaller but more numerous than those of *P. c. lalandei*.

All are easily grown in almost any soil and will succeed in shady as well as in sunny positions. When grown against walls, badly placed shoots should be removed or shortened in early summer after flowering when care should be taken not to remove any shoots bearing berries which will just be starting to form. Propagation is by seed in spring or cuttings in summer.

pyrethrum

PYRETHRUM. Hardy herbaceous perennials. 2 ft. Pink to crimson or white flowers in May and June. These are hardy plants making clumps of ferny leaves and with large daisy-like flowers on long stems in early summer. They are popular for cutting and make good border plants in well-drained soils and open sunny places. There are both single- and double-flowered varieties with a colour range from white and pale pink to crimson. Plant in spring or immediately after flowering and increase by division when replanting.

Pyrethrums enjoy fairly rich well-drained soil and sunny open places. In wet soil they are liable to rot in winter but this can, to some extent, be avoided by planting them along the summit of low ridges.

R

RAMONDA. Hardy rock plants. 4 to 6 in. Lavender or white flowers in May and June. These very attractive plants make flat rosettes of broad dark green wrinkled leaves, and from the centre of each rosette throw up several flower stems each terminating in a small spray of lavender or white flowers. They dislike damp collecting on the leaves and so are best planted on their sides in vertical crevices in a wall backed by soil or between large stones in the rock garden. They enjoy soil containing plenty of leafmould or peat and succeed best in places where they are not exposed to hot sunshine. Ramondas are increased by seed sown in spring or by leaf cuttings in June or July inserted by pushing the leaf stalk and the lower part of the leaf into a mixture of peat and sand.

ramonda

RANUNCULUS (Fair Maids of France). Hardy tuberous-rooted and herbaceous perennials. 8 to 24 in. Yellow, orange, pink to crimson or white flowers from May to July. Two very different kinds are commonly grown in gardens, the Turban Ranunculus, *Ranunculus asiaticus*, and Fair Maids of France, which is the double-flowered variety of *R. aconitifolius*. The Turban Ranunculus is a remarkable plant with flowers so double that they are almost globular. They are highly coloured in a variety of shades of yellow, orange, pink and red and are carried on 9-in. stems between May and July. The plant makes small clawed tubers which can be planted 2 in. deep, claw sides downwards, in October, November, February or early March, spring planting being preferable on all heavy soils. The Turban Ranunculus likes sun, warmth and good drainage. The tubers should be lifted each July and stored in a dry cool place till planting time. Increase is by division of the clusters of tubers.

Ranunculus aconitifolius is a herbaceous perennial with fibrous, not tuberous roots. It has deeply divided leaves and 18- to 24-in. stems bearing sprays of small fully double white flowers in May and June. It is a good border plant easily grown in any reasonably good soil and sunny or partially shady position. It can be increased by division in spring.

ranunculus

RESEDA (Mignonette). Hardy annual. 1 ft. Red and green flowers from June to August. Mignonette is a highly fragrant though not very showy flower which is botanically named *Reseda odorata*. It is grown from seed sown in March, April or May where the plants are to flower. Seedlings should be thinned to 6 in. or thereabouts. Mignonette likes a sunny place and will grow in practically any soil but it has a special liking for those containing lime or chalk.

reseda

RHODODENDRON. Hardy evergreen shrubs. Prostrate to 20 ft. Flowers in all colours from January to July. All the shrubs grown as rhododendrons in gardens are evergreen but botanically there are also deciduous kinds which gardeners know as azaleas. They are dealt with under that name in this book.

Rhododendrons will grow in most soils that do not contain lime or chalk. They can even be grown in such alkaline soils if they are well fed with iron and manganese sequestrols but this can be expensive. They like peat and leafmould and benefit from annual topdressings of either, which can be applied any time from October to April. Rhododendrons transplant readily, even when quite large, and this can be useful in the garden if rearrangement is necessary. October and April are favourable months for planting but they can be moved from the open ground during any reasonable weather in autumn or winter and can be planted out of containers at any time of the year. They do not need any pruning but if they become too big they can be cut back in April or May at the sacrifice of one year's flowers. It is desirable to remove the faded flower trusses each year to prevent seed forming.

Rhododendrons can be increased by layering in spring, by summer cuttings under mist, by grafting, usually on to seedlings of *Rhododendron ponticum*, and by seed. The seeds are very small and must be sown on the surface of peat and sand. Species usually come true to type from seed but garden hybrids may show considerable variation. Seedlings take several years before they produce any flowers.

There are very many wild rhododendrons or species, and literally thousands of hybrids or garden varieties. These have a great range in habit, height, flower form and colour so that there are rhododendrons for almost every place in the garden. Most kinds grow well in shade, particularly the dappled shade provided by trees not too closely planted, and so rhododendrons are often used for woodland planting. Many kinds, especially those known collectively as Hardy Hybrids, will also grow in sun though they do not like very hot dry places. The toughest of all is *R. ponticum* with mauve to purple flowers in May and June. This often spreads by self-sown seeds and is naturalised in many parts of the British Isles. Some of the dwarf species, such as *R. hanceanum nanum* and *R. pemakoense*, are very suitable plants for the rock garden.

Varieties are so numerous that only a few typical kinds can be mentioned. Hundreds more will be found listed in the catalogues of nurseries or on display at garden centres. Jenny is prostrate and has scarlet flowers in April and May; Elizabeth has similar flowers but is 2 to 3 ft. high; Blue Tit and Blue Diamond both have small lavender-blue flowers in April and May and grow slowly to about 3 ft.; Temple Belle has pink bell-shaped flowers on a 3- to 4-ft. bush in April and May. The Yakushimanum Hybrids have white or pink flowers in May and make compact bushes 3 to 4 ft. high; Lady Chamberlain Hybrids have clusters of tubular pink, salmon or orange flowers in June and are 5 to 6 ft. high. Hardy Hybrids such as Britannia, scarlet; Cynthia, carmine; Pink Pearl, pink; Susan, bluish-mauve; Purple Splendour, wine red; Mrs G. W. Leak, rose, crimson and brown; Sappho, white and maroon; Souvenir of W. C. Slocock, apricot and yellow and Loder's White, white, all bear their flowers in large erect trusses in May to June and make big rounded bushes 8 ft. or more in height; *R. loderi* and its varieties such as King George and White Diamond have pale pink or white flowers of great size, sweetly scented, borne on large open bushes in May. Tally Ho has scarlet flowers in June and July. The Arboreum Hybrids are tree like, growing slowly to 20 ft. or more with white, pink or red flowers from January to April but are not very hardy; this also applies to some of the very large-leaved species such as *R. sinogrande*, creamy white, *R. macabeanum*, yellow and *R. falconeri*, white, all April flowering. Nobleanum Hybrids with white, pink or red flowers from January to March also become tree like with age.

rhododendron – hardy hybrid

RHUS (Stag's-horn Sumach). Hardy deciduous shrubs or trees. 8 to 12 ft. Green flowers in July followed by crimson fruits from August to December. The Stag's-horn Sumach, *Rhus typhina*, is a small, open-branched tree or large shrub with long fern-like leaves turning to scarlet and yellow in autumn, and at the same season producing horn-like spikes of velvet-red 'fruits' which look more like flowers. These fruits are only produced from pollinated female flowers which are borne on separate plants from those which carry male flowers, so to have the fruits both sexes must be planted.

Rhus typhina will grow in any ordinary soil and sunny position and is readily increased by detaching rooted suckers in autumn.

RIBES (Flowering Currant). Hardy deciduous shrubs. 6 to 8ft. Pink, white or carmine flowers in March and April. *Ribes sanguineum* is a gay and vigorous shrub, one of the first to flower and the easiest to grow. Its short hanging trails of pink, carmine or white flowers start to open in March and continue throughout April. It soon makes a big bush, 8ft. high, and it will grow anywhere in heavy or light soil, chalk or peat, sun or shade. It can be increased by cuttings in autumn, and can be pruned after flowering as hard as is necessary to keep bushes from growing too large.

Ribes sanguineum

ROBINIA (False Acacia, Rose Acacia). Hardy deciduous trees or shrubs. 6 to 40ft. White or pink flowers in May and June. The False Acacia, *Robinia pseudoacacia*, is a fast growing thorny tree with ferny leaves and trails of white flowers in June, in form similar to those of a laburnum. It has several varieties including one, named Frisia, with yellow leaves and another, named Inermis, with no thorns and a much more compact habit of growth for which reason it is known as the Mop-head Acacia. This form seldom flowers but has been much used for street planting. Yet another variety, named *fastigiata* or *pyramidalis*, has erect branches forming a narrow column instead of a wide-spreading head.

The Rose Acacia, *R. hispida*, is a shrub which is sometimes grafted on to stems of *R. pseudoacacia* to form a small tree 7 or 8ft. high. It has foliage rather like that of *R. pseudoacacia* and larger pink flowers in May and June.

Robinia pseudoacacia will grow almost anywhere with a preference for sunny places and well-drained soils. Good drainage and warmth are more essential to *R. hispida* which is a much less robust species. Both can be increased by seed or by rooted suckers.

ROCHEA. Tender succulent perennial. 12 to 15in. Carmine flowers from July to September. *Rochea coccinea* is a showy succulent which makes a first-class pot plant for a cool or intermediate greenhouse. Its clusters of scented carmine flowers are freely produced in late summer. It should be grown in JIP.2, or equivalent compost, and should be watered fairly freely from April to September, sparingly from October to March. No shading is required at any time. It is increased by cuttings of firm young shoots in spring or summer. This plant is sometimes listed under its old name *Crassula coccinea*.

Rodgersia pinnata

RODGERSIA. Hardy herbaceous perennials. 3 to 4ft. White or pink flowers in July. The rodgersias all have handsome bronzy leaves and branching sprays of small, astilbe-like flowers in July. These flowers are white or pink in *Rodgersia pinnata* and *R. aesculifolia*, both of which have deeply divided leaves rather like those of a horse chestnut but much larger, and white in *R. tabularis*, which has rhubarb-like leaves. *R. podophylla* has the horse chestnut type of foliage and cream-coloured flowers. Their height is from 3 to 4ft. and they like damp soils but can be grown quite successfully in ordinary soil provided it is good, deep and not liable to dry out badly. All can be increased by division in spring or autumn.

ROMNEYA (Californian Tree Poppy). Hardy perennials. 6ft. White and yellow flowers from July to September. These lovely plants are half shrubby, half herbaceous. Their 6-ft. stems become firm and almost woody as the summer advances but are usually killed back to ground level in winter and a new lot appear the following spring. The flowers come in late summer and are huge white poppies each with a central boss of golden stamens. The foliage is blue-grey. Though there are several kinds, they do not differ much from a garden standpoint. All like sun and the best of drainage, and will thrive in very poor, gravelly soils. They can spread a considerable distance by suckers. Romneya are raised either from seed sown in spring or from root cuttings in winter, but are rather difficult to transplant, for which reason young plants are usually grown in pots until planting-out time in spring or autumn. They can then be transferred with minimum root disturbance.

romneya

121

ROSA (Rose). Hardy deciduous shrubs and climbers. Prostrate to climbing. Flowers in all colours except true blues and produced from May to October. There are so many different roses, varying in size, habit, flower form, colour and other ways, that many books have been devoted to them without exhausting the subject.

Broadly, they may be divided into wild roses or species on the one hand and garden roses on the other. The wild roses have single flowers and are grown mainly as shrubs or some kinds, such as *Rosa multiflora* and *R. filipes*, both white, as very vigorous climbers to cover screens or scramble up into trees. These wild roses mostly flower once each year whereas many garden roses flower on and off from June to October.

The garden roses may themselves be divided into climbers (including ramblers) with long flexible stems which can be tied against walls or fences or be trained around pillars or over arches, pergolas and arbours; and bush roses, which have shorter, stiffer, more freely-branched stems. Some of the latter are sufficiently large and vigorous to be grown, like wild roses, with other shrubs, but less vigorous bush roses are frequently massed in beds by themselves. Miniature roses are small in the size of their flowers and leaves and their overall structure.

Roses can be grown in any reasonably good soil and prefer open places with sun and free movement of air. They respond to generous feeding with manure or compost in late winter followed by occasional topdressings of a good compound fertiliser in spring and summer. They should also be sprayed occasionally from mid-April until September with both a good insecticide to keep down aphids and other insects and a good fungicide to prevent attacks of black spot, mildew, rust or other common rose diseases. Disease is usually less troublesome in town than in country gardens because sulphur in the air discourages the fungi which cause disease.

All roses respond to pruning though wild roses and vigorous shrub roses need less pruning than other kinds. Varieties that bloom only once each summer (non-recurrent roses) can be pruned in September. Roses that continue to bloom all summer (recurrent roses) are best pruned in February or March. Start by cutting out all diseased or damaged growth and also as much as possible of the older stems that have developed rough dark-coloured bark. This is all the pruning that wild roses and most shrub roses and vigorous climbers require. Bush roses can be further pruned according to the purpose for which they are being grown. If this is mainly for garden display, strong young stems (those made the previous summer) should be shortened by about a third and weaker stems by a half or two thirds. If large flowers are required strong young stems should be shortened by two thirds and weaker ones cut back to 2 or 3 in. or removed altogether.

Commercial rose growers increase roses by budding them on to stocks. This is a form of grafting carried out in summer. If such roses produce suckers (shoots direct from the roots or from below the point of budding) they must be removed as soon as seen as they will reproduce the stock or wild rose on which the garden rose has been budded. Gardeners often grow their own roses from cuttings taken in summer or autumn. Such roses are on their own roots and suckers need not be removed since they will produce flowers of the same type and quality as those from other stems. Wild roses can also be increased from seed sown out of doors in spring, but though garden roses can be raised from seed the seedlings may be very inferior to their parents.

ROSMARINUS (Rosemary). Hardy evergreen shrubs. 1 to 4 ft. Blue flowers in April and May. These are evergreen shrubs with aromatic foliage, and small lavender-blue flowers in spring. The Prostrate Rosemary, *Rosmarinus lavandulaceus*, is a trailing plant suitable for rock garden or dry wall but it is not very hardy and really only reliable where any frosts that do occur are light and of short duration. The Common Rosemary, *R. officinalis*, is a bushy, erect plant of which there are several varieties differing in height and shade. Severn Sea is relatively short, spreading and has bright blue flowers. Miss Jessop, also known as *R.o. fastigiatus*, is narrow and upright.

Rosa Dearest

All like warm, sunny places and well-drained soils and all can be increased by cuttings in July and August.

RUDBECKIA (Coneflower). Hardy herbaceous perennials and half-hardy annuals. 1 to 8 ft. Yellow or chestnut-red flowers from July to September. The coneflowers get their name from the fact that in many kinds the central disk of their daisy-type flowers is raised into a cone instead of being more or less flat and button like as in most daisies. This is particularly well marked in the popular variety Herbstsonne, a perennial 6 or 7 ft. high with yellow green-coned flowers in August and September. Golden Glow, an even taller perennial, has double yellow flowers, and Goldsturm is 3 ft. high, with orange black-centred flowers in August and September.

The annual rudbeckias are mostly hybrids 1 to 3 ft. high, with flowers in various shades from yellow to chestnut red. Seed is sown in March or April in a greenhouse or frame, temperature 15 to 18°C. (59 to 65°F.), seedlings are pricked out and hardened off for planting out of doors in May or early June about 1 ft. apart. The perennial kinds can be divided in spring or autumn. All rudbeckias are sun-lovers and will grow in almost any soil.

rosemary

SAGITTARIA (Arrowhead). Hardy perennial aquatics. 2 ft. **White flowers in July and August.** These are plants for the margins of pools in water not more than 12 in. deep. They have broad arrow-shaped leaves and spikes of white flowers, which are double in the variety *flore pleno*. Sagittarias should be planted in April or May in loamy soil and left undisturbed until overcrowded. Increase is by division at planting time.

rudbeckia

SAINTPAULIA (African Violet). Tender herbaceous perennials. 4 to 6 in. Purple, violet, pink or white flowers produced throughout the year. These are small and very free-flowering plants for intermediate or warm greenhouses. The leaves are deep green and velvety, the flowers, clustered on 6-in. stems, are violet-purple in the common form, but there are many variations from pale blue to pink and white, and some are double.

All are easily grown in a rather peaty compost, provided they can be given plenty of warmth—certainly a minimum of 13°C. (55°F.), even in the coldest weather and an average around 18°C. (65°F.). They will need some shade in summer but in winter should receive all the light possible.

When grown as house plants they benefit from the close rather moist atmosphere and extra illumination provided by a special 'growth cabinet', a kind of indoor frame or miniature greenhouse provided with fluorescent lighting. Under good conditions they will flower throughout the year. Propagation is usually by leaf cuttings but plants can also be raised from seed or increased by careful division in spring.

SALPIGLOSSIS. Half-hardy annuals. 1½ to 2 ft. Flowers in all colours from June to August. Salpiglossis has trumpet-shaped flowers in a wide range of colours, often with veinings of gold on a purple, rose or scarlet base. The flowers are carried in loose sprays on 3-ft. stems and are excellent for cutting.

Seed should be sown in a greenhouse, temperature 15 to 18°C. (59 to 65°F.), in February or March, seedlings being pricked out and eventually hardened off for planting out in late May or early June in good soil and a sunny, sheltered position. The plants should be spaced at least 9 in. apart. Alternatively, salpiglossis can be grown as a pot plant for the cool greenhouse in summer, in which case the young plants should be potted singly in 5- or 6-in. pots in JIP.2 or equivalent soil instead of being planted out of doors.

salpiglossis

salvia

santolina

annual
saponaria

SALVIA (Sage, Clary). Hardy herbaceous perennials, hardy or slightly tender deciduous or semi-evergreen shrubs and hardy and half-hardy annuals. 1 to 4 ft. Blue, mauve, purple, pink and scarlet flowers from May to October. The salvias are sages and sometimes show their relationship to the Common Sage very clearly, though the ordinary gardener will see little connection between the herb and the popular Scarlet Salvia, *Salvia splendens*, used as a summer bedding plant. This is a perennial but it is nearly always grown as a half-hardy annual, seed being sown in a well-warmed greenhouse, temperature 18°C. (65°F.), in January or February and seedlings potted singly in small pots and eventually hardened off for planting out in early June. This salvia likes sun and warmth but is not fussy about soil. Its spikes of vivid scarlet, pink or purple flowers are produced freely from July to October.

Salvia horminum is a hardy annual, 1½ to 2 ft. high with spikes of relatively insignificant flowers surrounded by showy purple, pink or white bracts. It is in flower all summer, is not fussy about soil, likes sunny places and can be raised from seed sown in March, April, May or September where the plants are to flower. Seedlings should be thinned to about 9 in.

Much more like the herb sage is *S. superba*, one of the best herbaceous perennials. It grows 1½ to 3 ft. high and produces slender spikes of violet-purple flowers in July and August. It will grow almost anywhere and seldom fails to make a good display. It is easily increased by division in spring or autumn. The Clary, *S. sclarea*, is less reliable as a perennial and is usually grown as a biennial, seed being sown in May or early June to give plants for removal to flowering quarters in autumn. The leaves are large and the mauve or lilac flowers are produced in 3- to 4-ft. spikes in summer.

There are also several shrubby salvias such as *S. grahamii*, a bushy, 3-ft. plant with scarlet flowers throughout the summer and *S. rutilans*, 3 ft. and magenta, but all need warm sunny sheltered places in well-drained soil as they are none too hardy. They can be increased by summer cuttings.

The Common Sage, itself, *S. officinalis*, has attractive spikes of purple flowers in summer and several varieties with coloured leaves such as *purpurascens*, purple and *tricolor*, purple, pink and cream. All are 1 to 1½ ft. high, hardy and easily grown in ordinary well-drained soil and a sunny place. They are increased by summer cuttings.

Finally, there is the Blue Sage, *S. patens*, a tuberous-rooted herbaceous perennial which is not very hardy and so may need to be lifted each autumn and over-wintered in a frame or greenhouse. The gentian-blue flowers are carried on 2-ft. spikes in late summer. This plant can be increased by careful division of the tuberous roots in spring.

SANTOLINA (Lavender Cotton). Hardy evergreen shrubs. 1½ to 2 ft. Yellow flowers in July and August. These are low-growing shrubs with aromatic foliage and small yellow flowers in summer. The most popular is the Grey-leaved Lavender Cotton, *Santolina chamaecyparissus*, best grown in its dwarf form which is known as *nana* or *corsica*. This is about 1½ ft. high, but can be kept to 1 ft. if it is clipped with shears each spring. It makes a fine silvery-grey edging plant for large beds. The Green-leaved Lavender Cotton, *S. virens*, is similar but has bright green leaves. Both can be carefully divided in autumn, or cuttings can be rooted in July.

SAPONARIA (Soapwort, Bouncing Bet). Hardy herbaceous perennials and hardy annual. 2 ft. Pink flowers from June to August. The most popular kind is the Rock Soapwort, *Saponaria ocymoides*, a sprawling plant for sunny banks, rock gardens or walls. It spreads rapidly and produces its abundant bright pink flowers in June and July. The Common Soapwort, *S. officinalis*, is a rather stiff herbaceous plant 2 ft. high with heads of pale pink flowers in late summer. There is a double-flowered form, often known as Bouncing Bet, that is more effective. Both these plants like well-drained soils and open places and can be increased by seed or by division in spring.

There is also the Annual Soapwort, *S. vaccaria*, a graceful plant with loose

124

sprays of pink or white flowers in summer. It is quite hardy and is grown from seed sown in March, April or September where the plants are to flower. Thinning is to 6 in. and a sunny situation is desirable.

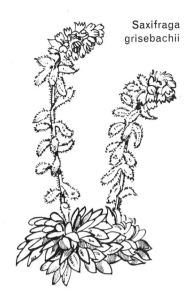

Saxifraga grisebachii

SAXIFRAGA (London Pride, Saxifrage). Hardy rock plants and hardy herbaceous perennials. 1 to 24 in. White, pink to crimson, or yellow flowers from March to July. There are a great many different kinds of saxifrages and they vary so much in appearance that it is not immediately obvious that they are related. From the garden standpoint four groups are most valuable—the Silver saxifrages, the Cushion saxifrages, the Mossy saxifrages and the London Prides.

The first two are plants for the rock garden or dry wall. The Silver saxifrages make flattish rosettes of leaves, often silvered all over or along the edges, and they produce clusters or sprays of flowers, usually white, though there are pink and even yellow varieties. One of the loveliest is Tumbling Waters with arching 2-ft. flower sprays in June. *Saxifraga cotyledon* is similar in appearance, but more erect, with white flowers which in the fine variety *caterhamensis* are freely spotted with red. *S. aizoon* has smaller rosettes and flower sprays which may be white, pink or pale yellow according to variety.

The Cushion saxifrages make low hummocks of usually greyish leaves which often have a hard and spiky feel. The flowers, which may be white, pink or pale yellow, are produced in early spring on 1- to 3-in. stems. Typical of this lovely group is Cranbourne, with flowers the colour of apple blossom. *S. burseriana* is white or pale yellow, *apiculata*, Elizabeth and Faldonside are all yellow, *jenkinsae* is deep pink and Myra cherry red.

In addition to these two major groups for the rock garden there are some others a little more exacting. *S. grisebachii* makes tight mounded rosettes of silver leaves from which in March and April come arching 6-in. flower stems clothed in velvet-red bracts. It is best grown in a pan of gritty soil in an unheated greenhouse or frame. *S. oppositifolia* makes carpets of small leaves studded in March and April with heather-purple or white flowers. It needs good drainage but plenty of moisture from May to August while it is in growth.

All these rock-garden saxifrages thrive in well-drained, gritty soils, preferably containing plenty of limestone chippings, and open places.

By contrast, the Mossy saxifrages thrive in any ordinary soils and do not object to shade. They make soft, low mounds of green leaves and carry sprays of white, pink or red flowers on 6- to 9-in. stems in April and May. They can be grown in the rock garden but are equally good for edging. Typical kinds are James Bremner, white, Winston Churchill, pink and Dubarry, crimson.

Saxifraga cotyledon

Saxifraga fortunei is another saxifrage that succeeds better in cool shady places and is an excellent plant for thin woodland. It has quite large bronzy leaves and foot-high sprays of white flowers in September and October.

The various forms of London Pride are very distinct in character from other saxifrages. In most nursery catalogues they will be found as *S. umbrosa* or, if the nurseryman is very up to date, as *S. urbicum*, which is considered by experts to be the more correct name. The Common London Pride has rosettes of green leaves and loose 1-ft. sprays of small pink flowers in early summer. It will grow anywhere in sun or shade and is a very useful plant to grow in places in which many less tolerant plants would fail. It has a variety with yellow-variegated leaves. A better plant for rock gardens is Elliott's Variety, often listed as *S. primuloides* Elliott's Variety. This is only 6 in. high and has deep pink flowers in May.

Almost all saxifrages can be increased by division in spring and most can also be raised from seed sown in a frame or greenhouse in spring, though it may be a year or two before seedlings attain flowering size.

SCABIOSA (Scabious). Hardy herbaceous perennials and half-hardy annuals. 1½ to 3 ft. White, blue, lavender, purple, pink to crimson flowers from June to October. There are two good kinds of scabious for the garden, the Caucasian Scabious, *Scabiosa caucasica*, a hardy herbaceous perennial with blue, lavender or white flowers on 2- to 3-ft. stems

Scabiosa atropurpurea

schizanthus

schizostylis

from June to October, and the Annual Scabious, *S. atropurpurea*, with white, blue, pink, red or crimson flowers on 18- to 30-in. stems all the summer. The Caucasian Scabious likes a well-drained soil and sunny place. It can be increased by division in spring or by seed in spring, but selected varieties, such as Clive Greaves, blue and Miss Willmott, white, cannot be raised true to colour from seed.

The Annual Scabious is grown from seed which may either be sown in March or early April in a greenhouse or frame, seedlings being pricked out and hardened off for planting out of doors in May or June, or it may be sown in late April or May out of doors where the plants are to flower, seedlings being thinned to 1 ft. It will grow well in any reasonable soil and open place.

SCHIZANTHUS (Butterfly Flower). Half-hardy annuals. 1 to 4ft. White, yellow, pink to crimson flowers from April to October. Though the schizanthus is hardy and can be grown out of doors in summer it is easily damaged by wind and rain and so is usually grown as a greenhouse annual. Plants are bushy and 1 to 4ft. high according to type, producing spikes of small butterfly-like flowers in a wide variety of colours and markings. Seed can be sown in March or April to give plants to flower from August to October; alternatively, seed sown in August or September will give plants to flower from April to June. In either case the seedlings should be potted singly in small pots and then moved on to 4-in. and finally to the 7-, 8- or 9-in. pots in JIP.1, or equivalent compost, in which they will flower. Plants should be carefully staked and should be kept throughout in a light, airy greenhouse with a minimum winter temperature of 7°C. (45°F.). Water is required fairly freely from April to September, much more sparingly in winter.

SCHIZOSTYLIS (Kaffir Lily). Hardy herbaceous perennials. 1 to 1½ft. Red or pink flowers from September to November. The kaffir lilies are related to the montbretias. The flowers are carried in spikes and provide valuable colour in autumn and even on into winter in sheltered places. *Schizostylis coccinea*, which is the scarlet kind, and its pink variety Viscountess Byng will grow in any reasonably good well-drained soil but need a warm sunny position. They are only reliably hardy in milder areas and may need a little winter protection where frosts are severe or prolonged. Increase is by division of the rhizomes in spring which is also the best planting season.

SCILLA (Squill). Hardy bulbs. 3 to 9in. Blue, purple or white flowers from March to June. The most popular kinds are small spring-flowering bulbs with blue flowers, easily grown in most soils and sunny or partially shaded positions and increased by division of the bulb clusters in late summer.

Scilla bifolia flowers first in March, is 4 to 6in. high and bright blue, purple or white. *S. sibirica* follows a week or so later, is violet-blue and about 6in. high. *S. tubergeniana* is similar in height and flowering time but light blue. The Peruvian Squill, *S. peruviana*, is a very different plant with a big more or less dome-shaped head of crowded violet-blue flowers on a stout 9-in. stem in May and June. It needs a warm, sunny place and its large bulbs should be covered with 2in. of soil.

Scilla peruviana

SEDUM (Stonecrop, Rose-root). Hardy herbaceous perennials, rock plants and hardy annuals. Prostrate to 2ft. White, yellow, pink or bronze-red flowers from August to October. The stonecrops are succulent plants, most of which are quite hardy and can be grown on sunny rock gardens, dry walls and banks. Most will grow in quite poor and dry soils Some, such as the Spoon-leaved Stonecrop, *Sedum spathulifolium*, and the Pink Stonecrop, *S. spurium* are quite prostrate; others, such as the Pink Rose-root, *S. spectabile*, and the Giant Stonecrop, *S. maximum*, are erect plants 1½ to 2ft. in height and more suitable for the herbaceous border than the rock garden. Autumn Joy is a fine garden hybrid with salmon-pink flowers deepening to bronze red as they age. It is 1½ft. high and flowers in September and October.

Almost all sedums are attractive in leaf as well as in flower and the flowers are usually pink, crimson or yellow. One of the smallest in leaf is the Spanish Stonecrop, *S. hispanicum*, a creeping plant with blue-grey leaves so small that the plant almost looks like a moss. This and similar small kinds can be planted in the crevices between paving slabs.

Most stonecrops can be increased by division in spring or autumn but one useful rock garden species, the Blue Stonecrop, *S. caeruleum*, is a hardy annual grown from seed sown in spring. It often spreads by self-sown seedlings.

Sedum spurium

SEMPERVIVUM (Houseleek). Hardy rock plants. Prostrate to 6 in. Pink or red flowers from July to August. These are all succulent plants making stiff rosettes of leaves, often of considerable beauty. The flowers, usually pink or red, are produced in clusters on thick stems but are not very attractive and it is for their foliage colours and shapes that houseleeks are primarily grown. Most kinds are hardy and suitable for planting on sunny rock gardens and dry walls. Many will thrive in very shallow soil and may sometimes be seen growing in the small accumulation of soil, leaves and debris that collects in the angles of tiles or old rocks.

The Common Houseleek, *Sempervivum tectorum*, has rather large rosettes, green in the original variety, but there are many colour forms, some with bronze-tipped leaves, some bronze or purple all over. The Cobweb Houseleek, *S. arachnoideum*, has much smaller, purplish rosettes covered with white, cobweb-like hairs.

All sempervivums can be increased by division at almost any time of the year and can also be raised from seed sown in a frame or greenhouse in spring but the coloured-leaved varieties may not come true to type from seed.

SENECIO (Jacobaea). Hardy or slightly tender evergreen shrubs or hardy annuals. 1 to 3 ft. Yellow, white, pink to crimson and purple flowers from June to August. This is a large and rather confusing genus which contains herbaceous perennials and annuals as well as shrubs. The colourful annuals known to gardeners as jacobaeas are varieties of *Senecio elegans* and may be found under that name in some catalogues. Though white is available it is the bright rose, magenta and purple forms that are most valuable, especially those with semi-double flowers. All are readily grown from seed sown out of doors in March, April or early May where the plants are to flower, seedlings being thinned to 6 or 8 in. apart. Jacobaeas grow 1 to $1\frac{1}{2}$ ft. high and like a sunny place with reasonably good, well-drained soil.

Senecio laxifolius

The best of the herbaceous kinds have now been renamed Ligularia and are described under that name in this book and here we are concerned only with grey-leaved evergreen shrubby kinds. Of these the most generally useful is *S. greyii*, a first-rate shrub about 3 ft. high with rounded grey leaves and sprays of small yellow daisy flowers in June and July. It is fairly hardy but may be damaged in very cold winters. *S. laxifolius* is very similar but is a comparatively scarce plant. *S. leucostachys* is considerably less hardy and needs a very warm sunny sheltered place. It has deeply-divided silvery-white leaves and white flowers that are not very attractive, and grows about 2 ft. high.

Finally, there is *S. cineraria*, a plant that suffers from too many names as it may turn up in catalogues as *S. maritima* or as *Cineraria maritima*. This is only half-shrubby and its soft stems usually get badly damaged in winter. It is grown mainly as a summer bedding plant for its very handsome grey-white deeply-divided leaves.

All the shrubby senecios can be increased by cuttings taken in July or August and rooted in a frame and it is wise to take cuttings of *S. leucostachys* and *S. cineraria* annually and over-winter them under cover in case the parent plants are destroyed by frost. Stems damaged by frost should be shortened to sound growth in March.

SIDALCEA. Hardy herbaceous perennials. 2 to 4 ft. Pink to carmine flowers in July and August. Sidalceas are useful border plants because of their long slender spikes of mallow flowers in July and August. All are in

sidalcea

Silene schafta

sisyrinchium

Skimmia japonica

shades of pink, from a light silvery pink to a deep rosy carmine, and heights vary from 2 to 4 ft. All are easily grown in almost any soil and a reasonably open position. They can be increased by division in spring or autumn or by seed in spring, and often spread freely by self-sown seedlings.

SILENE (Catchfly). Hardy annuals and rock plants. 2 to 9 in. White, pink or red flowers from April to October. The Annual Catchfly, *Silene pendula*, is an excellent plant for the rock garden. It is from 4 to 8 in. high according to variety, compact, with single or double flowers in various shades from pink to red, and white. It is grown from seed sown in March, April or May where the plants are to grow, seedlings being thinned to about 6 in. Alternatively, seed can be sown in a frame in September and the seedlings planted out in April for early flowering. It likes sun but is not fussy about soil.

The Mountain Catchfly, *S. alpestris*, and the Stemless Catchfly, *S. acaulis*, are both small rock plants for sunny places and well-drained rather gritty soils. The first has pink flowers from June to August, the second white in early summer, and they make neat hummocks or tufts of leaves. By contrast, the Autumn Catchfly, *S. schafta*, is a loose, tumbling plant with masses of rose-pink flowers in late summer. It will grow in any reasonably good soil and open position and is an excellent plant for covering banks or dry walls. All these silenes can be increased by division in spring.

For the German Catchfly, see Lychnis.

SISYRINCHIUM (Blue-eyed Grass). Hardy herbaceous perennials. 9 to 24 in. Blue, mauve or yellow flowers from April to August. The kind commonly known as Blue-eyed Grass, *Sisyrinchium bermudianum*, is a pretty little perennial, 9 to 12 in. high, with grassy leaves which seem to burst out near their tips into starry violet-blue flowers produced a few at a time from April to August. It is easily grown in almost any soil and fairly open place. More exacting is *S. grandiflorum*, with rush-like leaves and nodding, amethyst-blue flowers in April. It should be grown in a sheltered yet sunny place, in well-drained soil in the rock garden. Much larger than either of these is *S. striatum* with narrow leaves rather like those of an iris and stiff stems, 2 ft. high, closely set with pale yellow flowers in June. It will grow in any reasonable soil and prefers a sunny position.

All sisyrinchiums can be increased by division in the spring and also by seed sown in a frame in the spring.

SKIMMIA. Hardy evergreen shrubs. 2 to 5 ft. White flowers from March to April followed by red berries from August to March. The Japanese Skimmia, *Skimmia japonica*, has two sexes and only the females produce berries and then only if there is a male nearby for pollination. However, the male flower trusses are larger than those of the female and it is wise to choose male plants with care as some are more showy than others. *Fragrans* is one good male variety with scented flowers and *rubella* is another with purplish-red buds which are very decorative. *Foremanii* is a vigorous female and *rogersii* a shorter, more compact female. *S. reevesiana*, also sometimes listed as *S. fortunei*, is a dwarfer shrub which produces both male and female flowers so that a single bush will produce berries.

Skimmias grow from 2 to 5 ft. high, will thrive in sun or shade and practically any soil though *S. reevesiana* does not like chalk or lime. All kinds can be increased by layering in May or June or by cuttings in summer.

SOLANUM (Winter Cherry). Half-hardy shrubs. 1 to 2 ft. Orange-red berries from November to March. The botanical name of the Winter Cherry is *Solanum capsicastrum*. This small shrubby plant produces abundant crops of cherry-like orange-red fruits in winter and is popular for Christmas decorations. It is raised from seed sown in a greenhouse, temperature 15 to 18°C. (59 to 65°F.), in February or March, seedlings being potted singly, first in 3-in. pots, later in the 5- or 6-in. pots in which they will fruit. From June to September they may be placed out of doors or in a frame without lights, but should be returned to a moderately heated greenhouse before frost threatens. Water freely throughout and, when in flower, syringe frequently with clear water to assist setting.

SOLIDAGO (Golden Rod). Hardy herbaceous perennials. 1 to 6 ft. Yellow flowers from July to September. These are easily grown plants with sprays of tiny yellow flowers in summer or early autumn. They vary in height from varieties such as Golden Thumb, which is 1 ft., to Golden Wings, which is 6 ft. Two of the most popular are Goldenmosa, golden yellow and Lemore, primrose, both about $2\frac{1}{2}$ ft.

All solidagos will thrive in practically any soil and fairly open position and can be increased by division in spring or autumn. They often spread by self-sown seedlings but these may vary in size and quality from their parents.

solidago

SORBUS (Mountain Ash, Rowan, Whitebeam). Hardy deciduous trees. 25 to 35 ft. White flowers in May and June followed by red, pink or white berries from September onwards. All species of the Rowan or Mountain Ash, *Sorbus aucuparia*, have elegant leaves composed of a number of small leaflets, and small white flowers borne in large more or less flat clusters followed by similar clusters of berries. In the Common Mountain Ash these berries are red, in *S. hupehensis* and *S. vilmorinii*, the two Chinese species of mountain ash, they are white and pink respectively. There is a variety of *S. aucuparia* named *xanthocarpa*, which has yellow berries. *S. scopulina* is similar in colour to *S. aucuparia* but much stiffer, narrower and more erect in habit. Yet another kind, *S. discolor* (or Embley), is grown primarily for its brilliant autumn foliage.

All these mountain ashes are excellent garden trees of moderate size thriving in most soils with a special liking for those that are fairly light and well drained. They can all be raised from seed sown out of doors in spring but *S.a. xanthocarpa* may not come true from seed and is usually grafted on to the common kind.

The genus *Sorbus* also includes other species which are quite different in appearance and garden use. These are commonly known as whitebeams and they are grown more for their foliage than for their fruits. The Common Whitebeam, *S. aria*, has young leaves which are silvery grey all over but later become green on top, remaining white beneath. In the variety *lutescens* the upper surface of the leaves remains creamy white all summer.

Whitebeams have a special liking for chalk or limestone soils, do well in exposed places, even by the sea, and are handsome, easily grown trees. They can be pruned if necessary in autumn or winter. The wild forms are increased by seed sown out of doors in spring; the cultivated varieties by grafting or budding on to seedlings of the common kind.

Sorbus aucuparia

SPARAXIS (Harlequin Flower). Slightly tender corms. 12 to 15 in. White, yellow, orange, red to maroon flowers in April and May. These South African corms with gaily coloured flowers are just not sufficiently hardy to be reliable out of doors except in the warmest and sunniest places. Elsewhere they should be grown as pot plants in a greenhouse which must be sunny but need have no more than frost protection in the way of heating. Out of doors corms should be planted 2 in. deep and about 6 in. apart in October or November. Under glass corms should be potted 4 or 5 to a 4-in. pot in JIP.1 or equivalent compost. They should be watered sparingly at first, fairly freely as growth proceeds, but after flowering water should be gradually decreased until by July the soil is quite dry. The corms can then be separated out and kept in a dry place until it is time to start them again. Increase is by natural multiplication.

Sorbus aria

SPARTIUM (Spanish Broom). Hardy deciduous shrubs. 6 to 8 ft. Yellow flowers from June to August. Spartium is a tall, almost leafless bush with green rush-like stems and spikes of yellow fragrant flowers from June to August. It thrives in well-drained soils and sunny places and is particularly good near the sea. It can be raised from seed sown in spring. The habit is improved if the stems are shortened a little each spring.

Spiraea arguta

SPIRAEA. Hardy deciduous shrubs. 3 to 8 ft. White, pink to crimson flowers from April to August. All spiraeas are very easily grown in almost any soil and open position. They differ greatly in appearance and time of flowering. One of the earliest to flower is *Spiraea thunbergii*, a graceful 4-ft. bush with tiny white flowers clustered along the twiggy branches in April. There is an even better hybrid from this, *S. arguta*, sometimes known as Bridal Wreath or Foam of May. *S. vanhouttei* grows to 6 ft. and produces clusters of small white flowers in May and June. *S. japonica* is 3 ft. high and has flattish heads of pink flowers in July and August, but even better as a garden plant is a crimson-flowered hybrid from it named Anthony Waterer. *S. douglasii, S. menziesii* and *S. salicifolia* all have short pink flower spikes like bottle-brushes in July. All grow 5 or 6 ft. high. The best coloured variety is named Triumphans. *S. veitchii* is one of the tallest kinds, 7 or 8 ft. high, with clusters of white flowers carried along arching stems in June and July.

All these spiraeas can be increased by cuttings in July or August and many by detaching and planting up rooted suckers in autumn. Spring-flowering kinds can be pruned after flowering. *S. japonica* Anthony Waterer and the kinds with bottle-brush flowers can all be pruned hard in March.

STACHYS (Lambs' Ears, Betony). Hardy herbaceous perennial. 1½ ft. Red, purple or pink flowers from May to September. *Stachys lanata* is a hardy herbaceous plant with leaves and stems so densely covered with fine grey hairs that they feel soft, like an animal's coat. The purplish-red flowers are carried on 18-in. stems but are not particularly decorative and are best cut off. The plant itself mainly spreads along the ground and makes excellent ground cover.

Two other kinds of stachys are frequently grown in gardens under their former name betonica or betony. *S. macrantha* (or *Betonica grandiflora*) has showy 18-in. spikes of violet-purple or pink flowers in May and June. *S. officinalis grandiflora* is a creeping plant with 9-in. spikes of purple flowers in August and September. All these species of stachys can be grown anywhere and are increased by division in spring or autumn.

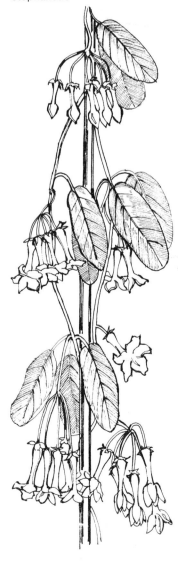

stephanotis

STEPHANOTIS (Madagascan Jasmine, Madagascan Chaplet Flower, Clustered Wax Flower). Tender evergreen climbers. White flowers produced throughout the year. This beautiful twiner with heavily fragrant white flowers must be grown in an intermediate or warm greenhouse. Its main flowering season is from May onwards through the summer but in a warm house it will continue to produce some flowers at irregular intervals all the year. It should be grown in JIP.3 or equivalent rather rich soil and should be watered freely from April to September, moderately from October to March if in a warm house, more sparingly if in an intermediate house. Shade must be given from direct sunshine from June to August inclusive. Canes should be provided for the stems to twine around. Propagation is by cuttings of firm young growths in spring in a propagator with bottom heat.

STRELITZIA (Bird of Paradise Flower). Tender herbaceous perennial. 3 to 4 ft. Orange and blue flowers in May and June. Strelitzia is a remarkable greenhouse plant with large paddle-shaped leaves and stiff 3- to 4-ft. stems terminated by purple, blue and orange flowers shaped rather like the head of a crested bird. It is not a difficult plant to grow in large pots, in either a cool or intermediate greenhouse, and in JIP.1 or equivalent compost. Alternatively, it can be planted in a border within the house. It should be watered and syringed with clear water generously from April to September but only moderately watered and not syringed at all in winter. Increase is by division in March, the best potting time. Strelitzias can also be raised from seed sown in warmth in spring.

STREPTOCARPUS (Cape Primrose). Tender herbaceous perennials. 1 to 1½ ft. Blue, pink, red or white flowers from May to September. The popular name is a poor one for there is nothing remotely primrose like about the trumpet-shaped blue (or occasionally pink, red or white) flowers carried in loose sprays on 12- to 18-in. stems in summer or early autumn. Though perennials, the hybrid varieties of streptocarpus are often treated as annuals and renewed each year from seed. For early flowering, seed is sown in a greenhouse in May and the seedlings are potted singly, first into 3-in., later into 4- or 5-in. pots in JIP.2 or equivalent compost. In winter they are kept in a cool or intermediate greenhouse and are watered sparingly, but in spring water can be given fairly freely, also daily syringing. For late flowering the same general procedure is followed, but seed is sown in January or February in a temperature of 15 to 18°C. (59 to 65°F.). Sometimes plants are grown from leaf cuttings taken in spring or summer.

streptosolen

STREPTOSOLEN. Tender evergreen climber or sprawling shrub. 5 to 6 ft. Orange flowers in June and July. This very showy greenhouse plant can either be allowed to sprawl over the edge of the staging or, better still, can be tied to wires strained beneath the greenhouse rafters. It will thrive in a cool house in JIP.1 or equivalent compost and can be increased by cuttings taken in spring or summer. It should be watered freely from April to September, rather sparingly from October to March. Very little shading is required at any time.

SYRINGA (Lilac). Hardy deciduous shrubs. 6 to 15 ft. White, mauve, lavender-blue to deep purple and maroon flowers in May and June. The Common Lilac, *Syringa vulgaris*, is a big bush, often 15 ft. or more in height, with light purplish-blue, sweetly scented flowers in May, but there are many improved varieties with larger, sometimes double flowers, ranging from white and palest mauve to intense reddish-purple or maroon. In addition, there are several other kinds of lilac worth growing, notably the Preston Hybrid lilacs, *S. prestoniae*, often referred to as Canadian Hybrids, and the Rouen Lilac, *S. chinensis*, both with smaller flowers in looser, more graceful sprays. There are several varieties of each differing in the colour of their flowers. The Preston Hybrids are not pleasantly scented but the Rouen lilacs are. Yet another useful kind is the Korean Lilac, *S. velutina* (sometimes called *S. palibiniana*), a smaller and much more slow growing kind, which may take many years to reach 5 ft. and has little rounded leaves and small clusters of bluish-lilac flowers. All are equally hardy and easily grown in almost any soil and reasonably open place.

syringa

Lilacs can be increased by layering in June or by detaching rooted suckers in autumn, but as nurserymen often graft the good garden varieties on to Common Lilac, care must be exercised when taking suckers from these as they will be of the common and not of the garden type. *S. prestoniae*, *S. chinensis* and *S. velutina* are also increased by summer cuttings and sometimes by seed, though seedlings of the first two may vary in colour. The flowering of lilacs is improved if the dead flower heads are removed.

TAGETES (Marigold). Half-hardy annuals. 6 to 24 in. Yellow, orange or chestnut-red flowers from July to September.** The marigolds are botanically varieties of tagetes but in seed catalogues only the Dwarf Marigold is usually listed as tagetes, other varieties being grouped under marigold. By contrast the Pot Marigold is listed under its botanical name Calendula and will therefore be found there in this book.

The two popular kinds of marigold are the French Marigold, *Tagetes patula*,

Tagetes erecta

Tamarix pentandra

Thunbergia alata

Thymus serpyllum

and the African Marigold, *T. erecta*; the first with yellow and chestnut-red flowers, the second all orange or yellow, but the two have been so much interbred that it is now difficult to draw any hard and fast line between garden varieties. Heights range from ½ to 2 ft. The Dwarf Marigold, *T. signata pumila*, is only 6 or 8 in. high and makes a neat dome-shaped plant covered in small single orange or yellow flowers.

All are half-hardy annuals flowering in summer and are raised from seed sown in a greenhouse or frame in March or April in a temperature of around 15°C. (59°F.). Seedlings are pricked out and hardened off for planting out in late May or early June. They prefer rather good rich soils and sunny places but will grow almost anywhere.

TAMARIX (Tamarisk). Hardy deciduous shrubs. 5 to 10 ft. Pink flowers in May and from July to September. These are hardy shrubs with plumy sprays of tiny pink or reddish flowers. They succeed best in well-drained soils and do particularly well in coastal districts. One of the loveliest is the Summer Tamarisk, *Tamarix pentandra*, which produces its pink flowers in July and August. There is also a rosy-red form. It pays for being hard pruned each April. The Spring Tamarisk, *T. tetrandra*, flowers in May and may be cut back fairly hard immediately after flowering. The French Tamarisk, *T. gallica*, pale pink and the English Tamarisk, *T. anglica*, nearly white, both flower in August and September and are often used as windbreaks near the sea. All tamarisks can be increased by cuttings in autumn.

THALICTRUM (Meadow Rue). Hardy herbaceous perennials. 1½ to 5 ft. Purple, mauve, white or pale yellow flowers from June to August. These are all very elegant plants, the foliage small and delicate, the flowers carried in little fluffy-looking heads or in loose sprays. One is known as the Maidenhair Meadow Rue, *Thalictrum adiantifolium*, because of its foliage. It grows 3 ft. high and has greenish-purple flowers in July; it is sometimes called *T. minus*. *T. aquilegiifolium* is also named for its foliage which is like that of an aquilegia or columbine. It has purple flowers in June and July and is 2 to 3 ft. high. *T. glaucum* is 4 or 5 ft. tall, has blue-grey leaves and pale yellow flowers in July. Loveliest of all is the Chinese Meadow Rue, *T. dipterocarpum*, 5 or 6 ft high, with nodding lilac and yellow flowers produced in open sprays in July and August. It has a double-flowered form named Hewitt's Double and also a white variety.

Most thalictrums are easily grown in almost any soil and open position, but *T. dipterocarpum* needs a well-drained soil and a rather sheltered position. It is best raised from seed in spring, except the double-flowered form which is increased by very careful division. Other thalictrums are increased by division in spring or autumn.

THUNBERGIA (Black-eyed Susan). Tender annual. Climbing. Orange, buff or white and black flowers from June to August. *Thunbergia alata* is a distinctive twining plant very suitable for growing in pots if each is provided with three or four canes up which the slender stems can climb. Seed must be sown in March or April in a temperature of 15 to 18°C. (59 to 65°F.), but after a few weeks no further artificial heat will be required and the plants can be grown on in a sunny greenhouse or, after the end of May, even on a sheltered verandah or balcony. JIP.1 or equivalent compost suits this plant well. The little flowers are trumpet shaped, orange, buff or white each with the circular black eye which gives the plant its popular name.

THYMUS (Thyme). Hardy alpines and perennials. Prostrate to 12 in. White, pink to crimson flowers from May to August. All the ornamental kinds are small perennials with aromatic foliage, suitable for rock garden, wall and paving. They are either completely prostrate, as in Creeping Thyme, *Thymus serpyllum*, or make neat little bushes, as the Lemon Thyme, *T. citriodorus*, or the Portuguese Thyme, *T. nitidus*, which is particularly compact and is in flower during May and June. There are numerous varieties of *T.*

serpyllum, one named *lanuginosus* in which the tiny leaves are covered in grey hairs, another named *coccineus* with crimson flowers and yet another, *albus*, with white flowers. There are also varieties of the Common Thyme, *T. vulgaris*, with yellow leaves—*aureus*, and white-edged leaves—Silver Queen. These are as useful for flavouring as the ordinary green-leaved form.

All thymes like sunny places and well-drained soils. The creeping kinds can be divided in spring, the bushy kinds increased by cuttings in summer.

TIGRIDIA (Tiger Flower). Slightly tender bulbs. 1½ to 2 ft. Yellow, orange, pink, red or white flowers from July to September. *Tigridia pavonia* is a bulbous-rooted plant for well-drained soils and warm, sunny, sheltered places out of doors, or for growing as pot plants in cool greenhouses. The flowers have three large petals and three much smaller ones and look rather like wide open tulips. They are in various bright shades of red, pink, yellow and orange usually with one colour spotted or blotched on another in the centre of the flower, hence the popular name Tiger Flower. These gay blooms are produced on 18- to 24-in. stems from July to September and though each flower is short lived there is a constant succession of them.

tigridia

Bulbs should be planted or potted in April or May and should be lifted in October for storing dry in a frostproof place.

TORENIA. Tender annual. 1 ft. Blue and yellow flowers from June to September. *Torenia fournieri* makes an excellent pot plant for the cool greenhouse. The little pouched purplish-blue flowers each with a yellow throat are freely produced all summer and good specimens can be had in 4- or 5-in. diameter pots in JIP.2 or equivalent compost. Seed should be sown in March or April, seedlings potted singly into 2½-in. pots in JIP.1 as soon as they can be conveniently handled and moved on into larger pots and richer compost when the smaller pots are well filled with roots. Plants should be watered fairly freely throughout and grown in a sunny place.

Tradescantia virginiana

TRADESCANTIA (Spiderwort, Moses in the Bulrushes). Hardy herbaceous perennials. 2 ft. Blue, purple, pink, red or white flowers from June to September. *Tradescantia virginiana* is the kind grown for ornament out of doors and it has numerous garden varieties. All have distinctive three-petalled flowers surrounded by long narrow leaves, whence the popular name Moses in the Bulrushes. These flowers are individually short lived (another popular name is Flower of a Day) but they are produced in constant succession on 2-ft. stems from June to September. The common kind is purple, but there are deep blue, lavender-blue, rose, red and white varieties. All are easily grown in almost any soil and place and can be increased by division in spring or autumn.

trillium

TRILLIUM (Wood Lily, Wake Robin, Birth Root). Hardy herbaceous perennials. 9 to 12 in. White, pink to maroon flowers in April and May. These are beautiful hardy plants for shady places and leafy or peaty soils. They have three-petalled flowers which may be pure white or rose, as in the Wake Robin, *Trillium grandiflorum*; deep maroon, as in the Birth Root, *T. erectum*; or white veined with purple in the Painted Wood Lily, *T. undulatum*.

All thrive in thin woodland or in shady rock gardens and can be increased by careful division in March.

TROLLIUS (Globe Flower). Hardy herbaceous perennials. 1½ to 2 ft. Yellow or orange flowers from May to July. The flowers of trollius are like very large globular buttercups. There are many garden varieties mostly flowering in late spring and differing mainly in the precise shade of yellow, but *Trollius ledebouri* flowers in summer and has orange blooms.

All like good rich soils and do not object to some shade. They thrive where the soil is rather damp and are excellent plants to grow beside a pool or stream, though they can also be cultivated quite successfully in a border provided this does not get too dry. Increase by division in spring or autumn.

trollius

Tropaeolum majus

TROPAEOLUM (Nasturtium, Canary Creeper). Hardy annuals and perennials. 8 to 12 in. and also climbing. Yellow, orange or pink to crimson flowers from July to September. The Common Nasturtium, *Tropaeolum majus*, is one of the most easily grown annuals which will thrive in any fairly open place however poor the soil. In fact rather poor soil can be an advantage since in rich soil plants grow so luxuriantly that the flowers are largely hidden by the leaves. There are climbing and dwarf forms and some with semi-double flowers, all in bright shades of yellow, orange, pink and red. Seed should be sown thinly an inch deep in April or May out of doors.

There are also perennial kinds, such as the Flame Flower, *T. speciosum*, which has small scarlet flowers in summer. Its creeping roots should be planted in spring or autumn near the base of an evergreen shrub into which its slender stems can scramble. *T. speciosum* does particularly well in places where the air is damp. It can be increased by division.

The Canary Creeper is also a species of tropaeolum, a climber with more slender stems and smaller flowers than those of the common nasturtium. The only colour is yellow. This plant is an annual grown as for *T. majus*.

TULIPA (Tulip). Hardy bulbs. 6 in. to 2½ ft. Flowers in all colours from December to May. These popular spring-flowering bulbs thrive in rather light but rich soils and sunny open places. Bulbs should be planted 4 or 5 in. deep in October or November and may, with advantage, be lifted in July when all foliage has died down and be stored in a dry, cool place until planting time. There are a great many different kinds and varieties, some, such as the Water-lily Tulip, *Tulipa kaufmanniana*, and the Early Double tulips, quite dwarf, others such as the Darwin and Cottage tulips, 2 to 2½ ft. tall. The Duc van Tols are the earliest to flower but need greenhouse protection. If potted in September, plunged out of doors under 2 in. of ashes until early November, and then brought into a warm greenhouse, they will bloom by Christmas.

kaufmanniana tulips

Water-lily tulips can be in bloom out of doors as early as March and are closely followed by the early single and early double varieties which are excellent for massing in beds. They are followed in April by the Mendel and Triumph varieties and also by Greigii varieties characterised by leaves which are striped longitudinally with chocolate. Then come Fosteriana Hybrids with very large flowers often in particularly brilliant colours, and Darwin Hybrids which are closely allied to them. The Darwins themselves flower in May along with the Cottage (or May-flowering) tulips, the elegantly waisted Lily-flowered tulips, the strangely shaped and sometimes bizarrely marked Parrot tulips, the green-striped or flushed Viridiflora varieties, the huge double Peony-flowered or Double Late tulips. Rembrandt tulips which resemble Darwins but have colours striped and flaked in the old-fashioned way, and Multi-flowered tulips with several flowers on each branched stem. In each group there are many varieties offering a wide selection of colours as well as some variation in height even within the group.

In addition to all these there are some delightful wild tulips or species, specially suitable for rock gardens, such as *T. clusiana*, the Lady Tulip, 12 in. high with red and white flowers in April; *T. eichleri*, 10 in. scarlet, March; *T. tarda*, yellow and white, 6 in., March, and *T. acuminata*, with narrow yellow and red petals, 18 in., May.

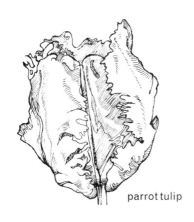

parrot tulip

URSINIA. Half-hardy annuals. 12 to 15 in. Orange flowers from June to September.** The brilliant daisy flowers of the ursinias are produced throughout the summer. Plants are raised from seed sown in a greenhouse or frame, temperature 15 to 18°C. (59 to 65°F.), in March or April, seedlings being pricked out and hardened off for planting out in well-drained soil and a sunny place in late May or early June. They should be spaced about 1 ft. apart.

One of the best is *Ursinia anethoides* with especially vivid orange flowers each with a central zone of chestnut red. It is about 12 in. in height.

V

VALLOTA (Scarborough Lily). Tender bulbs. 1½ to 2 ft. Scarlet or pink flowers in August and September. These are not true lilies but their trumpet shaped scarlet or pink flowers produced in clusters on top of a 2-ft. stem in September are distinctly lily like. The bulbs should be potted in March in 6-in. pots and if necessary may be repotted annually into larger pots, or the bulb clusters can be divided so that they can remain in 6-in. pots. Overpotting is not desirable as the bulbs flower most freely when a little overcrowded. Very little heat will be needed at any time, none at all in spring and summer and just enough to keep out frost in winter. The plants do not go to rest at any time but need far less water from November to February inclusive than during the rest of the year, when they are growing. They need maximum light at all times. The Scarborough Lily can be increased by division of the bulb clusters when repotting or by seed sown in a greenhouse, temperature 15 to 18°C. (59 to 65°F.) in spring.

VELTHEIMIA. Tender bulbs. 12 to 15 in. Yellow and red flowers from November to April. The value of the veltheimias is that they will flower in winter in a cool house (one with a minimum temperature of about 7°C. (45°F.). The tubular flowers are borne in short spikes rather like those of a small red-hot poker but the colours are much softer than in that popular family of hardy plants—pale or greenish-yellows combined with brick reds or reddish-purples.

Bulbs should be potted in August or September, one in each 4-in. pot in JIP.1 or equivalent soil. They should be watered moderately throughout the winter and spring but be kept quite dry from about June until August when they can be repotted. No shading is required at any time. Increase is by division of the bulb clusters at potting time.

VENIDIUM (Monarch of the Veldt). Half-hardy annuals. 2 to 3 ft. Orange and black flowers from June to September. These showy annuals have large orange daisy flowers, each with a central ring of black, in summer. Seed should be sown in March or early April in a frame or greenhouse, temperature 15 to 18°C. (59 to 65°F.), seedlings being pricked out and hardened off for planting out in late May in a sunny place. They are not fussy about soil. Heights vary from 2 to 3 ft.

Some handsome hybrids, known as Venidio-arctotis, have been raised between these plants and arctotis, with flowers in a range of unusual and beautiful shades of pink, orange, copper and wine red. They are sterile and so cannot be raised from seed. Instead they are increased by cuttings in spring or summer, but they flower so freely and continuously that it is often difficult to find any non-flowering shoots from which to prepare cuttings. However, shoots with flower buds can be used if the buds are removed.

VERBASCUM (Mullein). Hardy herbaceous perennials and biennials. 3 to 6 ft. White, yellow, bronze, pink to purple flowers from June to September. All the mulleins have long narrow spikes of flowers. Some kinds, such as the Common Mullein, *Verbascum thapsus*, and Broussa, *V. bombyciferum*, have large leaves densely clothed in silvery hairs as an additional attraction to their yellow flowers. Both are biennials to be raised each year from seed sown in May to give flowering plants the following year.

One of the smallest is the Phoenician Mullein, *V. phoenicium*, a perennial with 2-ft. purple spikes. There are numerous perennial garden varieties such

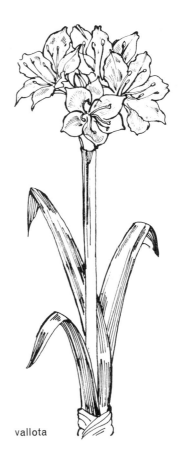

vallota

venidium

as Gainsborough, lemon, 4 ft.; Cotswold Beauty, amber, 3 to 4 ft.; Pink Domino, mauve-pink, 3½ ft. and Cotswold Queen, bronze 3 to 4 ft. All these perennial kinds are best increased by root cuttings in winter though they can also be grown from seed like the biennial kinds. The species will come true from seed but the garden hybrids will usually show some variation in height and colour. All mulleins like well-drained soils and sun and are first-class plants for hot dry places and rather poor sandy or stony soils.

verbena

VERBENA. Half-hardy perennials (usually grown as half-hardy annuals) and hardy perennials. 6 in. to 5 ft. Blue, mauve, purple, pink, red or white flowers from July to September. The most popular kinds are brilliantly coloured but rather tender trailing plants used for summer bedding. Though perennials, they are usually raised anew each year from seed sown in a greenhouse, temperature 15 to 18°C. (59 to 65°F.), in January or February. Seedlings are pricked out and hardened off for planting out in May or early June in a sunny place. Some selected varieties, such as the scarlet Lawrence Johnston, are raised from cuttings taken in August or September and rooted and over-wintered in a frame or greenhouse.

Verbena venosa, also sometimes known as V. rigida, is a hardy perennial 12 to 18 in. high, bearing spikes of purple flowers in late summer. V. bonariensis is taller and rather sparse in habit and has clusters of purple flowers. Both are increased by division in spring and they like sun and good drainage.

VERONICA (Speedwell). Hardy herbaceous perennials and rock plants. Prostrate to 3 ft. Blue, purple, pink or white flowers from May to August. The evergreen shrubs commonly called veronica belong to another genus, now named Hebe and are described under that name in this book.

veronica

Here, we are concerned solely with herbaceous plants from completely prostrate, mat-forming kinds such as Veronica prostrata, to middle-height plants such as V. longifolia, with narrow spikes of blue flowers. V. prostrata is excellent for sunny rock gardens or for establishing in the crevices in paving. In addition to the typical blue-flowered form there are pink and white varieties. V. incana is 12 to 18 in. high with grey leaves and deep blue flowers. V. spicata is similar in height with spikes of blue, pink or white flowers. All these are summer flowering but V. gentianoides, with shining light green leaves, produces its spikes of china-blue flowers in May and early June. All will grow in any reasonably good soil and open, preferably sunny place. All can be increased by division in spring or autumn.

VIBURNUM (Guelder Rose, Snowball Tree, Laurustinus). Hardy evergreen and deciduous trees. 3 to 10 ft. White or pink flowers from November to June. This is a big family of shrubs and one that can be very useful in the garden. Some species have both fertile and sterile varieties, which from a decorative standpoint are very distinct. An example is the British Guelder Rose, Viburnum opulus, which in its common form has flat heads of flowers in May and June in which only the outer flowers have large white petals. They are followed by shining currant-red berries. By contrast, V. opulus sterile has large white petals around all its flowers so that they build up into a big ball-like cluster. This is, in fact, the Common Snowball Tree and a great favourite with gardeners. Since there are no fertile flowers there are no berries.

Viburnum opulus

There is precisely the same contrast between the fertile and sterile forms of V. tomentosum. The variety mariesii is fertile and has flat clusters of flowers each ringed with white petals and they are carried along the length of spreading, often almost horizontal branches. It is a fine shrub to plant where it can be looked down on. The sterile variety V. tomentosum plicatum, is known as the Japanese Snowball Tree and has smaller but more numerous ball-shaped flower clusters than the Common Snowball Tree.

Then there are scented kinds, V. fragrans (now renamed V. farreri) has small pink and white flower clusters from November to April. V. grandiflorum and *V. bodnantense* have large deeper pink flower clusters during the same period. *V. carlesii* has white dome-shaped flower clusters in April and May and *V. carlcephalum* has creamy-white fragrant 'snowballs' in May and June.

All the foregoing are deciduous. One of the best of the evergreen kinds is the Laurustinus, *V. tinus*, a big, densely branched bush with dark green leaves and clusters of flowers, pink in bud and white when open, from November to April. It will grow in sun or shade and is an excellent town shrub. *V. rhytidophyllum* is even bigger, with larger wrinkled leaves and flat heads of creamy-white or dull rose flowers in May. Many more kinds are listed in the catalogues of shrub specialists.

All will grow in any reasonably good soil (the Laurustinus in quite poor soil). Most prefer sunny places and all can be increased by summer cuttings. Pruning is not essential, but the Laurustinus can be clipped in spring and summer if grown as a hedge and other kinds can be thinned or shortened after flowering if they grow too large.

Viburnum tinus

VINCA (Periwinkle). Hardy evergreen shrubs and tender perennials. Trailing. Blue, purple, white or red flowers produced throughout the year.
From the garden standpoint there are two totally different types of vinca. The hardy kinds are trailing evergreens which are very useful for covering the ground in shady places. Two good kinds are *Vinca major*, the Large Periwinkle and *V. minor*, the Small Periwinkle, both with numerous garden varieties, some with variegated leaves, some with double flowers or flowers of pink, purple or white besides the common blue. All flower from April to June. Less familiar but also hardy and ground covering is *V. difformis* with more starry paler blue flowers. These vincas will all grow in sun or shade in most soils and both *V. major* and *V. minor* and their varieties are very hardy. *V. difformis* is less hardy and may be killed to ground level in cold winters but usually shoots up again from the roots. All can be increased by division.

By contrast, the Madagascar Periwinkle, *V. rosea*, is a tender perennial commonly grown as a tender annual. It makes a showy pot plant for an intermediate or warm greenhouse and has red, pink or white flowers produced more or less throughout the year. Seed should be sown from February to April in a temperature of 18 to 20°C. (65 to 68°F.) and seedlings potted singly in 2½-in. pots in JIP.1 or equivalent soil and later moved on to 4- or 5-in. pots and JIP.2 or equivalent. Water freely in spring and summer, moderately in autumn and winter.

vinca

VIOLA (Violet, Pansy). Hardy herbaceous perennials. 4 to 9 in. White, yellow, orange, blue, mauve to purple and bronze-red flowers from February to October.
Because of the amount of interbreeding that has been carried out it is now extremely difficult to differentiate between violas and pansies; but traditionally violas are supposed to be more tufted and to have flowers mainly all of one colour or with rays of black, not large blotches of contrasted colours as in pansies. Now, however, there are frequent exceptions to these rules.

Though pansies are perennials they are usually short lived and old plants often do not over-winter well. For this reason they are grown either as half-hardy annuals or as biennials and raised anew each year from seed. If to be grown as annuals, seed is sown in a frame or greenhouse in January, February or March. Seedlings are planted out in April or May to flower from late May onwards. If grown as biennials, seed is sown out of doors in May or June, seedlings are transplanted 3 or 4 in. apart to a nursery bed and moved to their flowering beds in autumn or spring. Alternatively, cuttings can be rooted in a frame in September and over-wintered in the frame until April. The flowers are usually strongly marked with black on yellow, purple, blue or bronze red. They like good, rich soil and sunny places.

Both pansies and violas make good bedding or edging plants as they flower for a long time. Violas are quite hardy and will grow in any reasonable soil. They appreciate a little shade, but will also grow well in full sun. All can be increased by cuttings in September or by division in spring, but because of

single viola

double viola

pansy

the increase of soil-borne diseases which are liable to kill old plants in winter, violas are now usually grown like pansies as hardy biennials or half-hardy annuals.

There are also some wild or species violas well worth growing in the garden and these do behave as reliable perennials. *V. labradorica* has dark purplish-green leaves and violet-like flowers; *V. cornuta* is very vigorous and fast spreading and has blue, purple or white flowers. *V. gracilis* has deep purple or yellow flowers and *V. cucullata* small white violet-like flowers.

The garden violets, of which there are many varieties, are all derived from a species of viola named *V. odorata*. These fragrant flowers are also reliable perennials and can be grown either from cuttings made from the runners in early autumn, or by careful division of the roots in April. They prefer rather rich soils and cool, partially shaded places, but will grow almost anywhere. Out of doors they flower in spring, but if strong plants are placed in a frame in September, ventilated freely on fine days but protected at night and during frosty spells, they will give flowers during most of the winter. There are a great many varieties, some with single, some with semi-double and some with fully double flowers. The fully double kinds, known as Parma Violets, are less vigorous than the singles.

VISCARIA (Rose of Heaven). Hardy annuals. 18 in. White, pink or red flowers from June to August. This annual suffers from too many names and turns up in catalogues not only as *Viscaria oculata* or *V. elegans* but also as *Lychnis coeli-rosa*, as *Silene coeli-rosa* and as *Agrostemma coeli-rosa*. It is not even unknown for it to be listed separately under two of these names in the same catalogue.

The viscarias are pretty plants with thin, rather sprawling stems and an abundance of cheerful flowers. They are easily grown in any open, preferably sunny place and reasonably good, well-drained soil from seed sown in March, April or May where the plants are to flower. Seedlings should be thinned to about 6 in.

weigelia

WEIGELA (Diervilla). Hardy deciduous shrubs. 6 to 7 ft. Pink to crimson flowers in May and June.** At one time these popular shrubs were known as diervilla and may still be found under that name in some catalogues. The flowers are tubular, pink, rose or carmine and borne all along the arching shoots. Good varieties are Abel Carrière, Eva Rathke and Bristol Ruby, all about 7 ft. high. *Weigela florida variegata* has pale pink flowers and leaves broadly edged with creamy white. It is a first-rate variegated shrub.

All weigelas are easily grown in almost any soil and place, and can be increased by cuttings in July or in autumn. If desired, the flowering stems can be cut back to non-flowering shoots as soon as the flowers fade, and by this means flower quality can be improved and shrubs considerably restricted in size.

WISTERIA. Hardy deciduous climbers. Mauve, lilac, blue, pink or white flowers in May and June. These are vigorous and hardy twining plants with long trails of flowers in May and early June. They are admirable for sunny walls if trained on wires or trellis, or they may be planted to cover pergolas or large screens. Yet another possibility is to restrict them to a bushy or small tree-like habit by regular pruning and training.

There are two principal kinds, the Chinese Wisteria, *Wisteria sinensis*, with medium-sized trails of mauve flowers, and the Japanese Wisteria, *W. floribunda macrobotrys*, with longer trails of lavender-blue flowers. There are also varieties with white or pink flowers. All can be grown in almost any soil

wisteria

and sunny place but do best in fairly rich loamy soils. Once they have filled their allotted space they benefit from regular pruning, all side shoots being shortened to four or five leaves each July and further cut back to 2 or 3 in. in February. They can be increased by layering immediately after flowering.

Y

YUCCA (Adam's Needle). Hardy evergreen shrubs. 3 to 7 ft. Creamy-white flowers in July and August. These are striking evergreen plants with large rosettes of stiff sword-shaped leaves and, in summer, tall spikes of bell-shaped creamy-white flowers. They like sunny, warm places and well-drained soils but are really much hardier than is generally supposed. Perhaps the hardiest of all, and certainly one of the most beautiful, is *Yucca filamentosa*, with 3-ft. flower spikes. One of the largest is the Adam's Needle, *Y. gloriosa*, which is often over 6 ft. high and occasionally attains the proportions of a small tree. All can be increased by seeds or by detaching rooted offsets or suckers in March.

Z

ZANTEDESCHIA (Arum). Tender or half-hardy herbaceous perennials with fleshy roots. 2 to 3 ft. White or yellow flowers from January to June. The plant commonly known as arum by gardeners is botanically named *Zantedeschia aethiopica*. Though often referred to as a lily, it has no connection with the true lilies, nor does it resemble any lily. The flower is formed of a single spathe folded in the form of a funnel around a central yellow spike or spadix. In the Common Arum the spathe is white, but there are several other kinds, such as *Z. angustiloba* (usually called *Z. pentlandii* by gardeners) and *Z. elliottiana*, with yellow spathes.

Yucca filamentosa

All are usually grown in greenhouses, though the white arum is occasionally seen out of doors in mild places. A variety named Crowborough is hardier than most and so is particularly suitable for planting outside. All like damp soil and the hardier varieties are sometimes grown in ditches or along the sides of slow-moving streams.

In greenhouses, arums are grown in pots and a compost such as JIP.2. *Z. aethiopica* should be potted in July or August. Water sparingly at first then freely as the plants grow. For a while they can be kept in a frame, but as winter advances they need more warmth and, if early flowers are required, can be kept in a temperature of around 20°C. (68°F.). However, frost protection only will keep them going and they will then flower in late spring, after which the pots can be stood out of doors. The other two species are more tender. The fleshy roots of these are potted in February, watered sparingly at first and then more freely, and kept in a temperature of at least 13°C. (55°F.). Flowers are produced in the summer, after which the plants are dried off and stored dry until repotting time in February.

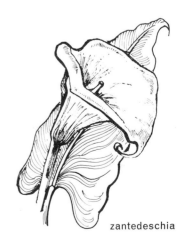

zantedeschia

All arums can be increased by division when repotting, but can also be raised from seed sown in warmth in spring.

ZEPHYRANTHES (Zephyr Lily, Flower of the West Wind). Slightly tender bulbs. 4 to 12 in. White, yellow or pink flowers from August to September. These are very attractive little bulbs with rather fragile funnel-shaped flowers in late summer, but they are only sufficiently hardy to be grown out of doors in warm, sunny, sheltered places. Elsewhere they must be grown in pots or pans which can stand out of doors in summer but need the protection of a frame or greenhouse in winter. Bulbs should be planted in March or April, 1 in. deep in well-drained soil or JIP.1 or equivalent compost. They need not be disturbed annually but can be left to spread until overcrowded when they can be lifted, divided and re-planted. If grown in pots keep almost dry from October to March but water fairly freely while plants are in growth and flower.

ZINNIA. Half-hardy annuals. 6 in. to 3 ft. Pink to crimson and purple, yellow or orange flowers from July to September. These are half-hardy annuals with brilliantly coloured flowers in summer. The colour range is from lemon and pink to orange and crimson and the flowers of good forms are large and double. Some have broad flat petals, some rolled or quilled as in chrysanthemums. There are also miniature varieties with pompon flowers to scale.

Seed should be sown in a frame or greenhouse in March or April, seedlings being pricked out and finally planted out in late May in fairly rich soil and a sunny position. The plants should be spaced at least a foot apart. Alternatively, seed can be sown in early May out of doors where the plants are to flower, seedlings being thinned to 1 ft. Most kinds grow about 3 ft. tall, but there are also dwarf races and some with small flowers. Zinnias succeed best in rather good, well-drained soils and warm sunny places.

zinnia